**W9-ARX-242**

# Praise for *Open to Hope*

"Most stories of loss and grief have a tendency to dwell within both, with little or no focus on looking for a way out. Not so with the stories contained in this anthology. Within them are insights for recovering joy. A remarkable collection I recommend to those who are grieving and are ready to move on."

—**Stan Goldberg**
Author of the international award-winning book, *Lessons for the Living: Stories of Forgiveness, Gratitude, and Courage at the End of Life*, and *Leaning into Sharp Points: How Caregivers Can Ease Their Loved Ones' Transitions at the End of Life*

"Losing a child is like being hit by a freight train. Only when people in grief realize that they are in physical as well as emotional shock can healing occur, and this book can be the next step in the process."

—**David Morrell**
*New York Times* best-selling author of *First Blood* and *Fireflies*

"How can we reach through the anguish of grief and embrace a life that once more has meaning and joy? There is no single answer to this question. Instead, there are a hundred answers, written in the lives and words of those who have loved and lost, and learned to live again. This book is a compendium of their wisdom."

—**Robert A. Neimeyer, PhD**
Author of *The Art of Longing* and editor of *Grief and Bereavement in Contemporary Society: Bridging Research and Practice*

"In this very readable book, the contributors in short vignettes share their own journeys. They are our best teachers. How to cope becomes real in each of their stories, as they find new ways to live and to find a place for their sadness in their changed lives."

—**Phyllis R. Silverman, PhD**
Coauthor of *A Parent's Guide to Raising Grieving Children: Rebuilding Your Life after the Death of a Loved One*
Resident scholar, Women's Studies Research Center, Brandeis University

"It cannot be said too many times or in too many ways that even our most profound losses are survivable. In this encouraging compendium of individual experiences of grief, the mourners share their unique ability to endure and ultimately transform their loss into a changed, but positive, meaningful and even joyful life...."

—Grace Christ, PhD, MSW,
Author of *Healing Children's Grief* and Coauthor of *FDNY Crisis Counseling*
Professor, Columbia University School of Social Work

"...[T]his book brings together a true community of people who... unselfishly share their most difficult journey in order help others find their way. Each beautiful story is a lesson in the miraculous ways that profound grief can very unexpectedly bring us to a place of peace, love and hope."

—Cori Bussolari, PsyD,
Associate Professor and Coordinator of Marriage and Family
Therapy Program, University of San Francisco

"*Open to Hope*... is a tapestry of interwoven stories of loss and healing that illustrates the uniqueness of the grieving process. The rich stories... offer something for everyone who has opened their heart and inevitably experienced grief and loss. A truly moving book."

—Kelly Taber Chasse, PhD,
Senior Clinical Social Worker, Bradley Hospital/Bradley School,
East Providence, Rhode Island

"The variety of stories and perspectives in this book offer a foothold for those on grief's journey. Every reader is certain to find something that resonates and echoes their own sorrow and their own hope for healing."

—Katherine Supiano, LCSW, FT,
Director, Caring Connections: A Hope and Comfort in Grief Program, University of
Utah, College of Nursing

"What makes this book a unique and important read is its humanity. Drs. Gloria and Heidi have put together a valuable book that is easy to read, yet powerful in its message. Written about the universal experience of loss, this book demonstrates the resilience of our capacity to grieve, mourn, and be human; a book that gives us hope."

—Richard Beck, LCSW, BCD, CGP, FAGPA,
Adjunct Professor at Fordham University Graduate School of Social Services,
internationally respected expert in psychological trauma

# Open to
# HOPE

# Open to
# HOPE

## Inspirational Stories
## of Healing After Loss

Dr. Gloria Horsley • Dr. Heidi Horsley
And the Open to Hope Contributors

With a Foreword by
Elisabeth Kübler-Ross Foundation

Published by the
Open to Hope Foundation

© 2011 by Dr. Gloria Horsley, Dr. Heidi Horsley, and the Open to Hope Foundation

Published by the Open to Hope Foundation
1485 Dana Avenue, Palo Alto, CA 94301

www.opentohope.com

Open to Hope Foundation helps people find hope after loss. The online forum at www.opentohope.com supports those who have experienced loss by helping them cope with their pain, heal their grief, and invest in their future. We encourage our visitors to read, listen, and share their stories of hope, love, and compassion.

ISBN: 978-0-9836399-0-9

All rights reserved. No part of this book may be reproduced without prior permission of the publisher. Printed in the United States of America.

To our lost loved ones

If you would like to apply to write about
grief, loss, hope, and healing for the Open to Hope
Foundation, please go to www.opentohope.com
and fill out the section under "Write for Us."

# Contents

## Part 1:
## Mending the Grieving Heart

## Part 2:
## I Wasn't Ready to Lose You

## Part 3:
## Rebuilding Your Lives

# Part 4:
## Let Hope Blossom

# Foreword

*You will not grow if you sit in a beautiful flower garden, but
you will grow if you are sick, if you are in pain, if you experience losses,
and if you do not put your head in the sand, but take the pain as a gift to
you with a very, very specific purpose.*

**—Elisabeth Kübler-Ross**

Who feels that devastating loss and the pain that accompanies it is a gift? In the beginning, I know I didn't.

In 2005, following the ten-year illness and subsequent death of my fourteen-year-old son, Austin, I began my relationship with overwhelming grief and loss. The journey has taken me on a ride that has had few highs and plenty of shattering lows.

When grief first became my proverbial dance partner, I felt that I was "leading," when in fact I was "following." I soon realized that I desperately needed guidance. I knew that if I didn't look for help and get it quickly, I was going to encounter years of missteps and out-of-sync movements, which would translate into depression and a mind-numbing lack of hope and faith in the future.

It was then that I sought out the work of psychiatrist, humanitarian, and hospice pioneer Elisabeth Kübler-Ross, MD. While reading her books *On Children and Death*, *The Tunnel and the Light*, and others, I began to ponder what the years ahead could possibly bring to someone who was as profoundly sad as I was. How would I ever be happy again?

What did I need to learn in order to have hope that this horrible grief would not consume my every waking moment?

After reading Elisabeth's thoughts on grief and bereavement, and life and living, I felt not entirely confident, but better in knowing that I wasn't alone in my despair, though at times I thought I would surely die from the pain of my grief.

I learned as well that I would indeed survive and that my intuition was right—I needed to reach out for help. Finally, I realized that I had to embrace this passage as some sort of gift and journey. But sometimes, I felt all I could do was try to breathe.

Through her books and her body of work, Elisabeth gave me a safe space to work through my own suffering by teaching me that I am not alone in my grief. Millions of people cry, grieve, and then cry some more. She also taught me that pain is a part of the greater journey of life.

In a desire to seek out sources of guidance for this dance with grief, I researched Elisabeth's Life, Death, and Transition (LDT) workshops and had a conversation with Larry and Anne Lincoln, who have been workshop facilitators for twenty-six years.

"Elisabeth knew that by connecting us to the universality of pain, we would have a better resting place for our own unique pain," said Anne. "She connected us, as well, through creating an environment that was emotionally safe." She did not "do the work," Anne explained. "In creating an emotionally open space for the workshop participants, they decided if or when to share their experiences with others, and the group environment became an opportunity for healing and hope."

The most extraordinary healing would take place at the workshops hosted by Elisabeth and her team of trained facilitators, Larry recalled. "In one workshop, a sixteen-year-old boy stood up and announced quite clearly that he intended to commit suicide the next time he had the opportunity, but that he was attending the workshop first, at the request of his mother.

"The workshop format required the young man to tap the shoulder of the person next to him when he was finished sharing his story. So that is what he did, never imagining what would happen next.

"As he was sitting down, the next man, in his mid-forties, stood up and began to share his story, that his own sixteen-year-old son had just committed suicide and he had come to the workshop to help cope with the profound loss," said Larry. "So for that one week, that man got to parent again, and that sixteen-year-old boy got to see the consequences of his intended actions."

He added, "Elisabeth had a unique ability to share a story that would connect ten people, then share another story that would connect thirty more people, and so on. It was incredible."

Through her Life, Death, and Transition workshops, global outreach efforts, and twenty-three publications in thirty-two languages, Dr. Elisabeth Kübler-Ross became not just the "Death and Dying Lady," but also the "Life and Living Lady."

Though Elisabeth passed away in 2004, her model of helping others through creating opportunities for sharing grief and subsequently hope continues to be embraced. Through organizations such as the Open to Hope Foundation, the Elisabeth Kübler-Ross Foundation, and others around the world, millions of people have access to quality grief and bereavement resources and programming every year.

The Elisabeth Kübler-Ross Foundation embraces the committed work of the Open to Hope Foundation and its cofounders, Dr. Gloria Horsley and Dr. Heidi Horsley. With radio shows, publications, videos, and its website, the Open to Hope Foundation connects grieving people in an open environment. Those dealing with loss, and the pain that goes with it, have an opportunity to share their innermost thoughts and feelings when and how they feel comfortable—which was one of Elisabeth's original goals in her workshops.

Heidi and Gloria are educators, innovators, and caring professionals, and their ongoing efforts are consistent with the groundbreaking work of Elisabeth so many years ago. Elisabeth was a pioneer in the fields of death and dying, grief and bereavement. In many ways, both Heidi and Gloria, through the work of the Open to Hope Foundation, are pioneers as well.

"I think my mother would applaud the work of Dr. Heidi Horsley and Dr. Gloria Horsley," said Ken Ross, Elisabeth's son and president of the Elisabeth Kübler-Ross Foundation. "The Open to Hope Foundation, through the use of contemporary communication methods, connects millions of people every week, while also keeping a careful eye on the most important factor—each and every individual who participates in their programming. Their innovative use of technology in the fields of grief and bereavement is groundbreaking and in their own way, Heidi and Gloria should be considered trailblazers, too, just like my mother. We are honored to participate in this publication and give it our full endorsement."

In *Open to Hope: Inspirational Stories of Healing After Loss*, Dr. Heidi Horsley, Dr. Gloria Horsley, and more than one hundred unique contributors share messages of hope and support through offering concise ideas to help the hurting, the suffering, and the grieving. Throughout the book, there are pointers for not just surviving, but thriving through the often tumultuous road to healing. Whether your grief is due to the loss of a child, a parent, a spouse, a sibling, or a friend, *Open to Hope* provides insight for communicating with family, neighbors, caregivers, and even complete strangers, as we all too often find ourselves at a loss for what to say or do to help another.

It is the hope of the Elisabeth Kübler-Ross Foundation that you embrace this book, *Open to Hope*, much in the same way you might open one of Elisabeth's books—with an open heart, an open mind, and a belief that hope is available where and when you least expect it.

Peace on your journey,

—**Dianne Gray**
Board Member
The Elisabeth Kübler-Ross Foundation

# Acknowledgments

A book like this comes together only through the dedication and selfless sharing of talent and energy from many, many people. Thanks to each of our Open to Hope authors, who have generously shared more than 2,500 wonderful stories and articles on www.opentohope.com. It was very challenging to select those who appear in this book. Thanks to Neil Chethik, our website's executive editor, and Heather Johnson, our Open to Hope Community Manager, for bringing these messages of care, healing, and hope together so seamlessly on our website.

Thanks to Stephanie Abarbanel for her tremendous editing efforts. Thanks too to Beverly McManus and Karen Lau for organizing and helping shape the book, and Karla Wheeler and the team at Quality of Life Publishing for their production support. A special appreciation to Dianne Gray, Ken Ross, and the Elisabeth Kübler-Ross Foundation for the book's foreword. We so appreciate the support of our husbands and families, and of course, we are grateful for our loved ones who have gone before us and who inspired each of us to do this work and to share their stories.

# Introduction

Whether a death is sudden or anticipated, losing a loved one shakes us to our very core, destroying our belief in a just, safe, and predictable world. Grief often changes us quickly, both physically and mentally. It is like being kidnapped and suddenly transported to a foreign land without luggage, a passport, or the language to make sense of what's happening. Even if you have a road map for getting through the pain and anguish, you still have to take the trip.

The purpose of this book is to help you find threads of hope that will assist your recovery and help you carry on. By sharing inspirational stories, personal experiences, and professional advice from contributors to the Open to Hope website, we hope that you will be comforted and inspired by learning how others dealt with their losses, what they saw as roadblocks, and how they handled them, as well as what it has taken for them to not only survive, but thrive. We want to help you resume leading the life that you were meant to live—a life of satisfaction and one driven by a belief in your own personal power for change.

We created the Open to Hope Foundation in 2008 to provide interactive forums with a simple mission: helping people find hope after loss. Our goal was to provide an "open platform" for grief experts and organizations to reach out and serve the grieving public with a combination of expert articles, news, research, radio, and video. Every day thousands of people who are looking for information and support visit our website, www.opentohope.com. They listen to our radio show, read our blogs, and read stories about what others experienced. The majority of our writers, radio show guests, and YouTube participants have been where you are.

We want you to know that you are not alone. We have been where you are and made it, and so can you. In 1983, Scott Horsley (Dr. Gloria's seventeen-year-old son and Dr. Heidi's brother) was killed in a car accident, along with his cousin Matthew, also seventeen. At first the pain was so bad, we didn't know if we would survive, and we certainly didn't think we would ever find hope again. This tragic loss profoundly influenced the course of both our lives and our careers. However, we not only survived, we eventually found the hope to build a future full of exciting opportunities and possibilities. If you lack the will and the belief that you will survive this blow to your heart, we ask you to lean on our hope until you find your own.

Some stories will resonate with you more than others, but it is our hope that you will find many glimpses of yourself or your situation in these pages, as well as the insight and information you need to carry on. Men and women tend to grieve differently, so we have included many stories from mothers and fathers, brothers and sisters, husbands and wives, sons and daughters. You will also hear from people of different ages and circumstances.

Perhaps most importantly, you will hear stories and advice from people in different places of recovery. Some of us are still in shock, while others have reached the point where we are looking for inspiration to begin rebuilding our lives. Some of us are wondering what to do when, after caring for a spouse, parent, or another loved one during a long terminal illness, we suddenly find ourselves with unwanted time on our hands. Some of us have lost a life companion, and others grieve for their beloved children, siblings, or friends.

We truly understand how hopeless, helpless, angry, and defeated you may be feeling right now. We also understand how contradictory your thought processes probably are. Especially early on, the fear of dying may be matched with the intense desire to join the one you have lost. You may think you are going crazy. These are probably not true suicidal thoughts, but rather a primal desire to be reunited. We recognize those waves of grief, the feeling that you can barely catch your breath, the pit in your stomach, and the yearning and searching in a crowded room for just one more glimpse of your loved one. We also know that if he or she walked into the room at this very moment, you would feel whole and sane again.

Your process of recovery is what is most important. The real story here is your story, the one that has knocked you down and forever changed your life, the one that shattered your world and may still leave you breathless and screaming for help. You are the reason that we are sharing stories of how others have walked the griever's path and found the hope to live rich, even joyous lives.

You will find an abundance of hard-won wisdom and insights in these pages. Some authors offer practical advice, including how to get through the holidays without your loved one, how and when to start dating again after losing your spouse, how to talk to your children about why their father or grandmother is no longer here, and how to parent after loss. Others address spiritual matters, such as what we should expect from God and how to keep our faith alive after a devastating loss.

Many writers talk through their anguish and pain. They also confront their guilt, shame, or anger—at the teenager who died of a drug overdose, at the ex-boyfriend who killed a beloved daughter, or sometimes at the person who is no longer here. Yes, there is agonizing sadness, but you will also find many, many moments of joy and renewal.

Over time, through reading, writing, and telling our stories about the loved ones we have lost, we have all succeeded in finding a new language and discovering new pathways to help us steer a course toward hope. We packed new luggage, applied for new passports, set new goals, and designed achievable maps for the rest of our life stories. It took time and energy, but we have found a "new normal" and are currently living happy and satisfying lives, and we know that with time and commitment you can too.

**—Dr. Gloria and Dr. Heidi**

# PART I

Mending the Grieving Heart

# Surviving the Unsurvivable

## Finding Spring Again after the Death of a Child
By Cathy Seehuetter

*W*e are finally at the end of what has often been a brutal winter. While gazing at the mountains of snow piled high in my front yard and the foot-long icicles hanging from my roof, it has been hard to imagine that spring would ever come. We have endured bitter cold winds that have chilled us to the bone and treacherous roads that we have cautiously traveled. The days have been long and dark. No matter how long I have been a native of the Upper Midwest, I know we all will be glad when it comes to an end.

As I described these thoughts about winter, I felt as if I was describing the days of my early grief. At that point, I did not believe that a day would ever come when I would thaw from the chill that had overtaken my body and mind. The bleakness of my existence during those first months after Nina died is almost too frightening to remember; it is so difficult to even conceive of that much pain. I was anesthetized from some of its cruelness by the protective blanket of numbness that blessedly shielded me from the gale force of such overpowering sorrow.

How could I ever feel spring in my heart again?

Spring had always been my favorite season. The air has a certain freshness to it that I would drink in. Simply put, it always made me feel happy and light of heart. Spring was our reward for surviving the freezing winter months that preceded it, and it brought a smile to my face and a bounce to my step.

However, it was in spring when my heart was irretrievably broken. It was during this exquisite season of warm, lilac-scented breezes and sun-kissed mornings when my sweet daughter Nina's life would end. I wondered if I would ever feel the same joy again. Rather than anticipate spring's arrival with gladness, I dreaded it with the knowledge that it contained the anniversary of her death.

The smell of the air and the look to the sky that I had once found exhilarating now brought me back to my darkest day. I know that anyone who has lost a loved one to death, no matter the season, understands.

Will spring come again to your life?

In the years since Nina died, has it come to mine? Looking back at my description of the winter of my early grief, I know I have come a long way from that time of desolation. I have found, especially after the first two years, that with each subsequent spring, I have rediscovered some of the pleasure I used to feel. I have learned that just because I find things to feel joyful about again, it doesn't mean I am dishonoring my daughter's memory. I now take her along with me in my mind and my heart. I try to retrieve memories of the dandelion bouquets she so carefully gathered and presented to me, the rides to the park in the Radio Flyer, our talks while sunning on the deck and, of course, shopping for spring clothes! Her favorite pastime!

I will always feel tenseness, apprehension, and sadness as May 11 draws near, but I no longer hold it against spring.

It is a slow, difficult journey, this grief pathway we travel. It is as treacherous as the roads we maneuver following a winter storm, never knowing when we would hit an icy patch on the road and be thrown into a tailspin. Yet we must travel it if we are to find any measure of peace and healing.

Please be patient with yourself as you are working hard to survive this winter in your heart. Trust that spring, though a much different one than the one we knew before our beloved child died, will come again.

---

Cathy Seehuetter's fifteen-year-old daughter, Nina Westmoreland, was killed in a drunk-driver accident in 1995. Cathy is the Minnesota Regional Coordinator and a former member of the Compassionate Friends' National Board of Directors, and has been published in *Chicken Soup for the Christian Family Soul*, as well as grief magazines. She also frequently speaks at grief conferences. Cathy lives in Minnesota with her husband, and has three surviving children and four grandchildren. Visit her articles at www.opentohope.com.

# Mustering the Courage
# to Face Our Fears
By Mary Zemites, MS

Recently, a woman who had lost her mother and father in the last two years expressed how tired she was of always feeling anxious and fearful. Her losses had brought home the fact that the people she loved were all going to die. It could be anytime and anywhere. The possibility of facing the loss of her husband or one of her children was constantly invading her thoughts. She was tired and stressed all the time.

Her words were all too familiar. They brought me back to the time between my husband's stage IV cancer diagnosis and his death three-and-a-half years later. When Greg's cancer was discovered, it had already spread to other organs. The doctor was understandably hesitant to share a prognosis of six months with a thirty-seven-year-old man, his wife, and his three young children.

Being youthful and otherwise strong, Greg fought for his life and even managed to rally for periods of time during those years. He was up and down, riding that roller coaster of cancer and chemotherapy. He bounced back quickly after the initial surgery and was back to work in just a few weeks. He tolerated the weekly chemo treatments pretty well, but after several months he would develop a complication, become quite ill, and be admitted to the hospital for care. He would recover, come home, go back to work, and the whole cycle would start over.

Every time he had a downturn, I was afraid. Would this be the time that he wouldn't recover? This fear was normal and realistic. The feelings of fear that troubled me more were the thoughts that occurred during the "good" times—when Greg was doing well, working a normal schedule, and involved with the family.

I kept worrying that this normalcy was just an illusion, and I was often overcome with dread and deep sadness that our future together most likely would not last long. It was debilitating. I desperately needed to find a way to face this fear and hold onto optimism, while still maintaining a realistic outlook on our situation.

I did manage to find an answer. One afternoon when the dread hit me, I thought about how much regret I would have later, when the worst did occur. I didn't want to look back when he was dying or had died and think, *Why didn't I appreciate life and feel happy when things were good?*

These were the days for rejoicing and thankfulness. They would end much too soon. I needed to squeeze every bit of joy and love out of them that I possibly could. I knew that I would have plenty of time to be horribly miserable later. I promised myself that I could wallow in it when he died. But I was not going to be miserable now!

Fear is paralyzing if we let it take control of our lives. Yes, we will all die someday, but in the meantime we must focus on the joy of living. Even faced with the knowledge of his impending death, my husband chose to take joy in his life and his family. He never wanted to be "written off." He wanted to live every day to the fullest.

Fear is an exhausting emotion. It takes up all of our energy. So here's the challenge: What good can we do with that energy? Are we afraid that we'll lose another loved one? Then carve out more time to spend with that person. Appreciate his or her qualities and try to find more joy in that relationship. Are we afraid of our own death? Then take that energy and help others who are already facing death. Volunteer at a hospice. Help out at a hospital. The dying have a great deal to teach the living.

Our courage is what will help us conquer the pain of death. Courage is not the absence of fear, but the choice to go forth in spite of the fear. *Courage is facing fear.* We must consider ourselves participants in life as long as we have this gift of life. Make a difference, live to the fullest, find joy—these are the things that will release us from the regrets of fear.

---

Mary Zemites's husband, Greg Jarczyk, died in 1992, leaving her with three young children, ages four to ten. This and subsequent family deaths inspired her to earn a master's degree from Arizona State University and reach out to those dealing with loss. In 2009, she founded a sympathy gift and grief resource website. Find her articles at www.opentohope.com.

# Will You Overcome Grief, or Will Grief Overcome You?

## By Jack Cain

Someone has died or you have experienced some other devastating loss, and grief has virtually taken over your life. It arrives in towering waves that engulf and own you, all at once. I can tell you this because I lived it.

Three people in my family died in a twenty-month period—all of unrelated causes. My son, Adam, committed suicide at age twenty-seven; then my wife, Lenore, died of ovarian cancer after having survived breast cancer four years earlier; and my daughter Stephanie died at age thirty-four of congestive heart failure, less than three months after the death of my wife.

There were only five of us to start with, and these battering blows left my daughter Nicole and I shattered. For a long time, people asked me how I survived them. I replied that I had no choice. It was either survive or jump off a bridge. I chose survival.

Three tragic experiences in my life could have virtually destroyed me. I deliberately chose not to be destroyed. Instead, I taught myself to overcome the grief that was consuming me and to bring my mind—and myself—back into the land of the living.

There is a certain strength that comes with knowing that even though the bombs of life are falling all around you, you aren't required to collapse; and you can use this knowledge as power that gives you the ability to rise above the ashes.

Because of my jangled mind, it took me some time to realize what I had really done to survive. It was no accident. I had a plan, born, I suppose, of desperation. The thing is, I didn't realize I had a plan until I was in the midst of using it.

Somewhere between the first and second year after my daughter died, I made a conscious decision that I no longer wanted, or needed, to have grief continue to control my life. I had chosen to regain my life. How did this come about?

I taught myself to live in the present, the *Now*, to leave the past behind and to not give currency to the feared future—a feared future that might never happen. I needed to do this in order to simply survive. If you are able to absorb this concept into your being, you will be able to say, as I do, that you can't believe how lucky you are, in spite of any misfortunes you might have had—which, after all, are in the past, not in the *Now*.

Living in the *Now* is to recognize this minute for what it is and what it means to you. To recognize the magic and grandeur of the moment. Appreciating what is right here, whether sensory or mental. To gather up all the positives in your life right now and draw them into you.

To be present in every living moment is to be here, *Now*. To be fully engaged in and focused on whatever you're doing or experiencing. Aware of what you're doing and who you're with, so that if you're sitting at a table talking to someone, you're not thinking about what you did yesterday or reading the titles of the books on the shelves around you or planning tomorrow's activities.

Eventually, together with Anne Berenberg, I made a road map that consists of ten steps. These steps, outlined in our book, *Now: Overcoming Crushing Grief by Living in the Present*, form the basis for leading the reader on a path out of his or her grief.

---

Jack Cain lost his wife, son, and daughter in a twenty-month period. In his book, *Now: Overcoming Crushing Grief by Living in the Present*, coauthored with his new wife, Dr. Anne Hatcher Berenberg, Jack describes his painful past and offers a ten-step program for regaining control after experiencing loss. Jack is a writer, a trained chef, and a photographer. Find his articles at www.opentohope.com.

# How Long is Too Long to Grieve?
## By Barb Roberts

Is there some magic amount of time to grieve a death, the breakup of a relationship or a family, the loss of a job, financial downturns, the loss of a pet? I'm talking about grief and loss, hurting, struggling, pain, sadness, anger. How long does it take to "get over" someone or something?

Would it be helpful for you to know that grief takes as long as it takes? People often ask me, "What is a normal amount of time to grieve?" I tell them there is not a formula for grieving. Certainly experience and coping skills can help, but I always get concerned when I hear someone say, "When you lose a spouse, it usually takes _____ years!"

The length of the grieving process often depends on the nature of the loss, whether or not someone is experiencing multiple losses, the willingness of those grieving to do their "grief work," and the willingness of family members and friends to give each other permission to grieve and to accept that there are no shortcuts in the grief process.

In the past, some would say that the griever must keep "a stiff upper lip." Part of the Christian message is that we certainly grieve, but we do not grieve as those who have no hope.

Grief does not express a lack of faith in God. Instead, it can lead us to a deeper understanding of our faith, our need for God, and His promise that He will be with us in the midst of our pain and grief, that He will never leave us nor forsake us.

Remember, grief takes as long as it takes. As you embark upon your own journey of grief, also remember that God wants to comfort you during the process.

---

Barb Roberts has been in the ministry of pastoral care for twenty-five years, where, having experienced grief and loss in her own life, she has been privileged to help those who grieve. She is a conference speaker and teacher on the topic, and published *Helping Those Who Hurt: A Handbook for Caring and Crisis*, including lists, step-by-step directions, scripture, and vignettes. Read her articles on www.opentohope.com.

# Lost in Widowhood
## By Catherine Tidd

*I feel so lost.*

How many times have we felt that way? How many times have we heard that from other grievers? How many times have we just wanted to pull on a T-shirt that says it, so we don't have to explain anymore why we're operating in such a daze?

We all go through these periods of feeling lost, as if we're floating out there in the world with nothing to anchor us. We make the best effort we can to find that connection—the Internet, support groups, counseling—something, anything to make us feel like we're still part of the world.

For some of us, these periods last longer than for others. It's discouraging, and when we see those who share a similar experience supposedly "getting on with it," we feel that we're failing in some way. That we're not living up to our grieving potential. That we'll never get that promotion from "new widow" to "widow once removed."

But I have a different idea.

When we lose someone, our perspective changes in a big way. The little things become just that—little. (That is, until a little thing comes along and completely runs us off the road. That's always fun!) Our connection with the world and the people around us does a complete 180. Spiritually (not necessarily religiously), our connection deepens. We seek out those who feel the same awakening because we suddenly feel a connection to them.

It's baffling to many of us that those with whom we find comfort are often not those people who have known us all of our lives, but complete strangers. We can't look at someone in pain in the same detached way we could before, because his or her pain was once our pain. And we feel it right to the core.

It's frightening, this opening of the spirit. It leaves us vulnerable and insecure. And when we used to feel that way—scared and exposed—whom did we turn to?

You guessed it—the person who's not here anymore. Talk about your double-whammy!

Sometimes I think that the people who are having the hardest time are the ones doing the most soul-searching. We all feel loss very deeply, but I wonder if the people who can't figure out what to do with certain areas of their lives—whether it's professionally, romantically, or just what to wear in the morning—are actually taking the time to really figure themselves out. They're not jumping into anything. Because jumping would imply that they have to land somewhere. And they're just not ready to do that yet, damn it!

The problem is, everyone around you is saying that you should be ready (mainly because the fact that you are still going through the grieving process makes them feel uncomfortable; it has nothing to do with you). They think you need to stop floating and join the real world once again. And it's almost harder when you reach out to people who have shared a similar loss who seem to be "getting on with it," because, in the back of your mind, you think that you're just not doing this right.

Sometimes I wonder if we are holding on so tightly to who we were, what we had, and what could have been so we can focus all our energy on that and let it take up so much space in our hearts that we don't have room for the new person who's waiting in the wings. It's not denial—or if it is, it's the sneakiest form. We know what's happened. We are fully aware of what we have lost. What we don't know is what happens next. And that's when we start floating.

I feel like I'm making this sound more magical than it really is. This "evolution of spirit" doesn't seem like it should come in the form of a ripped bathrobe and a bag of Oreos. When we wake up in the morning and feel like our entire body is made of lead, we don't think, "Wow, I feel like crap this morning. I must really be doing some soul-searching."

For me, I jumped into everything right after my husband died. It didn't occur to me that I needed to figure out who I was, whom I had evolved into, now that I was on my own. I wanted to get on with my life immediately.

What I failed to recognize was that my life was not the same anymore, that it was impossible to jump right back into my old life, because it had taken a permanent vacation. The rules that I had followed before didn't apply. This was a new game, and in order to play it, I had to change. And change takes time.

And that's really when I began to hurt.

I'll never forget it. I was going about one hundred miles an hour for six months after my husband died, and then, suddenly, I started to cry. And cry. And cry. I didn't want to do anything. All of the decisions I had been so desperate to make a few months earlier seemed as trivial as they were impossible. When I told my sister that I couldn't figure out what in the hell was wrong with me, she replied, "You've been moving too fast. And now you're being forced to sit down and deal with what has happened."

(Enter floating sensation and detachment.)

My point is, when you're feeling that lost feeling, try to look at it in a different way: that your damaged spirit is actually trying to take care of you while you figure out who you are.

For some people this takes longer than for others. Some of us will float back and forth between who we think we "should" be and that person we are actually evolving into, because sometimes that's two different people.

Just remember: the reason we feel lost is because we're hoping to be found.

---

Catherine Tidd is a widow and the founder of a free social support network dedicated to anyone who has lost a significant other. She is also a writer, a public speaker, and the mother to three entertaining young children. She earned her English degree from Rollins College in 1998 and lives in Denver, Colorado. To read more of her work, visit www.opentohope.com.

# "Reality Is Always Kind"— Moving Beyond Suffering

### By Byron Katie

I have a word for God: reality. I call reality "God" because it rules. It is what it is, and it's so physical—a table, a chair, the shoe on your foot, your hair. I love God. It's so clear, so solid; it's completely dependable. You don't get a vote in what it does, and it doesn't wait for your opinion or your permission. You can trust it completely.

You know that reality is good just as it is, because when you argue with it, you experience anxiety and frustration. Any thought that causes stress is an argument with reality. All such thoughts are variations on a theme: "Things should be different than they are." "I want . . ." "I need . . ." "He should . . ." "She shouldn't . . ." It always hurts when you argue with what is.

"What is" is a story of the past. The past is past. It happened, and you can't do a thing about it. Argue with that! The sane alternative is to ask, "What can I do from here?"

The past is a teacher, it's benign, it's over. But as long as people are living with an unquestioned past, they're living *in* the past. And it's a past that never happened in the first place. They're living in their story of the past. They're missing what's present right now, which is the real future. I never know what's going to happen. All I know about it is that it's a good thing.

People spend their whole lives dedicated to changing the past. It can't be done. Thinking that the past should have been different is hopeless and masochistic. "My mother should have loved me." "My child shouldn't have died." "The Holocaust shouldn't have happened." Comparing what happened to what you think should have happened is a war with God. (This is very difficult to hear when you're attached to concepts of right and wrong.) Some people even think that sadness is an act of loyalty, that it would be a betrayal of the people they love not to suffer along with them. This is crazy.

If my child has died, that's the way of it. Any argument with that brings on internal hell. "She died too soon." "I didn't get to see her grow up." "I could have done something to save her." "I was a bad mother." "God is unjust." But her death is reality. No argument in the world can make the slightest dent in what has already happened. Prayer can't change it, begging and pleading can't change it, punishing yourself can't change it, your will has no power at all.

You do have the power, though, to question your thought, turn it around, and find three genuine reasons why the death of your child is equal to her not dying—or even better in the long run, both for her and for you. This takes a radically open mind, and nothing less than an open mind is creative enough to free you from the pain of arguing with what is. An open mind is the only way to peace. As long as you think that you know what should and shouldn't happen, you're trying to manipulate God. This is a recipe for unhappiness.

Reality—the way that it is, exactly as it is, in every moment—is always kind. It's our story about reality that blurs our vision, obscures what's true, and leads us to believe that there is injustice in the world.

I sometimes say that you move totally away from reality when you believe that there is a legitimate reason to suffer. When you believe that any suffering is legitimate, you become the champion of suffering, the perpetuator of it in yourself. It's insane to believe that suffering is caused by anything outside the mind. A clear mind doesn't suffer. That's not possible.

Even if you're in great physical pain, even if your beloved child dies, even if you and your family are herded off to Auschwitz, you can't suffer unless you believe an untrue thought. I'm a lover of reality. I love what is, whatever it looks like. And however it comes to me, my arms are open.

This is not to say that people shouldn't suffer. They should suffer, because they do. If you're feeling sad or afraid or anxious or depressed, that's what you should be feeling. To think otherwise is to argue with reality. But when you're feeling sad, for example, just notice that your sadness is the effect of believing a prior thought. Locate the thought, put it on paper, and question it, for the love of truth, and then turn it around.

It was you who made yourself sad—no one else—and it's you who can free yourself. This is very good news.

---

Byron Katie guides people who are suffering through the powerful process of inquiry called *The Work,* where they radically shift their stressful beliefs and change their lives. She is the author of five best-selling books, including *Loving What*

*Is: Four Questions That Can Change Your Life; Question Your Thinking, Change the World: Quotations from Byron Katie;* and her latest, *Who Would You Be Without Your Story?* Find more on www.opentohope.com.

# Grief Reactions: The Four *R*s
## By Gloria C. Horsley, PhD, MFT, RN

Have you ever wondered why you feel so depleted both physically and mentally after a loss? I am not talking about in the hours or days that follow; I'm talking about weeks, months, and sometimes even years later. People often ask me how long grief takes. That is a hard question to answer, because recovering from loss is not a step-by-step progression. That being said, there are some markers that will help you to determine where you are in your grief work, as well as where you would like to go.

After thousands of interviews with the bereaved, I have identified four thought processes that I believe drive our reactions to grief. I call them the Four *R*s: Restitution, Reconciliation, Reality, and Reunion.

Depending on where you are in your recovery, your thought processes will influence the goals you set. And you *will* set goals. As humans we are hardwired to problem solve and set goals. We continually try to get a handle on our loss by telling our story to others, daydreaming, and dreaming about what's occurred.

As I talk about the Four *R*s, you may find that the goals related to your loss that you have set are outdated, unrealistic, or negative in terms of your future. It is only natural that you may begin to feel hopeless and helpless. But with time and a developing awareness of your thought processes, you will be able to free up the energetic force of hope. Once again, you will find yourself focusing on a life plan that includes a positive outcome for the future.

I do not see the Four *R*s as stages, in the literal or lineal sense. But I do believe that you can get stuck in one particular thought process, which holds you back from a life of hope and happiness that is your birthright. As I discuss these Four *R*s, see if you can identify them in your own recovery.

## 1. Restitution (Early Response)

Our initial response to loss is highly instinctive in that if we lose something, we want it back *now!* So we set a goal that has no pathway for success, and thus we are left feeling hopeless and helpless. "I want things the way they were." "I will get them back."

You have only one goal, and that is Restitution. You cannot let him or her go. You look at your wedding pictures, smell his clothes, visit her room, visit his grave, review events around the accident or illness, build websites, talk about her on Facebook. Every fiber in your body is in denial. You don't want to accept the fact that you live in a changed world and that you are a changed person.

As you struggle through the shock of loss, you are finally forced to come to terms with the fact that he or she is not coming back. You realize that the goal of having your old life back has no pathway to engage the energy of hope. How do you know this? His room is still empty, and she is not there to tuck you in bed at night, help with homework, play cards, or catch a ball.

## 2. Reconciliation (Life Goes On)

At this point we begin thinking about settling the accounts and balancing the books. Let's place the blame; let's figure out why this happened. Who, why, what, when, and how become endlessly looping questions. You and other survivors in your circle look to settle matters, square things up, and bring things back into harmony.

During the process of Reconciliation, survivors often look for goals related to the loss that they think are worthy of pursuing. There can be some very compelling Reconciliation goal possibilities, which may be destructive or constructive, depending upon your point of view. For instance, finding some person or institution to blame can provide what seems to be a new goal. The hope is that settling accounts will make us feel more in control and dampen our anger.

Some of these blaming goals can last for years and give focus to lawsuits and, in some cases, result in very positive community action. For instance, Candace Lightner (see page 119) helped strengthen laws against drunk drivers after her daughter was killed by one. But the results are seldom what we are looking for. More often than not, people don't get fired, go to jail, or say they are sorry in ways that heal us from our grief.

In the end, the goals of Reconciliation must give way to Reality if we are to live a fully happy and satisfying life again.

# 3. Reality (Searching for a New Normal)

Are you at the point where you have given up on the idea that you can reclaim your old life? Are you tired of your anger and resentment causing health issues? Are you weary of your own stories of how and why your loved one died? Are you tired of trying to balance the books by blaming yourself, God, and others? Are you beginning to feel that there must be more to life?

If your answers are "Yes," I ask you to take a leap of faith and join me in taking a hard look at Reality. This step can be a tough one to take, but it is necessary for your healing, and it is a life changer. How do I know? Because I have done it, thanks to my good friend Byron Katie, author of *The Work*.

Just suppose for a moment that in this world there are only three kinds of business—God's Business, Other People's Business, and Your Business. God's Business includes things like the rain and snow. Your Business includes things that refer directly to you, such as your responses to loss. In fact, the only time you really have control of your reactions to, and attitudes about, your loss is when you are in Your Business and are not second-guessing others. Other People's Business is related to everyone else in your life, including your lost loved one.

Ask yourself, "Whose business is it that my loved one met an untimely death?" Now that you have someone in mind, let's analyze your situation for a moment by looking at mine. In 1983 my son, Scott, was killed when his cousin Matthew lost control of his car. Is it my business that Matthew lost control on a rain-slick road and both he and Scott were killed? Was it Scott's business because he didn't tell him to slow down? Is it God's business because it was raining?

In order to fully heal, it is necessary to embrace Reality and stop second-guessing why things have happened, pointing fingers, and assigning blame. The Reality is that Scott and Matthew are dead and, after much contemplation and grief work, I have come to accept that seventeen years was a full life for them and they did not die an untimely death.

At this point, I ask you to embrace the Reality that your loved one lived a full life and that the date and time of his death are as they should be. When we argue with Reality we lose every time. How do we know our loved one should be dead? Because he or she is, and blaming yourself, others, or God does nothing but cause you to suffer. Instead, join me in Reality, a place where you will find peace, harmony, and possibility.

# 4. Reunion

If you have accepted the Reality of your loss, it is time to move into thought processes related to Reunion. This means not only taking your loved one into your new life and continuing your bonds, but also coming back to the new you.

After extensive interviews and analysis, Professor Richard Tedeschi has identified five different areas of personal growth after loss. One is *a sense of personal strength*. ("I'm stronger than I thought I was.") A second is *the recognition there are maybe new possibilities or opportunities*. ("I wouldn't have recognized this opportunity before taking my life on a new path.") A third is *deeper relationships with others*. A fourth is *a greater appreciation of life*, both the value of life and how precious it is. And the fifth is *spiritual development*.

There are thousands of examples of people who have found Reunion with their deceased loved ones through creative ideas and service. (See the section on Continuing Your Bonds, page 313.) There are as many creative ideas as there are people. I know that as your healing continues, you will think of ways to integrate your loved one into your life and identify your areas of post-traumatic growth.

I want you to use the Four Rs to free yourself up from goals that don't have a pathway for hope. I want you to reenergize yourself with goals that will again fire you up and drive you to make the world a better place in the name of what you have lost. As Byron Katie says, "Do it yourself and teach the world."

---

Gloria Horsley, PhD, MFC, RN, is an internationally recognized grief expert, psychotherapist, and bereaved parent. She and her daughter, Dr. Heidi Horsley, are the cofounders of the Open to Hope Foundation and cohosts of the "Open to Hope" Internet radio show. Dr. Gloria is a board member for the Compassionate Friends. In addition, she has authored a number of articles and written several books, including *Teen Grief Relief* with Heidi, and *The In-Law Survival Guide*. Find more at www.opentohope.com.

# How to Surrender to Grief
## By Louis E. LaGrand, PhD

"What you resist persists." It's an old saying in psychology that is especially applicable to anyone who is mourning the death of a loved one. In other words, trying to repress feelings, "be strong," or pretend you are doing well when you are not will guarantee that pain will spill out in unexpected ways. You will not only prolong the intensity of your grief process, you can be sure that you will add loads of unnecessary suffering to legitimate pain and sadness.

Contrary to popular belief, grief is a normal human response. It seeks expression when a person faces massive change due to a death or another major loss. The key words here are "normal" and "expression." Yes, the fear, despair, and lack of control are part of the experience and not signs that there is something wrong with you.

So how can you allow grief to work its magic by helping you accept the reality of the death of your loved one and find peace of mind? Here are five essentials used by millions of mourners who have found peace through expression.

1. Tell it like it is. It may be a hell for you. Do not suppress (consciously choose not to say what you feel) or repress (unconsciously bury certain thoughts and feelings) simply because you want to maintain the image of rugged individualism. Suppression and repression are two actions that often lead to reactive depression when grieving. It's healthy to admit you are hurting.

2. Cry when you feel like it, even if it continues for hours or days. Let the pain drain out through this natural response to the loss of someone cherished. If necessary, place yourself in the company of those who can be around pain and will not try to inhibit tears. Also, don't feel that you must cry. Some people grieve less through tears and talking, and more through thought and action.

3. Take time to be alone in a quiet setting, but don't isolate. Occasionally, you need time alone to think about the relationship with your loved one, or even talk to the deceased. But maintain your interpersonal relationships. In the long run, too much isolation is detrimental. Seek and accept help. We need each other.

4. Consider the possibility of an afterlife. Read about what others of all persuasions say about an afterlife, especially scientists. I have always liked Einstein's quote: "The probability of life originating by accident is comparable to the probability of the unabridged dictionary resulting from an explosion in a print shop." You might want to examine some of the literature about other mourners who were convinced they had a sign or message from a deceased loved one or a divine being. Find out why

millions believe that no one ever dies alone or grieves alone.

5. Let grief go through you at its own pace. When we choose to love, we automatically choose to grieve. There is no way out—only through. Make every effort not to resist grief. All relationships end in physical separation. However, although the person is no longer physically present, love never dies; it forever lives on. Follow your agenda for grieving and reduce contact with those who want you to follow their agendas. Accept the fact that the history of loss shows you will survive.

To summarize, there is a wide range of normalcy in grieving. Give yourself permission to openly mourn, feel the pain, and persist through it all. Beware of comparing yourself to others. Accept your feelings, as distasteful as they seem, as normal, normal, normal, especially after you have a good day and suddenly find yourself feeling the way you did early in your grief. Then continue on and treasure what you have—a way to peace, knowing that your loved one lives on through you and what you have learned from your experience.

---

Louis E. LaGrand, PhD, is internationally known for research on after-death communication phenomena and has authored numerous articles and eight books. His most recent book, *Love Lives On: Learning from the Extraordinary Encounters of the Bereaved*, is available in an e-book edition. He holds advanced degrees from Columbia University, the

University of Notre Dame, and Florida State University, and has counseled the bereaved for more than thirty years. Find his articles at www.opentohope.com.

# Can Your Faith Survive a Terrible Loss?

## By Barbara Francis

*Death of a loved one is an amputation. I fear the loss of memory.
No photograph can truly recall the beloved's smile. Occasionally, a
glimpse of someone walking down the street, someone alive, moving,
in action, will hit with a pang of genuine recollection. But our
memories, precious as they are, still are like sieves, and
the memories inevitably leak through.*

**—Madeleine L'Engle**

Jody, my best friend for twenty years, was gone, the most
unexpected turn in my nearly fifty years of living. I was left to
grieve, and I soon discovered that grief had a way of morphing.
Grief did not look or feel the same from moment to moment
or day to day. I cried constantly despite my efforts not to. I felt
mentally numb. And I battled for my faith.

I was in full-time ministry. I knew where Jody was—in
heaven. I'd see her again. She was fully whole now and would
never even want to come back. I knew these things. I had taught

and believed them for years. I should have been fine. But I was not fine and found it hard to imagine that I would ever be fine again. Life lost all its color, all its laughter. Everything seemed like bleak shades of gray and black. Hopeless. Vague.

In the weeks and months that passed, I gradually came to realize I could not/would not abandon the God who had loved me, forgiven me, and comforted me for more than thirty years. I knew Him too well. I cherished our relationship too much to throw it away like the flower arrangements that faded with age. I read books on grief and talked with others who were at different places in the grief process, all of whom helped me realize the importance of faith. I learned that mine was not a perfect faith, but it was one that would prevail.

The battle was difficult and the lessons hard to articulate. But I will try to share what I've learned with you.

Tragedy and loss can never be fully anticipated. I was not prepared for my loss then, and I will never be prepared for future losses. I am simply not the same as I was when Jody was alive. There is a hole in my life—the place Jody occupied—that will always be hollow and void. I wasn't finished doing life with her. I wish she were still here. My soul, however, has grown in the process.

I have had to learn to live with the principle I call coexistence. I have come to grips with the reality that loss and life, sorrow and joy, emptiness and hope, live side by side within me now. All these things coexist.

The unseen, eternal things mean more to me now. God is simply more a part of my life. I've been forced to grapple with His love and His goodness in light of my great loss. "Jody? You took Jody? You gave Jody and me this remarkable friendship. Why would you take it away?"

I've had to completely rethink God's sovereignty. "Couldn't you just have put your finger under that plane? It only missed getting over that mountain by one hundred feet! You did that kind of miracle in Idaho, why not in Arizona?"

I have learned that not all of my questions will be answered and that the greatest tribute to my friend is to go on living full on, full out for God. It's exactly what she would have wanted. Of this I am certain. He has been my Guide and my Captain, and He will take me through this great loss, as well.

---

Speaker and author Barbara Francis lives to bring God's message of healing love to hurting people. She has served with an international ministry for thirty-plus years, specializing in prayer and compassion, and has written numerous Bible studies and three books: *Following Him When I Can't See the End of the Road; Unexpected Turns: Leaning into the Losses of Life;* and *Grace and Guts: What It Takes to Forgive.* Read her articles at www.opentohope.com.

# "Grief Is an Illness" and Other Myths Surrounding Loss

By David Daniels, MD

Destructive myths abound concerning the loss and grief process. First, contrary to some views, there is no one "right" way to die or grieve. Our personality type makes a difference. Some of us go in peace, and some go screaming.

Many people don't go through all the steps in the dying process outlined by Elisabeth Kübler-Ross (*On Death and Dying*) or in the order she states: shock, denial, anger, bargaining, depression, and acceptance/resignation. By bargaining, she means asking for a favor or another chance, often based on the promise of good behavior. Depression is not inevitable, and some people don't feel angry.

With loving care and the receptive awareness and acceptance that go with presence, many people realize that life is each day and that wholeness is the goal, not postponing death. We can heal the heart while the body is dying.

There are myths about the grieving process, as well. The main ones are that grief is an illness, something to get better from, and that you grieve first and then come back to live life, as though grief and life are linear processes.

In truth, grief is a natural process. It lets us know that we care and love. The natural sadness of grief often comes in waves, unexpectedly. Trying not to grieve often causes persistent distress and even depression.

The natural process involves leaning into pain, not away from it, and releasing through the pain into love and life in each moment. Life and grief go hand in hand in a natural co-existence. These realizations, when truly lived, make both the death and grief process transformative rather than transfixing. These best or healthy principles about the dying and grief processes have been honored in both hospice and Anamcara (soul friend) care that goes back more than a thousand years.

---

D r. David Daniels, MD, is clinical professor of psychiatry and behavioral sciences at Stanford Medical School, a leading developer of the Enneagram system of nine personality styles, and coauthor of *The Essential Enneagram*. In private practice for more than three decades, David brings his knowledge of the Enneagram to individuals, couples, and groups, as well as to a wide range of applications. Find his articles at www. opentohope.com.

# Grief Happens: Taking the Risk to Bloom after a Loss

By Chris Mulligan, MS

L ife and death give us lessons to learn every day. If we're aware, we notice the lessons in the media, on bumper stickers, in conversations, and through our experiences. But what do we do with them? Do we heed them and heal ourselves by making different life choices? Or do we choose to stay stuck in a state that causes our own "death" in our grief?

Often, we become so accustomed to life's bombardment of information that we choose to view life from a surface level of involvement. We notice the signs: "Accidents Happen," "Divorce Happens," "S— Happens," "Change Happens." But one of the less visible and most uncomfortable signs that many choose to ignore is "Grief Happens." One problem is that the bereaved do not have placards giving us directions on how to get through the grief process.

Further, people who don't understand or prefer to disregard grief and loss sometimes cannot support those who are grieving. Therefore, to survive the experience, the bereaved

35

hopefully learn that they are ultimately responsible for their own grief process (and changed life) and that, as Henry David Thorueau said, "Things do not change, we do."

Many people do not realize that grief is not an event that occurs for a certain length of time and then reaches a final ending. Reality is, grief is a life experience that one endures and that lasts over a lifetime. The lack of acknowledgement of this can lead to tremendous pain for the griever when others make comments such as, "You should be over your grief by now," "You need to move on," or, "You're crying too much," or when others insinuate that you are mentally unstable because of your reaction.

Another life lesson from bereavement is that Grief Happens at all times and any time. Because grief is a lifelong process, we can be caught unprepared at any moment in our early grief process or beyond. We may think that we are progressing quite well, but the pain can surface at the most inopportune, most surprising times. All of us can expect these assaults on our hearts without notice or forewarning, because grief cannot be controlled.

Depending on how your loved one died, you may find yourself re-experiencing the trauma of the moment of death, the moment you found out about the death, or your reaction. It is common to relive those events during bereavement. But since grief cannot be scheduled, many find themselves overcome when their pain resurfaces during pleasant or normal activities. While walking down the street or watching television or a movie, you see a person, hear a comment, taste a food, or smell a fragrance, and grief unexpectedly envelops you.

With time, the frequency of these episodes may diminish. But you need to know and accept that because grief is centered in the heart and is a part of who you are now, an unforeseen reminder of your pain may wash over you at any moment.

I have survived many of these moments since my son Zac's death on October 1, 2000, but I was totally taken aback recently when a song sung in church transported me back to my grandmother's funeral forty years ago. I had tears in my eyes and could not sing. It made me realize that Grief Happens anytime, anywhere. I am a different person because of my grief, and this is my world now. Further, I know I need to take responsibility for how I live my life differently, and I must be aware of the lessons I have learned from the deaths I have grieved.

Yes, Grief Happens. Grief will be with us the rest of our lives, and it will change who we are. But we can also choose to be aware of and learn from the lessons that grief teaches us. I think Anaïs Nin's comment about change supports what the bereaved learn through the life lessons of grief: "There came a time when the risk to remain tight in the bud was more painful than the risk it took to blossom." I wish you the strength to blossom in your grief.

---

Chris Mulligan's son's death challenged her twenty-five years of experience as an adoption social worker, her MS in clinical child, youth, and family work, and her beliefs and values. Their continuing relationship and ongoing communication changed her and introduced her to a new life of gifts, gratitude, and growth. *Afterlife Agreements: A Gift from Beyond* details these changes and the development of this new relationship. Read more at www.opentohope.com.

# "It's *Not* Going to Be OK,"
# She Said

### By Robin Moore, MBA

Looking back on it now, the bright curve of my life turned gently downward after my daughter was born, fell sharply as my husband was diagnosed with stage IV cancer, and waggled as we fought his illness for a year. After the second surgery, through the fourth and fifth chemo regimens, my line flattened into a basin. After he died, our hearts grieved the loss, and we struggled to adjust to everyday life.

Caregiving and anticipating loss were, in a way, worse than the pit of grief. Adjusting and struggling for air in the year after his death were very like that horrible period of desperate blindness and denial that we took on during the final, rapid, unpredictable, often petty depredations of a horrible disease.

So it's hard for me to say in what part of this low period a trusted friend helped me see some light. She cut through my fog by saying one of the darkest, least supportive things you can say. Maybe it was tough love, or maybe it was just her sharing an honest view with someone who really wanted her eyes to stay closed.

She might have started with "Hang on a minute," but it was a single phrase that entered my tired ears: "It's *not* going to be OK."

I blinked.

"You won't come out of this experience just fine, and neither will your little girl. This will have a huge effect on your lives. It will change you both and you will never be entirely 'better.'"

How dare she tell me that the platitudes I'd been spouting a moment before, the hard work I was doing to keep myself afloat, were not valid? *We won't be OK?*

This woman knows me very well. I trust her authority in the ways of humans. I sat there, eyes smarting, in shocked silence.

"What I mean is, this is a major loss. It's not simple and it's never going to go away. But you *can* affect how you'll come out of the experience. You can develop the tools to survive and even flourish; you're already far along in creating and using them. And at this point, you have to do it for yourself and for your child. But it's not going to happen automatically. You'll have to do it, and from now on, you'll have to do it on your own."

My face smarted. "But I'm sure we'll be OK. I mean, surely we'll heal. Things have to get better."

"Yes, things will get better. Your life will go on, and you will probably be happy again. You might even be stronger and better off. But nothing will be the same. An event like this will leave scars. Your injuries have been hurting you for years. You can't just 'fix' them. Don't you have some scars now—a big one on your arm?"

"Yes." I started to exhale and concentrated on listening.

"Can you remember how you got that one?"

"Yes."

"Does it still hurt? Does it hold you back now?"

Today, the scar was nothing, a vestige of a lesson, but over. "No."

This momentary exchange was a fulcrum, one of several tiny thought shifts that changed everything. My friend's first words shattered all my comforting rationalizations, forcing me to see that our future would be shaped by my choices and my actions. I became conscious, for the first time, that I deeply believed someone would stride up one morning (but after coffee) on a great white horse and save us.

This belief lasted through my husband's illness—the FDA could approve one of the two drugs in the pipeline! Or maybe we'd score a miracle! And it persisted during the months and months (at least twenty-four of them) when all I could do was sleep, eat, take basic care of my family, and show up at a few appointments designed to keep me afloat—therapy and a support group. I was waiting for someone else to do the hard part, and I had no idea what that would be.

Remembering what a scar means and how it lasts—hearing that there was no way out without injury—helped me discard any fantasy about a hero or even his trusty steed. I was alone and still responsible for my daughter. I started to imagine what I could do if I stopped waiting.

Sometimes, you do need to rest in order to heal. But that time was over for me. Who knows why I was able to listen that day. I don't recommend being so uncomforting to *your* friends.

But somehow the smack-upside-my-head of these hard words opened my ears to what was already around me. I started to hear new ideas from my peers at my support group, other folks also living with grief and raising children with no time off: Viv started a new workout, Elena took an evening out with girlfriends, Frank wrote a personals ad. Options, small steps, maybe tiny: each and every one of them was possible for me, too.

I could feel myself starting to climb the hill, neglected calf muscles again pumping good blood to my heart. I didn't know where I was going, but it hurt so much that I knew I was moving up.

*This piece was first published in Thin Threads.*

---

Robin Moore, MBA, is a writer and social media consultant with twenty years of experience. She writes a popular blog about her experiences raising her young child after the death of her first husband, a well-known visual artist. She has built several online communities for grieving people. She is remarried and enjoys her work creating products and solutions with select partners. Learn more at www.opentohope.com.

# Don't Just Heal Grief, Transform It
## By Tabitha Jayne

There is a tendency in our society to talk about healing loss as if it is a physical wound. It reduces loss to nothing more than an illness to be cured. Our objective is to heal it as quickly as possible and get back to normal.

This approach has failed us in our understanding of loss and made us miss its real nature. This has created a society that is reluctant to express loss, and we thus keep the pain inside of us, instead of letting it go.

Transformation is the real nature of loss. It shows us that we don't need to heal anything. We can take our loss and change it into something more, something better for ourselves. It means that not only do we let go of our loss, but we gain something far greater in return.

We become just like caterpillars entering the cocoon stage. By going into the darkness of our loss and accepting it rather than fighting against it, we can emerge brighter and lighter than ever before.

Transforming loss means you become aware that life is too

short and incredibly precious, and you have a responsibility to live fully and die without regrets. Transforming loss means changing fundamental aspects of your life. It means acknowledging and experiencing deep and sometimes painful emotions. It means facing demons and letting them go. It means discovering your hidden dreams about what you really want for your life.

Transforming loss can be uncomfortable. Yet in loss, we are already uncomfortable. Transforming loss requires that you accept it and explore it. This takes courage. It is far easier to heal loss and continue living as you did before.

There is a tendency to tap into unresolved past painful experiences. If we don't take the time to acknowledge these and let them go, we stay forever trapped by them like the caterpillar on the plant's leaf. It also requires us to be brutally honest with ourselves, become aware of behavior that doesn't work in our best interests, and change it.

By choosing to transform loss, you create a statement of intent, one that says, "I deserve the best for myself." Transforming loss can increase happiness and health. It can give you the opportunity to find your true purpose and fulfill your wildest dreams.

Ask yourself this: Do you wish to live your life as a caterpillar? Or are you prepared to metamorphose into a butterfly and experience everything that life truly has to offer?

---

Tabitha Jayne's seventeen-year-old brother, Peter, died suddenly in 2002. From this experience she developed a deep interest and passion in both understanding grief and loss and how to live fully after the loss of a loved one. She now works with the bereaved, sharing what she's learned from loss and helping them to transform their grief, live fully, and thrive after loss. Find her articles at www.opentohope.com.

# The Art of Longing

## By Robert A. Neimeyer, PhD

This poem arose from a conjunction of events—the recent death of my mother-in-law, the last surviving parent on either side of our family—and my driving for hours through a deep Canadian winter to offer a grief workshop in Brockville. The periodic bursts of long "O" sounds echoed for me the howling wind, and the endlessly receding landscape evoked the landscape of memory and our yearning for return. The sensory pull between the strong draw of the past and my forward momentum found expression in the evolving imagery and hinted at an essential tension in grieving.

## The Art of Longing

Those of us who have driven
the long cold road alone
have watched the thin line
of trees, frosted white,
slipping behind
like memories.
We know the pull

of something unseen
beyond the reach of dry eyes,
fixed, blinking
at the distant mist.
We ride the road
with our lonely ghosts,
unwavering in their devotion
like penitents at the altar
of our grief.
This is how we perfect
the art of longing,
learn to nurse the hurt,
refuse the fullness
of this world.
For now, we keep driving,
lean into the dimming light,
lean further toward
winter's receding horizon,
and away from arrival.

---

Robert A. Neimeyer, PhD, is a professor of psychology at the University of Memphis, where he also maintains an active clinical practice. Bob has published twenty-five books and serves as editor of the journal *Death Studies*. The author of more than three hundred articles and book chapters and a frequent workshop presenter, he is currently working to advance a more adequate theory of grieving as a meaning-making process. Read his articles at www.opentohope.com.

# Gratitude as the Antidote to Grief

By Joanne Cacciatore, PhD, MSW, FT

G rief is a potpourri of paradoxes. In brokenness, there can be wholeness. In darkness, there can be light. In egoism, there can be selflessness. In despair, there can be hope. In a world of injustice and suffering, there is often, eventually, gratitude.

This isn't just psychobabble; for many, it is their survivalist reality. It is the only way that so many bereaved have moved beyond mere suspension. Those who allow themselves to experience gratitude are often able to transcend their former place in the world. They have reached a threshold of joy and passion that they would never have known had it not been for their loss.

These are individuals who, despite incapacitating trauma and turmoil, manage to find gratitude. This is not a magical moment of epiphany for many. Rather, it evolves over time and with intense cognitive effort. I believe that finding gratitude—even crumbs or morsels at first—requires emotional maturity, practice, and mindfulness.

It requires us to first focus on the self—to take personal

responsibility for our own suffering and to turn toward the pain. It is a paradigm of approaching rather than avoiding. We acknowledge our suffering, tell and retell our story, and know ourselves intimately. It requires us to acknowledge that there can be healing and growth in our suffering and encourages patience as we slowly evolve toward post-traumatic growth. It is a place where we silence our minds, respect our bodies' response to the grief, and are gentle with ourselves.

It commands intentionality and tolerance in the face of the insufferable pain that radiates from the tips of our hair to the tips of our toes, the agony that causes every cell in our bodies to ache. As Hemingway said, the world breaks us all, and some are stronger in those broken places. We may reach out for help from others, sometimes strangers, and we are able to accept the outreached hand with grace.

Then, when we are ready, we move beyond the self and we turn our hearts outward. We see the suffering of others. We acknowledge others' pain without the fear of losing or diminishing our own suffering. We learn to sit compassionately with another, abandoning for a moment our own grief's narcissistic exigency. We widen our circle of compassion for the suffering of all beings. We begin to truly see the world through others' eyes.

We recognize the acts of kindness, courage, and sacrifice that others have offered along our journey, and extend that droplet of hope to another, honoring even ill-fated attempts to comfort. And we eventually reconsider exchanging alienation, anger, and resentment for tolerance, empathy, and acceptance.

We seek gratitude daily, even for the "small" things in life, like a dandelion dancing on the warm breeze, apple trees in the spring, or a fiery sun setting against a mountainous silhouette—

or, perhaps, a simple kind word of support from a friend.

Like threads in a garment, grief runs in and out of our daily lives from the instant of death, one moment often indistinguishable from the next for many days and months. There is a time for this. There is a time to wallow in the mud, a time to pause for the entangling. The garment is unraveling, and grief has patterned your life, against your will, in an unfamiliar mosaic. Yet gratitude can truly help us to heal from our suffering when the time is right to reconvene and rejoin the world of the living.

And when that time comes, revisit the expectations of the human condition. Take the time to fill your heart with gratitude. You can be grateful for what you have without taking away from that which you have lost.

So tell someone who has helped you how grateful you are for his presence in your life. Hug someone you love and tell her three things you admire about her. Write a letter or send a card to someone who is making a difference in your community. Leave an anonymous gift for a teacher, doctor, or other "carer." Reach out to another person in mourning. Let gratitude hang in the shadows, parallel to your grief. It is not magic, but it is transformative.

When we allow the experience of gratitude, the heart may still be broken, but the heart is also most full, most whole, and most complete. Menachem Mendel of Kotzk, a Hasidic rabbi and leader in the nineteenth century, said, "Where is God to be found? In the place where He is given entry." Where is gratitude to be found? It also can be found in the very place where you have given it entry.

D r. Joanne Cacciatore, PhD, MSW, FT, is an expert in traumatic death and child death in families. She is founder and CEO of the MISS Foundation and is a consummate teacher; she is a researcher and professor at Arizona State University. Joanne is also an acclaimed public speaker, teaching mindfulness-based psychosocial intervention to medical professionals worldwide. She is a mother to five children, "four who walk and one who soars." Find her articles at www.opentohope.com.

# Helping Others Help You

---

## Caregivers: Be Gentle with Yourselves
By Karla Wheeler

W hen someone we love is terminally ill, it can be the most challenging time in our lives physically, emotionally, socially, and even spiritually. But if we can learn to be gentle with ourselves, newfound energy awaits us on all levels.

## Go Gently, Go Gently
This became my mantra, the phrase that kept running through my brain when my fifty-four-year-old husband of thirty years was dying of cancer. I'd be stuck in traffic, late for an important doctor's appointment about Gerry's latest X-rays or CT scans.

My heart would pound as I willed the stoplight to turn green, knuckles clenched around the steering wheel. Then I'd take a deep breath and say aloud to myself over and over again, "Go gently. Go gently. I will go gently about my tasks this day." Instead of racing into the doctor's office, I would try to walk normally, silently chanting my calming mantra.

## Physically Exhausted

Oftentimes we are exhausted physically, not sleeping well, forgetting to eat or eating whatever's handy, especially junk food. We know we should be eating properly so we can keep up our strength, but who has time to plan a balanced meal, go grocery shopping, or cook?

Tempted to grab a handful of cookies or chips, I'd try my best to remember to stop, take a deep breath, and repeat my calming phrase, "Go gently. Go gently. I will go gently about my tasks this day." My task at that moment was to be gentle with my body, feeding it something useful, rather than forcing it to deal with the excess sugar from cookies or an infusion of salt from chips. So I'd put down the junk food and reach into the fridge to grab a piece of cheese or a handful of baby carrots.

## Emotionally Drained

Unless someone has walked a mile in our shoes, no one fully understands the emotional toll of knowing that a loved one's time with us is limited. Will he live another month? A week? Will he hang in there until his brother arrives tonight from out of town?

Emotionally, we become frantic one minute, numb from anticipated grief the next. Sometimes our hearts ache so much that we think the pounding in our chest must mean that our physical heart is injured, too. How can one person cope with the roller-coaster ride of feelings that plague our every waking hour?

## Ask for Help

When we're going through these increasingly demanding times, many people around us want to help, but they don't know what to do or say. Having been through the terminal illness of not only my husband, but also my parents, I've learned it is OK to ask for specific help from friends, neighbors, and coworkers. In fact, they will be so grateful to know they can help lighten your load!

Ask your neighbor to do your grocery shopping. Rely on friends to take care of your children after school or during regular sleepovers. Lean on a coworker to take your car in for an oil change or pick up your dry cleaning. Let everyone know that casseroles (in containers that don't have to be returned) are welcome any time. Don't be shy about saying which recipes are your family's favorites.

## Be Gentle

Most importantly of all, don't beat yourself up when you can't be Superman or Superwoman. We are human beings, not human doings. So during this time of enormous emotional upheaval, take more time to be with your loved one, rather than doing things nonstop. And when you feel you're at your rope's end, gently whisper a healing mantra to yourself, whether it's "Go gently, go gently," or another phrase that brings you calm amidst the storm. And if the angels at hospice are helping to care for your loved one, ask them for other ideas to help get you through each day. You are not alone. Help and support surround you at every turn.

---

Karla Wheeler has been an expert in hospice care and grief support for more than twenty years. A former newspaper reporter and editor, Karla is the founder of Quality of Life Publishing Company, dedicated to helping hospices provide compassionate care to terminally ill patients and their families. She is the author of *Afterglow: Signs of Continued Love* and other gentle grief support books, and is a board member of the Open to Hope Foundation. Find more at www.opentohope.com.

# How to Help Our Friends Help Us When We're Grieving

By Joy Johnson

*When the goddess emerged from the cave of her sorrow she*
*wept anew, for there was no one there to greet her.*
**—Ancient Greek myth**

One widow said it well: "You find out who your friends are!" Many people think that illness, death, and other tragedies bring people closer together. Actually, the opposite is more often true. Stresses build, relationships have changed; anger, guilt, sadness, and all the other emotions that come with grief seem to attack everyone at different times and in different ways. Recognize that your family and friends will be grieving differently.

+ They don't know what you need.

+ They don't know what to say.

+ They are probably afraid of their own feelings.

+ They want you to feel better so they'll feel better.

+ Most of them are uncomfortable around grief and loss.

There are many times when you will have to take the lead. Audrey's eighteen-year-old son killed himself. Three weeks after his death, she took her seven-year-old daughter to church to get ready for the Christmas program. As she walked in the door, thirty women working on costumes became suddenly silent. Audrey sighed. She turned to the friend who had carpooled with her and said, "Our pastor said we would have the burden of making people comfortable. I guess I'll start now," and she walked to the nearest table and simply opened up her arms for hugs. Voices rang out and she was immediately surrounded by loving arms and heartfelt tears.

Take the lead! If no one calls you to meet for lunch, call somebody new. Want to see a movie? It may take six or seven calls, but find someone or go alone and have your own popcorn. Even though it's hard, make a list of what you want to do and go after it.

You will hear a lot of stupid things. People worry about what to say to you. They're afraid of saying the wrong thing, reminding you of bad memories and hurting you, so they try to make it better and often fail miserably. As one bereaved mother said, "At least they gave me lip service and didn't ignore me."

Another had words of real wisdom: "When people say how I'll feel better soon and that at least I have other children or good memories or it could have been worse and he's in a better place, I'm not ready to hear it. In a few years, I may look back and think how most of those sayings were true, but not yet." When people give you clichés and obviously don't understand, it may be helpful just to say, "Thank you, I'm just not there yet."

Prepare to be surprised. You are likely to be surprised at who among your friends and family steps up to the plate and who disappears into the shadows. People you hardly know will contact you and tell you their stories and know how you feel. Others will not invite you to their parties and will ignore you completely.

People are afraid of grief. And you may be surprised at your own reactions to friends and family. Aunt Doe (no cousin ever called her "Aunt Doris") was gentle and, as my mother said, "Never said a bad word about anybody." But after Aunt Doe's husband died, mother said something and Aunt Doe let her have it with both barrels. Mother was astounded. "That just wasn't Doris," she said over and over again. "That just wasn't Doris." My mother didn't understand about grief.

Some families have seagull grievers. "They fly in, usually from out of town. They make a lot of noise. They bother everybody. They make a crappy mess, then leave and make somebody else clean it up," a friend said. It is your grief and your life that are important here. Find the help you need, whether it's legal, spiritual, emotional, or medical, and take care of yourself. It's not your job right now to take care of everyone else. It's your job to make sure you grieve in healthy ways without interference.

Find a support group or a good listener. In the beautiful book *Tear Soup*, an old and wise woman named Grandy suffers a great loss and has to make tear soup. She calls together other people who are also making tear soup for a BYOS (bring-your-own-soup) dinner and they all share their tear soup. The last sentence on that page is vital. It says, "And they became Grandy's new best friends."

Your funeral director, pastor, local hospice, or hospital social work department should have a list of local support groups. You don't have to say anything when you go. You can share at your own comfort level, and you will learn a lot from people who have walked the walk. Louise said, "I walked in and they were gathered around having coffee and laughing. I thought, 'How can they laugh when I'm in such pain?' But way back in my head, a little voice said, 'Lou, someday you'll laugh again, too.' That group saved my life." And if the first group isn't a fit for you, try another. If there is no group in your area, find a friend, family member, or someone who will listen to you without criticizing or telling you what to do.

You will hear, "Call me if you need anything," or "Let me know what I can do." Those are caring statements. The problem is, it puts the burden of contact on you, the griever. Never be afraid to ask for what you need. Never be afraid to find new friends, and every night before you go to sleep, say a quiet "thank you" to those friends and family members who are there for you. Some nights it will be a short list, but gradually it will expand into an impressive collection of love and support.

---

In 1977, Joy Johnson and Dr. Marvin Johnson founded Centering Corporation, an organization that provides education on grief and loss. Joy has written or edited 150 books and has presented more than five hundred workshops at grief seminars. She is the author of *Keys to Helping Children Deal With Death and Grief* and a novel, *The BOOB Girls: The Burned Out Old Broads at Table 12*. Read her articles at www.opentohope.com.

# Ten Ways to Comfort the Grieving Heart

By Kelly Buckley

*Sometimes I wish I were a little kid again.*
*Skinned knees are easier to fix than broken hearts.*

**—Author Unknown**

I've been thinking about all the different ways I have been comforted over the past eight months since my son Stephen died. I have been blessed and surrounded by so many people who envelop me with love and protect my healing heart. Every day I am reminded that I am not alone. And with each reminder, I feel Stephen's love. It is as if his essence has been dispersed across the globe, and different people give me a little piece of him when I need it the most.

That being said, I want to share my Top 10 list of simple things that you can do if you are comforting someone who is grieving. Based on my own experience, these are the things that have helped me the most. I will approach the list like Dave Letterman and start at Number 10, but unfortunately, I have no drumroll. So, as you read each one, tap on your desk and make your own.

## 10. Understand the power of a handwritten note.

There is something about seeing someone's cursive writing in ink on paper, sent via snail mail. It says, "You matter enough and are worth the extra effort." I have been deeply touched by e-mails, even text messages. But a handwritten note is a tangible piece of comfort.

## 9. Validation is not just for parking passes.

When someone hurts from the pain of grief, she needs to feel that the pain is being validated, recognized. For me, I needed to feel that Stephen's life had impacted others as much as it had changed me. It was so important for me to hear from others, who validated my feelings of loss, shared their own, and, in so many words, told me, "Yes, he was as special as you thought he was." If you are comforting someone, don't hold back. Tell him or her how this person impacted your life.

## 8. Don't wait for an invitation to help.

In the early days, I wore a pair of lead boots and a lead sweater, and I had rocks in my pocket. It was physically difficult to move because of the pain. The heartache, the hurt, had taken its toll. But I was blessed because I had friends, neighbors, and family who simply showed up. They did not wait for an invitation or a request for help. They just rang the doorbell and handed me a casserole dish, or flowers or a card, or gave me a hug. If you know someone who is hurting, jump in, ring the doorbell, and let him know he is not alone.

## 7. Check in with them on key dates and occasions.

Christmas, Valentine's Day, birthdays, and so many more. Key dates serve as milestones for people who are grieving. I call it the year of "firsts"—the milestones of time that serve as further confirmation of the finality of death, in a physical sense. I can't sugarcoat it; they are not easy. On December 26, I laid in my bed staring at the ceiling, thinking, *Whew, thank God we made it through that one.* Check in on key occasions and milestones, and recognize them. Understand, especially in the year of "firsts," that these days can be so lonely and painful.

## 6. Lasting memorials.

Memories endure, but the details fade with time. The impact of a life can be articulated clearly in the immediate days and weeks following the death of someone special. But then ten years pass and people move on and stop talking about him, and you are left to remember his spirit quietly, within your own family circle. I know this because I have grieved the loss of my parents and understand the passage of time changes things. That is why lasting memorials mean so much. I was humbled by how Stephen was remembered. North Carolina State Hockey retired his jersey, and the team and the Carolina Hurricanes changed the name of a yearly tournament from the Canes Cup to the Stephen Russell Memorial Tournament. And in a sense, my book is also a lasting memorial to his life.

But no matter how you do it, a lasting memorial can be such a source of comfort for those who grieve. It serves as a confirmation of their loved one's contribution to the community, what he loved, who he was. Think about ways to create lasting memorials—scholarships, donations, writing. A life lived is one worth remembering.

## 5. Don't be afraid to be honest with them if they need some extra help.

There are so many terrific resources that help people every single day with their journey through grief. If you feel your friend or family member needs some extra support, don't be afraid to make the suggestion. Encourage participation in groups such as the Open to Hope Foundation and the Compassionate Friends. And, if needed, suggest they find a "grief lady" of their very own. Sometimes the perspective and wisdom of a professional can make all the difference in processing the painful emotions of loss.

## 4. Invisibility is for the movies, not grief.

OK, I must stand on my soapbox for a minute because this one really affected me in my own personal journey. Two things happened with regards to "invisibility." First, some people could not face me. So they didn't. They ran for the hills. They did not know what to say, so they felt it was best to stay away. I understand; it is hard. But I am still here, and I still need you as a friend—now more than ever. Second, some people abruptly just stopped talking about Stephen, as if he had never even existed. We would be having a conversation, and it was obvious that they were fumbling over their words, trying to find a way to talk to me without mentioning the fact that I ever had a son named Stephen.

*News Flash:* I need you to feel comfortable talking about him, because he is still my son and I am still his mother. Trust me, it hurts more when you avoid the subject and don't recognize that he is still part of who I am. He may be in heaven, but he is still part of me. If you are comforting someone, please recognize the person who died and the loved ones left behind.

## 3. Understand that loss and grief continue after the funeral.

The casserole dishes have been returned, the flowers have wilted, and life's routines have resumed. Work, parenting, chores, fun—all seems normal, right? But the hurt continues, privately and quietly. As I mentioned, those special days can trigger a pain that returns you to the early days of loss. Remember this as you comfort someone. She may look fine, laugh, and be on time for that meeting, but within her chest sits a broken heart that is still mending. Be mindful of that fact and be the kind of person who treats a friend with extra care as she heals.

## 2. Talk less, listen more.

When something bad happens to someone you care about, you want to find the perfect words of comfort to make it all better. But the truth is, there are no words that will make this better. Your words of love and support can comfort and ease the pain, but no words will be able to take it away. I see grief as a journey, and with each painful step the load lessens, as if you were dropping pebbles from your pocket on each bend in the trail. So don't get caught up with trying to find the right words. Keep it simple. Say things like, "I'm so sorry, I'm here for you," or "If you need to just talk, I am a phone call away."

As the saying goes, you have two ears and one mouth, so listen twice as much as you speak. Because when someone is grieving, she needs to talk through her feelings. Be there to listen, and stop worrying about the right words.

## 1. Love, love, love.

I wrote my book on gratitude because people loved me. I made a choice to find the good in the worst of situations. And do you know what I found? When I looked for the good, I found it all around me. By opening my heart to it, I was able to let it into my life. People, in simple and quiet ways, loved me. Some knew me, and some were strangers. But they just loved me. They showed me that there is more good in this world than bad, no matter what the evening news tells you.

And the more love I let into my life, the closer I felt to Stephen's spirit. If someone you know is hurting, give her a little taste of love today. Show her that love is all around her, and make her feel less alone on her grief journey. Today, I am thankful for all the people in my life who showed me comfort in all the right ways and who loved me harder than I thought possible. They showed me that life is still beautiful, even in loss.

---

As a Canadian healthcare executive, Kelly Buckley witnessed others journey through loss. But nothing prepared her for the unexpected death of her twenty-three-year-old son, Stephen. She found solace in daily gratitude, even in the pain of loss. She wrote about this life-changing journey and her son in her first book, *Gratitude in Grief*. She lives in Charlotte, North Carolina, with her husband, Brady, and son Brendan. Find more at www.opentohope.com.

# Listen Closely—It's the Sound of Someone Healing

### By Catherine Tidd

I always thought that going through a profound loss would make someone an expert on loss. I mean, we always work with what we know, right?

You would think after experiencing the death of my husband that I would be one of those people who knew what to say when someone else was going through something similar. That I would have some magical words of comfort. That I would finally know the secret handshake that gets you into the National Grievers Society and thereby bestows upon you everything you need to know about healing others. That I wouldn't be as stupid as some of the people I have encountered during my meandering walk through the Grief Canyon.

Yup, you'd think.

But because of the experience I've been through, it makes me more self-conscious than ever that I'm going to say the wrong thing. If there's one thing I know by now, it's that what one person finds comforting will make another person want to smack you. So, most of the time, I just try and keep my trap shut.

Earlier this summer (Father's Day weekend, to be exact), I got a double helping of grief. After jollying my kids through Father's Day, I came home to a memorial service going on next door, because my very sweet neighbor had passed away a few weeks earlier. He went into a doctor's appointment on a Tuesday and was diagnosed with cancer, and by the next Tuesday he was gone.

We were all shocked, to say the least.

Anyway, I always think it's important, when it comes to this sort of thing, to just show up. Growing up, my parents explained to me that nothing is more important at a funeral than a butt in every chair. Meaning: Even if you didn't know the departed very well, show up. Fill the church. Crowd the house. Nothing makes us feel better than knowing that hundreds of people thought so much of our loved one that they decided to come over and pop open a beer with us.

I don't know, that could be a Southern thing. There's really nothing we like better than a good funeral. That's where you usually find the best food.

After my exhausting Father's Day with the kids, I trudged over to my neighbor's house for (hopefully) a quick glass of wine and what I hoped would be a short but meaningful hug. And in my attempt to keep my foot out of my mouth (so that I could drink more wine), I started asking my neighbor questions about how she and her husband met, how long they'd been married—general things like that.

And then something interesting happened.

My neighbor's face suddenly lit up (as much as it can when you're fighting against the riptide of grief) as she told me their story. She talked on and on about meeting him in college and how crazy and fun he was. She shared stories about raising their kids and talked about the relationships they had with everyone in the room. After a while, she asked me to go with her to watch a slideshow that someone had put together of their life. As I followed her into the living room, the most obvious thing hit me.

We all just want to tell our story. She just wanted to talk.

Not about his illness. Not about what had happened. But about the life they had built together. And about a person who would never be forgotten.

In everyone's attempt to "say the right thing" in times of grief, they're ignoring a very simple fact that would save everyone a lot of aggravation.

They don't have to talk at all.

They just have to ask one simple question about the person who is gone. And listen.

I realized that the most healing time I had after my husband was gone was just sitting around with friends while they asked me questions about us and our life together. Even in my darkest hour, I enjoyed strolling down Memory Lane with anyone who would take the time to listen. Don't we all? I *love* it when people ask me how I met my husband. I love it when they look at pictures of me in my younger and more attractive days and ask what we were doing then. I love it when they ask me if all my kids were fathered by my husband. (Yes, someone really asked me that question. And if you had ever seen my husband and my kids together in a picture, you would never wonder. They're all little clones.)

This realization has been such an "aha" moment for me: That listening has more healing powers than saying something that you think is comforting while making the other person feel like she'd rather be walking barefoot on glass than listen to me.

It's probably something that everyone else has known for years, but I'm always a little behind on the grief learning curve. So the best thing you can do is smile politely, nod your head, and listen to me ramble about this latest lesson I've learned.

Because it will just make me feel better.

---

Catherine Tidd is a widow and the founder of a free social support network dedicated to anyone who has lost a significant other. She is also a writer, a public speaker, and the mother to three entertaining young children. She earned her English degree from Rollins College in 1998 and lives in Denver, Colorado. To read more of her work, visit www.opentohope.com.

# We're Strengthened When We Say, "I'm Here"

By Tony Falzano

I recently attended calling hours to support a close friend who had suddenly lost her cousin to cancer. When I arrived, I joined the end of the receiving line and proceeded to view a television monitor, which displayed a memorial of the deceased.

After a short while, the line turned into the large viewing room. It was then that I noticed a young woman sitting toward the back of the room by herself. I watched as she slowly bowed her head and started to cry. Then she searched her pockets for a tissue. Just when she realized she had none, an older woman walked over and sat beside her. "Here, Jamie," I heard the woman say as she offered a handful of tissues.

They spoke for a moment and then Jamie started to sob. The older woman put her arm around Jamie, who buried her head in the woman's shoulder and released her feelings. I heard the woman say two words to her: "I'm here."

I turned slightly so as not to stare. I had certainly seen someone cry on another's shoulder in the past, but this time was different. I learned something from watching these two women.

The older woman's words, "I'm here," were showing me a benefit to crying that I hadn't seen until that moment.

Though there's a taboo or stigma that crying shows signs of weakness, that it's embarrassing and draws attention, there are benefits to it. Weeping counters grief's often raw, deep, cutting pain. Crying is normal and therapeutic. Crying stabilizes and should be welcomed. Like a volcano that waits to erupt, the body often waits to let go of the emotional energy that has built up during a time of grief. We surrender tears in an effort to surrender the pain, tension, and bottled-up feelings. We also let go of stress and toxins when we release tears.

Furthermore, the body goes from an electrified and energized state to one of calm and relaxation. Breathing returns to normal, the heart rate slows down, and the body becomes quieter. And it proves that old saying—you *do* feel better after a good cry. It's one of the best things we can do when we are upset.

But what I realized that day by watching these two women was that crying not only has benefits for the person who's shedding the tears—it also has benefits for the person who is consoling. The older woman was taking a position of strength. She acted as the caregiver and, in that moment of Jamie's helplessness, she was the one who could be leaned on. That's important, because at some point we all want to be of service in these circumstances. This woman was able to fulfill that role, and I could see she was doing so with honor.

The two sat there in a conversation that used no words but said plenty. One person said, "I'm out of control." The other answered, "I'm in control and will take care of you. You are important." One said, "I need to let go and be submissive now." The other stated, "I am strong for you and think nothing less of you." Finally, "I feel nothing but pain." The ultimate response, "I feel strong and capable of carrying you to the other side of this time."

Crying brings people together and allows relationships to deepen. A bond forms between letting go and holding on. It's in these moments that crying makes all of us feel better. The act of crying gives the person who cries an opportunity to let go, because someone else will be there to catch her. And the "catchers" are there with arms open wide, honored to serve in a time of need.

When someone is grieving, we often will say, "Let me know if I can do anything for you." When someone lets out his tears and feelings within our arms, we answer that call. It's not a pleasant time, but what an honor it is to keep vigil with someone who is temporarily out of control and out of hope.

I reflected more on what I witnessed while working my way to the family at the end of the line. Eventually, I reached my friend. Upon seeing me, she said how glad she was that I was there. She threw her arms around me and her tears started flowing a little harder. There was silence as she held onto me, quietly weeping. As we embraced, I simply responded, "I'm here."

---

Tony Falzano writes about the healing power of music. His articles can be found in many major grief publications. Tony also writes music that is listened to by individuals grieving loss. His albums, *Just a Touch Away* and *In Abba's Arms*, contain beautifully orchestrated, instrumental music designed to be a companion to those searching for healing and hope. Find more on www.opentohope.com.

# Six Questions to Prepare You for "How Are You Doing?"

## By Sharon Greenlee, MS

It's been more than six months since my husband died, and people still ask: "How are you doing?"

If you've lost a loved one, you're familiar with that question. I wonder how you've responded. Do you really tell them, or do you offer a polite cliché? I found myself practicing various responses so as to not be caught off guard and either melt into a pile of tears or sound stoic and cold in my efforts to stay together.

As a counselor in private practice I have worked with many grieving clients, and I have worked through my own prior grief losses. It isn't easy! It *is* work, and it takes time, tears, patience, and self-care to experience and try to understand the emotions that surround a grievous loss.

In my case, it means putting myself in the "client chair" (figuratively speaking), as I ask myself six questions. They're the same questions I ask clients, whose answers help me assess their progress. As I journal my own responses, I'm able to do the same gentle assessment on myself.

If you are in grief recovery, you may find solace and greater self-understanding as you answer these questions. If you answer "yes" to questions one through four or "no" to five through six, you may want to journal your responses and share these thoughts with a trained grief professional.

1. Do you find it difficult to find peace and acceptance with the circumstances surrounding the person's death?

2. Is there something that needs forgiving, or is there still unfinished business between you and the one who died?

3. Do you have unmet needs that feel insurmountable?

4. Are you unable to find your own sense of identity as a result of your loved one not being with you?

5. Compare your previous reactions to loss and disappointments with your recent loss. Are you within the range of what you would call "healthy-normal" for you?

6. Describe either the optimism or the pessimism that you are feeling in your belief that you will eventually find peace of mind after this loss. Are you mostly optimistic in spite of your current pain?

None of us will be able to avoid the well-intended "How are you doing?" We can either keep practicing responses and use a cliché or discover our grief truth for ourselves. Who would have guessed it might require answering six questions in order to answer one?

As a licensed counselor, author, and consultant, Sharon Greenlee works in staff development and grief after-care for hospital staff, schools, funeral directors, hospice staff, and caregivers. She facilitates bereavement groups and has worked with cancer patients, suicide survivors, and bereaved children and their terminally ill mothers. Sharon has written *When Someone Dies* and grief-related articles. She has a private counseling practice in Fort Collins, Colorado. Read her articles at www.opentohope.com.

# Calming the Emotional Storm

## The Hard Work of Dying
### By Stan Goldberg, PhD

Imagine that you're preparing for a thirty-day trip to a foreign country and you're limited to taking only what can be carried in a backpack. Your decisions on what to take or leave behind will determine the quality of your experience. Too many items and the weight will be burdensome. Not enough of the right ones and you might be forced to neglect some basic needs.

We make decisions of this type daily. We take what's important, leave behind what isn't. But we tend to be oblivious to the importance of these decisions for possibly the most momentous journey of our lives—our death.

As a bedside hospice volunteer in the San Francisco Bay Area for the past seven years, I've found that the ideas and emotions people carry with them through life often determine the quality of their death. During one visit, a patient named Joyce leaned back in her chair and softly said, "You know, dying is such hard work."

For two months her physical condition had been steadily declining, and I assumed she was referring to her pulmonary problems. She paused, then said, "I'm not talking about what's happening to my body." Pointing to her head, she continued, "The hard work is what's happening up here."

Although specific end-of-life issues were as numerous as the number of people I served, the type of "hard work" expressed by Joyce and others mostly fell into four categories: the difficulty of simplifying the present, forgiving the thoughtlessness of others, wanting desperately to be forgiven, and letting go of the dreams that would never be fulfilled.

## Simplifying

Many of my patients experienced a stimulus overload as they got closer to dying. For example, the CEO of a multinational company had difficulty deciding what he would have for breakfast. A professor who had spent his life analyzing language had problems following simple conversations. A carpenter who built houses couldn't complete easy manual tasks. For patients with dementia or other neurological problems, the difficulties were clearly organically based. But for many others, I believe the hard work of dying involved an information-processing problem: too many issues and not enough time to come to terms with them.

For many, their decision to limit the number of people who could visit was helpful, although often misunderstood by relatives and loved ones. For others, cutting back or eliminating lifelong interests reduced the overload. And for some, not talking about highly emotional issues was effective.

Anne, a well-known poet, chose a unique way of simplifying her life: she gave herself a going-away party. She invited friends to her hospice facility. After they all told her how knowing her had changed their lives, Anne called each person individually to her side. In a whisper she said something and then gave each person a poem on a sheet of paper. When all were given away, she turned calmly to everyone and softly said, "Now, I'm ready to die." When Anne described the party to me, I asked if she could recite one of her poems. With a smile she said, "I can't. I don't own them anymore."

## Offering Forgiveness

The pain people experienced from their past often followed them into their deaths. I had been visiting Marie weekly for five months. Every visit began and ended with the story of her co-workers' cruelty, spoken with a freshness you'd expect from a recent event, rather than something that had occurred more than fifty years earlier. Until she went into a coma, Marie regularly repeated the story in detail and painfully relived the emotions it generated. For her and many others, the inability to forgive the unskillful acts and words of others made the time leading up to their deaths emotionally difficult. But for some people, such as Ned, it never was too late to forgive.

I started visiting Ned almost every day after he expressed a fear of dying alone and asked me to be with him when it happened. Sometimes my visits lasted only a few minutes when he was heavily medicated but still showed no signs of actively dying. At other times I stayed for hours as he alternated between rambling and lucid thoughts. His AIDS-related dementia began rapidly increasing after three weeks.

"Carl, I'm so glad you came," Ned said to me, with his head still on the pillow. I could see that his eyes weren't focusing and I had no idea who Carl was.

"It's me, Ned. It's Stan."

"I thought you wouldn't come back."

"I told you I would."

"I know it's been hard on you," he said barely above a whisper.

"No, I enjoy coming to visit you."

"You were right telling me to leave."

"Ned, it's me, Stan."

"I shouldn't have asked you to take me in. I didn't have the right to ask anything of you. A father shouldn't do that to his son."

I didn't know what to say as he waited for me to respond. I knew continuing to insist I wasn't his son wouldn't make any sense. Given his level of delusion, I didn't think he would believe me. It appeared that he needed his son right there, next to him. I asked myself if I should become part of his delusion; if ethically I had the right to do that. I also was concerned, in the unlikelihood that his son or wife would visit, how they would react to someone impersonating Carl. Or what if friends came and Ned told them about a visit from a son he hadn't spoken to in years? There obviously wasn't time to ask anyone's advice.

"It was all right what you did, Dad," I said.

"No, it wasn't. I haven't seen you or your mom in fifteen years and here I am, asking you for a place to stay. Asking you to care for me. You were right telling me to get out of your life."

As I struggled to find my next words, his eyes seemed to focus, and he said, "I forgive you."

Then, just as quickly as the delusion began, it ended in a peaceful look as he drifted off to sleep. I didn't know the effect of my decision until the day of his death. When I entered his room, a woman was crying as she sat by his side. I could tell by Ned's breathing and fixed gaze that he was in a coma and actively dying. She introduced herself as a friend and said that Ned had been lucid for a few minutes in the morning and told her that his son had visited him. "Then," she said, "he just smiled and peacefully lost consciousness."

## Asking for Forgiveness

Jean had abandoned her children and husband when her daughters were teenagers, twenty years before I met her. Now, dying of emphysema, the only thing she wanted was her daughters' forgiveness. However, despite knowing she was dying, they had refused to see or talk to her. I suggested we write a forgiveness letter. Jean agreed, on the condition that "They get it after I die." For three weeks, she dictated and I wrote. After many starts and stops and numerous crumpled sheets of paper, we finally had something she felt good about. All her hard work was contained in two sentences. "Please forgive me. I love you." It was enough to give her some peace before she died.

## Unfulfilled Dreams

Fortunately, not all dreams go unfulfilled. Sometimes completing a simple thing can provide immense comfort, as it did for Vince. He was seventeen, a high school senior with cystic fibrosis, and had more unfulfilled dreams than he had memories. Vince, his family, and all his caretakers knew that he wouldn't live long enough to attend graduation, so his mother and his school's principal arranged for a "pre-graduation" graduation at the hospice.

Vince, propped up in bed, breathing through an oxygen mask and dressed in full regalia, was presented his diploma by the principal as a small group of us applauded and cried. That one simple event may not seem significant in comparison with the sheer number of dreams that wouldn't be fulfilled. But I think his memory of it—which was supplemented by a photograph posted next to his bed—made his death easier two weeks later.

## Don't Wait

From my hospice friends I've learned much about living and dying. In serving them, I've come to believe that the baggage I'll tote with me to my death will determine its complexity and quality. I've seen what happens when you wait too long to simplify. When you forget to luxuriate in the present moment. When you don't forgive the thoughtlessness of others. And when you're too afraid to ask for forgiveness.

From my friends, I've learned the importance of doing all of these on a daily basis. Nothing profound, just simple routine things like appreciating every moment I'm alive. Telling my family and friends that I love them. Expressing gratitude for even the smallest kindness shown to me. Being accepting of the unskillful words and actions of others. And asking for forgiveness when I screw up, which still happens more then I would like.

Stan Goldberg is a Professor Emeritus of communicative disorders at San Francisco State University. Stan has published ten books and numerous articles, and he presents workshops around the world. He is currently working on a book that focuses on how helping loved ones die can reduce grief. His latest book is *Lessons for the Living: Stories of Forgiveness, Gratitude, and Courage at the End of Life*. Read his articles at www.opentohope.com.

# He Was More Than the Way He Died

### By Debra Reagan

"My son died of a drug overdose." This is one of the most difficult sentences I have ever spoken in my life. Every time I opened my mouth to speak these words, my throat felt as though it were closing. I wanted to be truthful about his death in the hope that someone else could benefit from this tragedy. I also felt I owed it to family members to be honest with myself and with others. Oh, but the pain was so deep and heavy.

There were times when I privately wished the cause of death had been different. I imagined another cause would not have had the same level of shame and guilt attached. I wondered if perhaps I would not have felt the same level of isolation if the cause had been different.

I now believe that no matter the cause of death, the pain of losing a child is basically the same for all parents. With this in mind, I believe we each must learn to process the factors that make our loss unique.

Five years before Clint's death, we battled the challenges and struggles that come along with mental illness and drug addiction. Our lives were turned upside down by chaos and confusion. Soon after my son's death, it seemed I could only recall every argument we had ever experienced. The tapes continued to play in my head, each time focusing on a decision I now questioned.

These thoughts added to my pain. Weeks grew into months, and I continued to view myself as the worst mother on earth. I couldn't remember anything positive I had ever done. I had heard that talking and sharing were an important part of the healing process. Yet I held all these thoughts inside. I was so ashamed; how could I share these feelings with anyone?

I remember rejecting my first positive memory. Then I realized how unfair I was being with myself. From that moment forward, when a negative memory came to mind, I forced myself to recall a positive memory from our history as mother and child.

Soon I began to accept the truth: We had shared far more wonderful memories than negative ones. And most of all, even during the difficult times, we were being a typical family responding typically to a stressful situation. Slowly, I began to understand that each of us had done the best we could with what we knew and understood at the time. It was unfair to judge myself with any new information I had gathered after his death.

Eventually, I found my voice along with a level of peace. I no longer feel the same anger and guilt. I know that had Clint lived and matured, we would have worked past our struggles. Now it is up to me to work past these for both of us. I am learning that with time and healing, I can honor all my feelings. Drugs are no longer in the forefront of the memories of my precious son. My son's life was more than the way he died.

D ebra Reagan's son Clint died in 2005 at the age of twenty of an accidental overdose and bronchial pneumonia. She is cofounder and president of Listening Hearts, a non-profit organization designed to help bereaved mothers. She lives in east Tennessee with her husband of thirty years. They have one surviving son, Blake. Read her articles at www. opentohope.com.

# Say Good-bye to Guilt

## By Doris Jeanette, PsyD

Family members frequently feel guilt when someone dies. Mothers feel especially responsible for their children. No matter what the rational reason for the death, they feel as if it is their fault. And children can sometimes carry guilt into their adult years, thinking they had something to do with the death of a loved one.

Guilt is one of the worst experiences known to humans. It ties you up in knots and makes you feel unworthy and miserable. Guilt is the result of thinking that you have done something wrong. The reason you think this way is because you judge yourself, or someone else judges you, as "wrong" or "bad."

When you "feel guilty," you are pulled in different directions at the same time, with no resolution possible. There is no way out of guilt's sticky, stale energy. You feel as if you have committed a "sin" and you need to be punished. Guilt is awful. It is a losing battle, an inner conflict where no matter what you do, you feel bad.

When you look at the emotional energy dynamics of guilt, you can clearly see that it is a lose-lose situation. So, as soon as you realize you feel guilt, you want to move out of it. It is not helping you, and it does not help anyone else.

You may be surprised to learn that guilt is not a real feeling. Psychologically speaking, "feeling guilty" is a conditioned response, not an authentic feeling. This means you learned to experience guilt; you were not born with it! You were taught to feel bad and thus guilty when someone judged you. This is how you learned to judge yourself.

Never make your life's decisions based on guilt. If you have done something you really regret, apologize for it and stop doing it. Take responsibility for your behavior in all situations and notice how different this healthy behavior is from guilt.

For example, if for some reason you had some real responsibility for a person's death, you can take responsibility for the facts instead of punishing yourself forever in the pit of despair. Outside professionals can give you realistic feedback so you come to terms with reality. The act of taking responsibility allows you to do what you can to correct the situation and move on.

So how do you rid yourself of guilt? Become conscious of the difference between an authentic feeling and a conditioned response. With awareness, you can learn how to sense the sticky lose-lose energy of guilt and say good-bye to it.

Once you recognize guilt, you want to move out of guilt as soon as possible and find ways to win and move forward. One of the best ways to feel better is to forgive yourself or others. Cease the judgment that you or anyone else is wrong. Once you do this, you will be able to let go and feel your authentic emotions and feelings so that you can heal your heart.

Be aware that making anyone else "wrong" has the same effect as making yourself wrong. How you relate to others is how you relate to yourself. This means if you make someone else wrong, you are making yourself wrong. This is why you feel so miserable.

You will feel relief from guilt the moment you stop judging anyone as wrong. Forgiveness is really nothing more than giving up your own judgment.

Say good-bye to guilt and say hello to feelings, healing, and a more loving future.

---

Doris Jeanette, PsyD, is a licensed psychologist with thirty-five years of experience healing broken hearts. As director of the Center for New Psychology and founder of a website where she mentors and trains people in holistic psychology, she invites you to subscribe to her free newsletter "The Vibrant Moment," which inspires thousands every week. Find her articles at www.opentohope.com.

# The Healing Power of Forgiveness
By Mary Zemites

When we suffer the death of someone we love, we experience mental, emotional, and physical distress. In this fragile state, it is likely that we will feel resentment, indignation, or anger. Sometimes these feelings may be the result of a perceived offense or difference with someone we know—even, perhaps, with our deceased loved one.

During the final stages of my husband's illness and after his death, I remember being surprised at the support and kindness of many people, some of whom I hardly knew. I was also surprised by the absence of support and inappropriate remarks made by family and friends. One family member told me with great urgency that my children didn't stand a chance. Her claim was that children of single parents are "always problems and in trouble."

Other comments, such as, "It's a blessing that his suffering is over," seemed flippant. Didn't they know that any young father would gladly suffer in order to watch his children grow up? Everyone who suffers a loss experiences similar situations.

When we think of forgiving others, it may seem an impossible task in our distressed state of mind. We think, "I'm angry. I'm hurt. I'm offended. Why should I have to forgive? I'm the injured party!"

It takes great effort and strength to forgive. We are tired and emotionally spent. It is easier to push grudges out of our consciousness or to nurture them into anger in order to focus our emotional energy. The problem with avoiding forgiveness is that it is detrimental to our healing.

It has been my life experience that what goes around, comes around. I know I have made countless blunders in my life—conscious and unconscious—and I always have the expectation of being forgiven. So it is only right that I should forgive others. But that doesn't make the task any easier.

It may be surprising to learn that we can benefit greatly from forgiving others. In fact, we benefit far more than those we forgive. Studies show that people who forgive are happier and healthier than those who hold resentments. This information is not new. The ancient Buddhist religion views forgiveness as a practice to prevent harmful thoughts from causing havoc on one's mental well-being. Buddhism recognizes that feelings of ill will leave a lasting effect on our karma. And Judeo-Christian philosophy places great importance on forgiveness as a path to redemption.

Forgiveness is a vital step in the healing we need to recover from the loss of someone we love. The Christian ethicist and theologian Lewis B. Smedes wrote, "If you've been hurt, do you deserve to go on hurting? Or do you deserve to be healed?" So, the question of forgiveness is whether we and our future are worth it. I think we are. And this makes forgiving easier.

As we begin the process of forgiveness, we should be conscious of these common misconceptions:

Forgiveness will make us feel better right away. (In reality, making the decision to forgive will be only the beginning of a slow but ultimately satisfying process.)

Forgiveness will only make the other person feel better. (The forgiven person often doesn't even feel the need to be forgiven or know he or she has hurt you.)

In order to forgive, we must tell the other person. (As above, the forgiven person often doesn't know or care to be forgiven.)

To forgive means to forget. (We may never forget the actions that we have forgiven.)

A clergyman once spoke about the difficulty of forgiveness by citing a personal example. After being grievously wronged, he felt the urge to run his car over the perpetrator. As he worked to find forgiveness, he imagined lightly braking, then braking completely, and even stopping and waving. As he reached true forgiveness, he could imagine stopping and even offering the person a ride.

While this example might be comical, it illustrates how we must work on the process of letting go of our anger. Forgiveness is a process. It does not happen instantaneously. It is a journey of the heart.

We must internalize these truths as we deal with forgiveness:

- Forgiveness involves the mind, emotion, and will.
- Forgiveness requires a conscious conviction or need to forgive for our own benefit.
- Forgiveness attempts to understand the other person.
- We must desire to forgive.
- We must choose to forgive.

If we keep in mind that it is ourselves who will reap the

greatest rewards of forgiveness, we can find the strength to take these steps. And these steps will move us forward on our journey of healing.

---

Mary Zemites's husband, Greg Jarczyk, died in 1992, leaving her with three young children, ages four to ten. This and subsequent family deaths inspired her to earn a master's degree from Arizona State University and reach out to those with loss. In 2009 she founded a sympathy gift and grief resource website. Find her articles at www.opentohope.com.

# Nine Steps to Self-Forgiveness
## By Fred Luskin, PhD

The process of forgiveness can be a liberating experience, one that if practiced proactively can lead to a wonderful quality of life. But as challenging as it may be to forgive another person, sometimes the hardest person to forgive is yourself.

You have the gift of choice. You can forgive or not forgive yourself or someone else, and no one can stop you. This ability to forgive is a powerful manifestation of the personal control we each have over our own lives. What is critical to remember is the importance of exercising that choice to forgive so that you can bring peace and healing to yourself and your relationships.

1. Know exactly how you feel about what you did. Be able to articulate the specific wrong you have committed and the harm it caused. Tell a couple of trusted people about your experience and your feelings.

2. Understand forgiveness. Forgiveness enables you to feel at peace even though you did things you wished you had not. You do not have to reconcile with the person you have hurt and what you did may not be OK. Still you can make peace with yourself.

3. Self-forgiveness can be defined as the recognition that everyone, including yourself, makes mistakes, that blame and shame can be replaced by making amends and developing better ways to behave, and that your grievance story can be changed and relinquished.

4. Recognize that your primary distress is coming from the hurt feelings, thoughts, and physical upset you are experiencing right now, not what you did two minutes or ten years ago.

5. At the moment that you feel upset, practice stress management by breathing slowly into and out of your belly while focusing on someone you love.

6. Give up demanding things from yourself or your life that did not happen. Recognize the "unenforceable" rules you have for how you should have behaved. Remind yourself that every single human being makes mistakes. Remind yourself that no one is a failure: Each of us is only someone who was unable to do something correctly at a particular place and time.

7. If you have hurt others or yourself, instead of mentally replaying the hurt, look for ways to sincerely apologize, make amends where possible, and when necessary change your behaviors so you won't make the same mistake again.

8. Appreciate your good points. Take time out of each day to acknowledge the kind and loving things you do.

9. Change your grievance story of failure and regret to reflect your heroic choice to learn, grow, and forgive yourself.

---

D r. Fred Luskin is the bereaved parent of twenty-year-old Anna. He holds a PhD in counseling and health psychology from Stanford University. He is a Senior Fellow at the Stanford Center on Conflict and Negotiation, speaks at conferences across the country, and has published two best-selling books on the topic of grief. Dr. Luskin is on the Board of Directors of the Open to Hope Foundation. Read more at www.opentohope.com.

# Young Widow Overcomes Her Death Wish

By Michele Neff Hernandez

It is an odd and frightening sensation to wish you were dead. After my husband died, I fervently wished I could die, too. The first time I read that grieving people sometimes fantasize about death, I was relieved. My entire life I had appreciated the gift of life; to suddenly and frequently wish it away was a disconcerting and lonely experience.

When my husband, Phil, was hit by a car, the initial shock provided a buffer to the complicated emotions that would gather to haunt me in the days and months to come. As the buffer of shock wore off, I was struck daily by the realization that Phil wasn't coming home. It felt like the movie *Groundhog Day*. Every day I woke up with the expectation that the day would somehow go differently, and I would discover that Phil wasn't really gone. Day by day, the reality of his death ate away at my desire to live.

There is a difference between wishing to be dead and being suicidal. My death wish did not come from a desire to stop living. It didn't even come from a desire to stop hurting, though the pain was so intense at times I hoped it would kill me. My death wish came from a desire to be with Phil again. His physical absence was like a phantom pain in a limb that was no longer attached.

My death wish became a part of my daydreams. Jogging up a street, I would mentally challenge cars to run me over. On a plane I would imagine a fiery crash that I didn't survive. Hiking in the mountains, I looked for wild animals that might want to make a meal of me. Driving alone in the car, I visualized my car flying over any ledge I passed. Every brush with imagined death was followed by the disappointing result of still being alive—continuing to jog down the street, landing as expected at my destination, a safe return from hiking adventures, and no crash over the nearest ledge. The longing I felt to be with him was a constant ache; the only cure I could imagine was joining him wherever he was.

As time marched on, the call to live gradually grew stronger. In the early part of my grieving, I desperately held on to two reasons to live: my kids needed me, and our family and friends would be so sad if I were gone, too. All my reasons for wanting to live were about someone else; if it were up to me . . . beam me up, Lord! There was not one personal reason that I could think of to continue living.

But healing has a way of sneaking up on you. Eventually, I recognized that my husband lived his life fully every moment. He had an awareness of the value of life that influenced his daily choices. Reflecting on how he lived his life reminded me of the gift that life is, and he became a role model for me.

As I have begun the process of creating a life for myself without him, I have had to find reasons to live that are my own. I want to be a mother to my children. I want to make a difference in my community. I want to weave my husband's spirit into the fabric of the person I am becoming. I want to bask in the joy of being in love again. I want to experience the adventure that life still holds for me.

The woman my husband married died with him. Grief has changed me, but I am proud of the woman who is emerging from the ashes of loss. Life is a gift to me in a way it never was before. The nuisances of life don't bother me as much as they once did. Age-old adages such as "take time to smell the roses" actually mean something to me now.

The world can't be the same place it was two years ago, because Phil isn't in it. Somehow that comforts me. What I am learning is that though many things around me are radically different, I can still be a whole, happy, grateful person. Ironically, my death wish has become a steely will to truly live. Phil would be glad to hear that.

---

Michele Neff Hernandez's husband died in 2005. Since then, she has reached out to other widowed people as the founder and executive director of the Soaring Spirits Loss Foundation, which provides peer-based grief support programming worldwide. Michele is the creator of the Camp Widow program, a motivational speaker, a freelance writer, and the proud mom to three amazing kids. Read her articles at www.opentohope.com.

# How to Release Regret
## By Irene Kendig

Recently, I was talking with a man who'd been caring for his dying father. "I left him to take care of some personal business," he said. "I knew I shouldn't have gone because something inside told me not to go, but I didn't listen. My father died while I was gone."

Regret.

The word originates from Old French—*regreter*, which means "bewail (the dead); feel sad, repentant, or disappointed over something that has happened or been done, especially a loss or missed opportunity."

"If only I'd been a better sister, brother, wife, husband, mother, father, daughter, son, friend...."

"If only I'd said *a*, *b*, or *c*."

"If only I hadn't said *a*, *b*, or *c*."

Get the picture?

Take a moment to think about something you regret, something you didn't do that you think you should have. Choose something meaningful, something with substance. Get a clear image or sense of it. Now tune in to your thoughts. What do you tell yourself about it? Say it out loud. Don't read on until you've said it out loud, because I want to point something out. OK, now please tune into your feelings: How do your thoughts make you feel?

As you thought about the regret, did you notice that your mind automatically assumed things would have turned out better if you'd done whatever it was you didn't do?

We assume an untruth when we're in the throes of regret. We assume that what we regret—the thing we should have done but didn't—would have turned out better than the actual outcome. But how can we possibly know that with certainty? We can't.

Next time you catch yourself in regret, remember that you're making a huge assumption. Truth be told, you don't know how things would have turned out. Our minds, however, tend to idealize what isn't in lieu of what is. "If only . . . " is the accompanying refrain.

Here are some conscious assumptions/affirmations that I make, which you may find helpful, as well:

+ **Life is occurring in divine order regardless of my judgments about it:** Facilitates me in owning and releasing my judgments so that I can embrace what is.

+ **I am free to perceive that everything that happens is ultimately for my highest good:** Allows me to view the glass not just as half-full, but as always full.

+ **We're 100 percent responsible for our own experience:** Provides me with the power to cease blaming and change.

+ **Every event provides an opportunity to grow spiritually:** Facilitates me in looking for and discovering value and growth in the most challenging of circumstances.

Our feelings are generated by our thoughts, and our thoughts are generated by our beliefs. If you want to feel differently, you have to think differently, and in order to think differently, you have to challenge and change your beliefs. Releasing what no longer serves you—assumptions, limiting beliefs, conditioned patterns, misinterpretations, and judgments—allows you to grow spiritually.

And guess what? When you change within, life has a way of showing up differently. Outer experience is a reflection of inner reality. Now, I'm not advocating that you shouldn't grieve when a loved one transitions. On the contrary, if you're present to sadness, give yourself permission to cry all of your tears. But living with regret is unnecessary suffering.

I began this article by sharing a story about a man who'd been caring for his dying father. I could hear the regret and guilt in the way his voice lowered and trailed off. Can you see how regret was showing up in the way I just described? In his mind, things would have turned out better if he'd been there when his father transitioned. In his mind, that's how it should have happened. But, I ask you, how can we possibly know that with certainty?

"It was wrong of me to have left. I should have been there for him."

"Let's take this out of the arena of right or wrong," I said. "From a spiritual perspective, we can't judge it because we don't know. What if, on some level—and for the highest good of all concerned—you and your dad agreed that his passing would play out this way? What might your soul want you to learn from the experience?"

He paused. "I guess my soul would want me to learn to listen to myself."

"What a beautiful gift your father's given you. Would you be willing to accept it, receive it, and be thankful for it? If I were a gambling person, I'd bet that's what he'd want for you."

"But he died alone."

"I have a friend who was by herself when she transitioned. She told me, through a medium, that it was precisely the way she wanted it. She didn't want to share the experience with anyone in physical form. Would you be willing to consider the possibility that it was how your father may have wanted it, too?"

"That never occurred to me."

"And although we all make the transition from physical to spiritual on our own, are we ever really alone? I don't think so."

The session continued a bit longer, but can you feel the energy start to free up? The next time you find yourself deep in regret, remember to question your assumptions. No matter what you've done—or haven't—you are lovable and worthy . . . and all is well.

---

Irene Kendig is the national award-winning author of *Conversations with Jerry and Other People I Thought Were Dead: Seven Compelling Dialogues That Will Transform the Way You Think about Dying and Living.* An accomplished speaker, workshop facilitator, and self-acceptance coach, she assists clients in identifying the judgments, misconceptions, and limiting beliefs that are the source of unnecessary suffering and facilitates healing through compassionate self-forgiveness. Find more at www.opentohope.com.

# The Gift
## By John Pete

When we lose a loved one, we are confronted with a life-changing event that forces us to accept that our lives will never be the same again. As a grief counselor and someone who has experienced my own profound losses, I have read all the textbooks and witnessed the common stages of denial, anger and guilt, bargaining, and depression, as well as the slow journey to true acceptance.

There is no other experience in life like losing a loved one. And during a time of volatile emotions, it is easy to be hurt and angered by those who do not understand what you are going through. However, there is another perspective to consider when experiencing these feelings, one that can bring you peace and healing.

Rather than directing anger at those around you who are trying to help but are saying all the wrong things, or at those friends who have faded from your life altogether simply because they do not know what to say, direct your anger where it can help you. It is OK to be angry that loved ones are suddenly gone and never coming back. And it's OK to be angry that you are left to pick up the shattered remnants of your life and then are expected to somehow magically piece them back together and move forward. However, directing anger at the people around you will not help you.

Instead, consider telling these people, in person or in writing, how you feel and what they can do to support you, then move on. This will allow you to direct your energy where it belongs—on your situation. And this in turn will help you to focus on working through your feelings and seeking the answers that will help you to cope and understand what your loss means to your life, which will lead you to a path of healing.

You may be feeling anger that you are soon expected to smile again and to heal from something you cannot imagine ever recovering from. And yet, we can truly be thankful for every single moment we had with our loved ones and reaffirm to ourselves that most of us would do it all again, even knowing the outcome. Renowned grief coach Aurora Winter says that this revelation was a turning point in her own healing, following the loss of her young husband.

There truly is a spiritual gift to be found within the insurmountable pain of loss, although it is a gift that is often difficult to accept. Consider that love has no boundaries in life or beyond, and we can never fully measure the depths of the bonds of love unless we know what it is to lose it. And when we look beyond the confines of this life, we realize that life is temporal, and so is the pain that it brings. However, love stays with us forever.

---

John Pete is a certified grief counselor and founder of a grief website he started in 2006 in response to a need for an online community providing peer-support for coping and healing following loss. He is currently developing a series of grief-related courses and frequently blogs about grief, spirituality, and healing. Read his articles and find out more at www.opentohope.com.

# PART II

I Wasn't Ready to Lose You

# Losing Your Child

---

## Dawn to Dusk: One Father's Marathon Love
### By Nicole Alston, MSW

One can never be sure what to expect of Marathon Sunday's weather in New York City. For spectators that Sunday, November 5, 2006, the temperature was seasonably brisk. But for the runners, like my husband, Paul, and his running mates, the weather was perfect. Although this would be Paul's second marathon, this event marked the first organized fund-raiser for the Skye Foundation and the first marathon for Team Skye. The team was comprised of a special group of fathers recruited by what I would describe as divine serendipity, as their lives had been either touched or directly impacted by black infant death.

After months of training, Paul and the team left for the start in Staten Island at dawn. I said a prayer for the team, praying for protection and strength, especially for Paul, whose knee had never been the same after a freak accident on the basketball court a few years earlier. The cheering squad of family and friends left later that morning. We dispersed ourselves throughout New York City, at different points on the race's course.

At mile eight, it seemed as if Paul and Team Skye were progressing through the course almost effortlessly. I, along with my mother-in-law, my sister, and her husband, headed uptown to mile twenty-one. But it would be several hours before I would see Paul again, a lot longer than I had anticipated. Most of Team Skye had passed mile twenty-one, but there was still no sign of Paul. Even with my slowest estimate, I thought Paul should have reached mile twenty-one by now.

Finally, my mother-in-law yelled, "There he is!" And then, through the sea of runners, we saw him. Paul was limping terribly; his pained look made it clear that he was in agony. He stopped to tell us that his knee had given out at mile fourteen, his legs were hard to move, and he had been limping for the last seven miles.

Knowing Paul's proclivity to finish what he starts, I figured that it would be a long shot, but I had to say it anyway: "Babe, really, you can stop if you want. You have absolutely nothing to prove; you are already my hero." His mom agreed, "That's right, you're my hero, too."

Paul responded to my invitation without words; with a quiet and steely determination, he limped away from the sidelines to rejoin the race. I started walking with him.

As we walked the last five miles of the marathon together, Paul and I didn't say much. I can only remember him saying once, "Daddy's tired. Daddy's really tired," and I knew that he was focused on Skye, the foundation, and finishing the course. Paul later told me that he equated giving up the race to giving up on our daughter, which for him was non-negotiable.

Despite the thousands of runners and spectators around us, it seemed as if Paul and I were in our own private bubble. My thoughts about the last year seemed to drown out what was happening with the race. I thought about our own personal marathon and the complex grief experience that followed Skye's birth and death. I thought about how many times I had not completely understood the difference between Paul's style of grieving and my own.

My emotions after Skye's death were visible and intense, but had I interpreted this to mean that Paul was not as impacted by her death? With every step Paul took, I realized that although our expressions of grief may differ, it did not mean that Paul was affected any less by our baby's death than I was.

Only an enduring love for Skye kept Paul in the race. As dusk settled, Paul took his last steps of the marathon. I watched him with tears in my eyes and promised myself that one day I would share this story with fathers worldwide.

Family, friends, and Team Skye runners were reunited at the finish line, celebrating the team's accomplishment. And in the midst of the celebration, I could almost imagine our one-year-old Skye cheering wildly for her amazing father.

---

Nicole Alston's firstborn daughter, Skye, was stillborn in 2005, leading her to establish The Skye Foundation in her honor. Nicole has spoken to audiences internationally and serves on various state and national boards, focusing on improving birth outcomes and providing compassionate care to families experiencing reproductive loss. She received her master's degree in social work from Columbia University. Read more at www.opentohope.com.

# The Death of a Grandchild Is a Double Loss

## By Sherry Van Pelt

April 11 was my second-born grandson's birthday. Conner would have been sixteen this year. Oh, the fun age. The sixteenth birthday, to me, is when you no longer feel like you are a child but are not quite an adult. You aren't quite sure where to go with those feelings you have inside you. Also, the child changes physically.

But I will never get to see those changes in my grandson. As a matter of fact, I never got to share any birthdays with him, as he was stillborn. To this day, we do not know what happened, but he stopped breathing shortly before he was born. No reason was ever given.

I can still feel the pain of the horrific chain of events that day. As a grandparent, I wasn't sure what to do first. Where is there a handbook written on what to do when your grandchild dies? You are in such grief and complete shock yourself when you are given the news of the death of the baby—your grandbaby!

I remember sitting on the edge of the bed completely stunned at first, thinking this can't be happening. Michelle's pregnancy was so normal; what went wrong?

The medical staff had taken my daughter into the operating room to do an emergency C-section, and when the doctor came out to give us the unbelievable news, I wrapped my arms around my son-in-law, David, and sobbed with him. Later, we went together to see Conner in his bassinet and just wept. The pain in my heart was so deep as I watched his daddy hold him; he shook with grief.

Suddenly, my mind whirled as I thought: What do I do now? And what do I tell my daughter when she wakes up?

After a while, I called my husband and the other grandparents. While I sat and waited for my daughter to come back to her room, I prayed and prayed for God to give me the strength to help her through this. You see, a grandparent has the pain of losing a grandchild, and then there is also the enormous pain that you have for your own child. I don't know which hurts worse.

When Michelle came out, she and David cried like I've never seen anyone cry before. It tore me up inside. It took my breath away. I felt smothered. Then my daughter reached out to me and we hugged. She asked me, "Why?" Again, I had no answer. All I could do was hang onto her tight and give her my love and support.

On the day we lost Conner, I remember seeing all the people in the hospital walking around. Some were talking and laughing, others were having lunch in the café or leaving in their cars, and I just wanted to yell, "Hey, stop, I just lost my grandson! You need to stop and grieve with me! Can't you see I am hurting?!" But the world goes on around us.

The pain at times was overwhelming. I felt helpless. I wanted to fix the problem, but I couldn't. There are some things not even a parent can fix. But with my faith intact, I went forward and was there for my daughter at all times. I respected the times when she just needed to be alone, too.

But I also remembered to grieve for my grandson. You have to. You will go through many grieving steps, and you need to take each one as it comes. Your grief won't go away overnight, and don't let anyone try to tell you that it will, whether you are the parents or grandparents. Also, friends console the parents, as they should, but oftentimes they forget the grandparents are grieving tremendously. People forget that a grandparent grieves twice—once for the grandchild she lost and again for her own child who is hurting.

I wasn't upset with anyone. That's just the way it is. I am thankful I was raised to have strong faith in God, and that is what I relied on.

---

Sherry Van Pelt lost her best friend in an accident at age thirteen, and since there were no support groups for grief, she put her feelings and thoughts on paper to cope with her loss. Years later, when her grandson died, she again used writing to deal with the pain and wrote the book *Dear Conner, A Grandmother's Pain*. Two years later she lost a granddaughter. Read her articles at www.opentohope.com.

# Giving Up on Having It My Way
## By Jenny Hander

I knew I had turned the corner on grief the moment I lost it all, the moment I let my hopes, my dreams, my world fall apart.

For six months, I refused to accept that my infant twin daughter was gone. I couldn't see how life would be possible without her. I had always envisioned a grand way of living and was convinced that living an extraordinary life was no longer an option for me after my daughter's death. I felt I deserved something better, something more than a life of grief. So, as a woman of faith, I chose to believe that if I prayed hard enough, God might make it such that I would wake up one morning and realize her death had all been just a really bad dream.

For six months, I chose to fight my grief. I felt that if I truly accepted my daughter's death, grief would claim victory over my life, and that was a life to which I did not want to succumb.

But one day it all became too much. I was exhausted from battle. I couldn't find a way for my life to be great again, so I gave up my way—my wants, my hopes, my desires—and turned to the One who promises to make my life great in spite of my circumstances.

It happened in an instant. I woke up one morning too emotionally exhausted to look in the portable crib beside my bed to see if my twin daughter had returned. Instead, I walked to the opposite side of the house and fell to my knees in defeat. I surrendered all I had to the Creator.

Accepting that she was really gone—that her death was, in fact, meant for my life—was one of the hardest things I have ever done. It was also the moment I knew grief would not take victory over my life after all. Faith offers a life of hope. Since placing my faith in the plans God has for my life, I have been able to claim true victory over grief!

---

Author and speaker Jenny Hander seeks to enlighten and uplift audiences by exposing the truth of God's Word in light of hurt, disappointment, and loss. As a bereaved mother, Hander once deemed all hope for an extraordinary life gone. However, Hander's faith in God has since allowed her to discover a life more abundant than ever before. Hander is the author of *A Place of Peace* and resides in Texas. Find more at www.opentohome.com.

# The Burden Basket: Why Some Prayers Go Unanswered

By Judy Wolf

In the children's hospital in Salt Lake City, there is a small meditation room where one can have a quiet "heart-to-heart" talk with God. Families are encouraged to release worries about their children's health by writing a note to God and placing it in a Native American "burden basket." Periodically, the chaplain burns the notes, a symbolic letting go of one's burdens, turning them over to God.

In 2001, I became a devout member of the Burden Basket society when my oldest son, Joe, then thirteen, was hit by a car while crossing the street to accept a ride home from church. "God, whatever it takes, please save my child," I wrote. I was not above begging, pleading, negotiating, or making outlandish promises to seal the deal.

My prayers went unanswered. Or, more precisely, I did not get the answer I desperately sought.

Joe's body survived the accident, but he never recovered any meaningful function because of severe brain injury. He "lived" for three years, requiring total care twenty-four hours a day, ultimately dying of pneumonia. We tried everything to restore his consciousness—surgeries, therapies, drugs, stimulation, and even some alternative approaches. Still, we had no miracle . . . just a very surreal, quiet, long good-bye to our beloved son.

In the years since his death, I have revisited the mystery of the Burden Basket many times. Why are miracles granted to some and not to others? When a child's life is saved, families gush with gratitude and, at times, a prideful certainty that their prayers were the tipping point. Joe received hundreds of prayers from dozens of different faith communities. I don't begrudge another's miracle or their exuberance, but I would give anything, literally anything, to have Joe alive today.

After his death, I struggled to make sense of our prolonged and painful loss. I wrestled with "God, why?" in prayer and meditation. I poured out my heart, uncensored. After my sobbing subsided, I learned to listen deeply.

As an interfaith minister, I sometimes companion newly bereaved parents. I journey with them as they struggle to reconcile their loss even as I continue to wrestle with mine. I've come to learn that we all find solace in different ways. Some rely on a faith with a formal plan for salvation and reunion. Others come to accept life on life's terms, relying more on a philosophy than a theology. For still others, it remains an unanswerable mystery.

The question of "why?" no longer haunts me. What if the death of a child is something that just happens, despite our best efforts? What if it's not God deciding to save this one or that one? What if life, by design, is a risky proposition? Nobody is immune from illness, injury, disease, or death, no matter how loved, no matter how heavily prayed for, no matter how young or undeserving.

Life in a physical body is fragile, sacred, and precious. It is also "real time."

Joe's short life was his gift to us. If I dwell on his death, I miss the much larger gift of his life and consequently my own. I didn't die with Joe; I am still here. I hold his heart tenderly in my heart, the sweet memory of his life never far from my thoughts. Today is my precious gift. Today I choose to honor his life by living my own.

---

Judy Wolf's son Joe was struck by a car in 2001, sustaining a severe brain injury. He never regained consciousness but survived for three more years after the accident. To stay emotionally and spiritually afloat through the crisis, Judy enrolled in an interfaith seminary. She was ordained an interfaith (nondenominational) minister and serves families who are suffering the critical illness, injury, or death of a child. Read more at www.opentohope.com.

# Taking Action to Save Others
## By Candace Lightner

In 1980, I lived in a suburb of Sacramento with my three children, including my thirteen-year-old twins, Cari and Serena. One day, Cari and her friend Karla were on their way to a Catholic school carnival, which was right down the street from our house. Both girls were walking inside the bike lane when a car hit them from behind. Cari was thrown one hundred and twenty-five feet and left on the road to die while the driver kept going.

Several days later, the driver's wife, who was a very Christian woman, called the police and turned her husband in. Before he killed Cari, he had just been released from jail several hours earlier from another drunk-driving crash. He had totaled his car so he was using hers, and when he came home, she noticed the car had obviously been in another wreck. She asked a friend of hers, who was a California highway patrolman, if there had been any accidents over the weekend, and he replied that a thirteen-year-old child had been killed by a hit-and-run driver. She told him that her husband might have been responsible.

Now, you may be wondering why he was still driving, given that he had hit someone two days earlier. Unfortunately, that's the way the laws worked in 1980. They were just not enforced. It is hard to believe, but he was driving with a valid California driver's license even though, if I can remember, he had several prior drunk-driving arrests and convictions. Drunk driving wasn't taken seriously or treated as a crime. And that was one of the things that I set about to change, which I did. We've come a long way since then. Times have changed.

The day after Cari's funeral, I learned from a patrolman that the man who had killed my daughter had been drinking and had a rap sheet as a drunken driver. I asked, "How long will he get in prison?"

The cop kind of laughed. "Prison? Lady, you'll be lucky if he sees *any* jail time."

I was so angry I started Mothers Against Drunk Drivers, now Mothers Against Drunk Driving (MADD). And it worked. MADD just took off, and there was no stopping it. I was a crusader with a cause. I was angry for a long time and with good reason. Soon, I incorporated Cari's death and her life as part of my life, and it became one, so to speak—it's who I am and what I'm about.

I think the reason MADD became so successful was because I didn't know any better. People would say, "You can't do this," and I'd say, "Sure I can. Why not?" I had no concept. I was incredibly naïve. I felt the need to reach out, to save another life and not let this happen again. I wanted to save my other children.

But eventually I got burned out. I wasn't seeing my children because I was on the road seven days a week, twenty-four hours a day. Going to Washington to help get tougher federal legislation passed against drunk driving was a good way of dealing with my anger, but it probably was not the best way of dealing with my grief. So after five-and-a-half years with MADD, I left.

That's when I discovered that I had never fully grieved Cari's loss. I went to a wonderful therapist and realized that I had put the painful part of grieving Cari's death on hold, mainly because it was so painful. When I would run into people and I was obviously grieving, they'd say, "But it's been five-and-a-half years!" People confuse the list of Kübler-Ross's stages of dying with grieving over the death of a loved one. Everybody thinks you go through this at this time and that at that time, and that's not true. I think people need to just do what comes naturally.

I don't get angry at all anymore, but there are times even after thirty years when I still grieve and I'm still sad. In my opinion, grief comes in three stages—the beginning, the middle, and the rest of your life.

If I had to give a newly bereaved person one piece of advice it would be: Mourn. Grieve. Do what you need to do. Don't worry about whether it's normal or not, as long as you're not hurting yourself or someone else, and you can still function. Don't try to put it off. I know it's painful. Don't worry about crying in front of other people, and if you need help, ask for it.

---

Candace Lightner transformed a personal tragedy into a crusade against drunk driving. While walking down a quiet street, her thirteen-year-old daughter Cari was struck from behind and thrown one hundred and twenty-five feet in the air by a driver with numerous previous drunk-driving convictions. She founded Mothers Against Drunk Driving (MADD), a grassroots organization dedicated to curbing alcohol-related traffic deaths. Find out more at www.opentohope.com.

# When the Heavens Go Dark
By John French

*Out beyond the silence of eternal night,*
*within the void of voiceless echoes,*
*between the folds of dark and light.*
*In somber streams of starlight.*
*In the waves of ebb and flow.*
*Heaven exceeds eternal planes.*
*Though, it remains closer than we know.*

There was a time when the stars were a great source of inspiration and contentment for me. Their slow, predictable progression seemed to calm some of the anxiety brought on by a chaotic world. The incomprehensible distances and incalculable numbers were a humbling reminder of my insignificance, while at the same time, the vastness and complexity made me feel as if I were a part of something great.

It recently occurred to me that over the last six months, since my son's death, I have not acknowledged a single star, and even the moon has escaped my view—which, to be honest, doesn't surprise me, considering my mood has been steadily waning.

The death of my son not only decimated my world, it enveloped every aspect of my life.

My universe imploded the moment his heart ceased to beat. So now when the galaxy does cross my mind, it only perturbs me. It no longer exacts a sense of awe, nor does it bring me any peace. It only serves to remind me that the singularity of an individual is expounded by the gravity of death. And the loss of a child is beyond the scope of any conceivable horizon.

I can only describe it as a black hole of sorrow in which every emotion is compressed and compounded in the vacuum of grief. It is an inescapable vortex that drags me down and wears me thin.

I don't think anyone would dispute that our children are the center of our emotional cosmos. My world certainly revolved around my son. When that hope is extinguished, you live in perpetual oblivion where nothing sparks your interest or distracts you from your pain.

In some strange way, it's disheartening to see that the world is persevering and that the heavens are unchanged. It's so contrary to what we are going through. Even if the stellar array were suddenly extinguished, it would not compare to what we have already experienced. In fact, it might give us some comfort, because only something of that magnitude could begin to convey to others the horror and isolation that we are enduring on a daily basis.

But despite the fact that I am overwhelmed by the bleakness of my own encroaching future, I am compelled to make an attempt to turn the darkness into something we can all reflect on.

The lack of physical interaction does not detract from the effect that our children have on our lives. In fact, it enhances them greatly. Clearly, love is still the most powerful force in the universe. It transcends death and grows exponentially with each passing moment. The tears of loss refract the full spectrum of bliss, through which we can envision all that should have been. One day, we will look beyond the darkness and see that only such an intense source of joy could have brought such pain to light.

My love eclipses the sun in both mass and intensity.
It is not diminished in the evening,
nor does it rise at dawn.
It is infinitely brilliant and all encompassing.
It is so boundless that it defies the limits of comprehension
and exceeds all expectations.
It is so great that it envelops my every thought,
and surpasses means of measure.
Somehow, it overwhelms the void that your absence produces,
and diminishes the relevance of time.
It propels me through my bleakest moments,
and sets my mind adrift.
Even now, when my hope is exhausted
and my longing is unfathomable,
your effect on my life is undeniable and astounding,
awe-inspiring and incredibly influential.
You are the light of my life, I will forever delight in calling you
my son.

(A tribute to Brandon French,
5/24/92–8/16/09)

John French's son, Brandon, died at the age of seventeen in August of 2009 from an undiagnosed heart condition. Brandon's sudden death has inspired John to share his writing with the world, in the hope that something beneficial will stem from his mourning. John lives in Highland, Michigan, with his wife of twenty-one years, Michelle, and his daughter, Veronica. John's articles can be read at www.opentohope.com.

# Eighteen Years Later, Father Confronts Daughter's Killer

By Lew Cox

In October 2005, I attended a California State parole hearing for the slayer of my daughter, Carmon. She was twenty-two years old when she was murdered in 1987 in Los Angeles. The drive from Tacoma, Washington, to the Soledad Prison in central California was a philosophical time that gave me the chance to reflect on the ramifications this crime has had on my family.

The person who murdered Carmon was charged with first-degree murder after being at large for two weeks. In the winter of 1989, the District Attorney's office accepted a guilty plea of second-degree murder with a life sentence, with the possibility of parole after fifteen years of hard time.

This would be the first time that I would face Carmon's killer. When he was sentenced for his crime, I was not informed by the LA District Attorney's office that I had a right to attend the sentencing and give an impact statement. At this point, I wasn't sure what emotions I still had stuffed down that I had not dealt with.

## The Hearing

The purpose of a parole hearing is for a convicted felon to establish a realistic parole plan that proves to the Board of Prisons that the public would be safe if this person is released. The hearing opened with the following people present: two parole board commissioners, the inmate, his attorney, the DA, a prison–victim advocate, and me. There were two prison guards standing behind the offender at all times.

When the commissioner asked the inmate's attorney if his client was going to speak, he said yes. However, when the commissioner asked him to talk, the inmate responded by saying that he wasn't going to talk about the crime. He was told if he wasn't willing to talk about the murder, the hearing wouldn't go well for him. I believe he wasn't willing to talk about how and why he killed my daughter in front of me. Since he refused to speak about the crime, the commissioner could not proceed with the questions about the murder.

I was the last person to speak at the hearing after the Los Angeles County DA read a letter from the LA Police Department stating their reasons for not wanting this killer released. The DA then stated why his office did not want him released, as well.

## Impact Statement

I had been waiting eighteen years to give my impact statement. This was a surreal moment for me. I couldn't believe that I was actually sitting a few feet from my daughter's killer. I was about to find out what kind of emotions I still had stored up inside. As I gazed into his eyes, with my jaw quivering and my voice cracking, I spoke to him and the commissioner about the moment I received the call from my son that Carmon had been murdered. I talked about the father-daughter relationship we had, including teaching her to water-ski, drive a car, and fly an airplane.

## My Emotions

Halfway through my statement, my voice became paralyzed. I was saturated with emotions. Tears were rolling down my cheeks. I wasn't sure if I was going to be able to pull myself together and complete what I had to say. Then, I asked the Lord to give me the strength to continue. It took more than a minute for me to regain my composure and resume speaking. That minute seemed like an eternity.

I said, "We cannot change what has happened to Carmon. I am not Superman. I cannot turn back time. But my family and I are gravely concerned that if this man is ever paroled, he most likely will kill again if he is rejected by another woman."

We know that he was not high on drugs or alcohol the night he killed Carmon, because he didn't use them. He murdered her in pure rage and in a brutal fashion, by shooting her six times with a pistol. First, he shot her four times in the back. She was able to turn and fight for her life, and then he shot her two more times in the chest.

Finally, I told the commissioners, "We do not want another family to have to go through what the Cox family has had to endure because of his fatal actions." Then the commissioners broke to discuss their decision to grant or refuse him parole.

## The Decision

After a five-minute recess, the hearing resumed. The lead parole commissioner was very direct as he faced the inmate. He told him that parole was denied. Among many things, they believed that his crime had been committed with extreme cruelty, and he lacked sympathy for shooting and killing a young woman. He had expressed no remorse for his crime.

The commissioner asked him if Ms. Cox had attacked him. He said that she attacked him after he shot her, and the reason he shot her was because he was afraid that she might take the gun from him and shoot him. That statement did not go over very well with the commissioners. The hearing concluded and the commissioner set his next parole hearing in two years. It seems that I will have to deal with this man's parole hearings every two or three years for the rest of my life.

In January 2007, my two other daughters and I attended his third parole hearing. He was once again denied parole and was given an additional three years before he can petition for another hearing.

---

Lew Cox is a survivor of the 1987 murder of his twenty-two-year-old daughter, Carmon. He is founder and executive director of Violent Crime Victim Services in Tacoma, Washington, which provides direct services to co-victims of homicide. Lew is a Certified Trauma Service Specialist and a Certified Victim Advocate Specialist. He is the coauthor with Robert Baugher, PhD, of the book *Coping with Traumatic Grief: Homicide*. Read more at www.opentohope.com.

# Shadow of Grief Still Lurks Twenty Years Later

By Robert Thompson, MD

*Although we know that after a loss the acute state of mourning will subside, we also know we remain inconsolable and will never find a substitute. No matter what may fill the gap, even if it is filled completely, it nevertheless remains something else. And actually this is how it should be. It is the only way of perpetuating that love which we do not want to relinquish.*

**—Sigmund Freud**

This year marked a milestone regarding my son's death that I noted but did not celebrate. This was the year that Paul has been dead longer than he lived. To use an overused but nonetheless accurate word to describe my feelings, it felt "surreal."

Thinking about it further, I realize that the whole experience of my son's death was surreal. From the moment of the first phone call through the funeral, memorial service, and the dark days that followed, it all had an unnatural feeling.

The first year's goal was to function, and somehow we did that. But after that first year, we had to learn to live and love and laugh again, and those are harder tasks. It's hard to laugh when the vulture of death is sitting on your shoulder and harder to love when acute pain wells up in you at unexpected moments. Yet that is what we must do for our own sakes, the sakes of our partners, and truly for the good of everyone whose lives we touch. And most of all, we must do it for the child who has left us. And yet even now, we live in the shadow of our pain and awareness of our loss.

In a book first published in 1986, *Beyond Endurance: When a Child Dies*, Ronald J. Knapp describes six characteristics that parents who have suffered the loss of a child hold in common. His conclusions are not the result of theories formed in an academic vacuum, but rather research based on extended interviews with 155 families over a five-year period. In my opinion, it is still one of the most compassionate and best longitudinal studies of what parents experience after the death of a child, regardless of whether the death occurs suddenly and unexpectedly, or is the result of a prolonged illness or due to murder or suicide. One of the six characteristics is a term coined by Knapp, "shadow grief."

Shadow grief is a form of chronic grief. Knapp describes it as a painful awareness of the child's death that never goes completely away and that prevents us from fully experiencing the joys of living. While we function normally, shadow grief "is characterized by a dull ache in the background of one's feelings that remains fairly constant and . . . on certain occasions comes bubbling to the surface . . . always accompanied by a feeling of sadness . . . ."

By now, we have learned to choose those with whom we share stories of our child's life and perhaps the circumstances of his or her death. Such sharing on our part is not easily borne by everyone, so we pick and choose and sometimes move on to new friends. Our wish is not to burden others with our sadness. Yet the sadness engulfs us and affects who we are. Even if we are not defined by it, we are shaped by the grief and cannot run from it any more than we can run from our shadows.

Just as we can see our shadow better on some days than others, we are more aware of the shadow of our grief some days than others. On some days, it becomes very plain and bright, and at other times we say "good morning" to the grief and it recedes for the rest of the day. But the pain is always there, following us even if we and others can't see it. Shadow grief has become part of us and we of it.

Now, almost twenty years after my son's death, I embrace the shadow of my grief. Partly this is because it's there and I can no more deny it than I can deny my son's life, and partly because the pain serves to remind me of him and brings back memories that I find pleasant. I no longer care if others want to hear the story of my sorrow, and I don't feel any compulsion to share it unless there is genuine interest on their part. What once was important to me has become less so as I weave the tapestry of my own life. My son lives in my memory of him, and my grief shadow is his grief shadow, too. Grief over an uncompleted life snatched away in its prime.

Very recently, I was in the north woods just before sunrise, sitting on a stump and watching a brown creeper spiral down a large white pine tree. As the sun rose higher behind me, I watched my shadow lengthen on the ground. I thought about my son and the times we spent in the woods together, and the joys and humor that we shared with his brothers. Those memories, like my shadow, are always there and always comfort.

With apologies to the psalmist, "Yea, though I walk through the valley of the shadow of death" . . . I will live my life.

*This article was previously published in* Living with Loss *magazine, "Living in the Shadow" by Robert R. Thompson, MD, Spring Issue, by Bereavement Publications, Inc, in the Healing the Body, Mind & Spirit Column, 2009.*

---

D r. Robert R. Thompson's youngest son, Paul, was killed in a traffic accident in 1989 at the age of eighteen. After retiring from a long-acclaimed medical career in public service, Dr. Thompson decided he could help others who have lost children by describing the healing journey that he and his wife, Martha, took after Paul's death in his book, *Remembering: The Death of a Child*. Read more at www.opentohope.com.

# Valentine Poem from a Dad to His Beloved Girl

By Alan Pedersen

One day in early February of 2007, I was driving near my home in Denver, listening to a local talk radio show. One of the hosts was setting up a commercial for a flower company he represented by saying that his young daughter was now at an age when he was going to send her flowers for Valentine's Day.

As he talked glowingly and lovingly of his daughter and his excitement about sending her a beautiful bouquet of all different-colored roses, it got me thinking about my Ashley. I began to imagine how wonderful it would be if I could send her roses on Valentine's Day, as well.

Ashley was my only daughter; she died in 2001 and this year she would have been twenty-four years old. The pain of not being able to shower her with gifts came flooding back to me. I had been in a writing slump, but when I went home that evening I kept thinking about roses and Ashley and Valentine's Day. I wrote this poem that I am happy to share with you.

# A Dozen Roses

If I had a dozen roses, I know just what I'd do
I'd give each one a name that reminded me of you
The first rose I'd call sunshine, because you brighten every day
The second would be beauty, the kind that never goes away
The third rose would be priceless, like those
hugs you gave to me
I'd name the fourth rose silly, oh how funny you could be
Rose five of course is patience, something you
have helped me find
The sixth rose would be memories, the gift you left behind
The seventh and the eighth rose would for
sure be faith and grace
Nine would be unique because no one can take your place
The tenth rose, well that's easy, I'd simply name it love
Eleven would be angel, I know you're watching from above
I'd think about that twelfth rose, and I'd really take my time
After all these roses are for you, my Valentine
I'm sending them to heaven in every color that I know
So twelve I'll name forever, that's how long
I'll love you so.

---

Alan Pedersen's eighteen-year-old daughter, Ashley, was killed in an automobile accident in 2001. The tragedy led this award-winning singer/songwriter to write and record several CDs that share his message that grief and loss offer the opportunity for ordinary people to accomplish extraordinary things, and that healing begins when we give of ourselves. Alan plays his original music and speaks to grief organizations throughout the United States and Canada. Find more at www.opentohope.com.

# Losing Your Sibling

## A Survivor's Story: Aftermath of a Brother's Death
By Leigh Cunningham

Two a.m., Wednesday, March 17, 1979: a deathly knock on our front door disturbed our sleep and divided lives into two parts—before Paul and after Paul.

I was sixteen. Paul was two months past his seventeenth birthday. His driver's license was two months old, as was his motorbike. My mother had bought it for him for his birthday, with justified reluctance. But he was persistent, and who could resist his charms?

Two policemen delivered the news. My mother responded by rocking back and forth frenetically like an autistic child. My younger brother and I watched on, in horror and disbelief, feeling heavy with fear and despair as if the roof had collapsed upon us; in many ways, it had.

We went outside and walked the length of our street, arms around each other, no tears or words. It seemed symbolic that the rain should fall as it did—a soft, gentle rain that seemed to be saying good-bye—and it cast a beautiful yet somber shroud under the light from the street lamps as we strolled past.

I wondered about Paul's tall, lean frame splayed on the asphalt on that coast road, alone, with a steel rail piercing his chest—and ours. I wondered if, as his spirit ascended, he had stopped for just a second to glance back to see what he had done to us. And if he had stopped for that second, why didn't he turn around?

Surely, he could see the anguish and the broken lives scattered like autumn leaves, shriveled and colorless. A good-bye would have been nice, and perhaps an apology: "I'm sorry for what is to come, for the decades of unrelenting grief and regret. I'm sorry that lives will be destroyed because I am leaving you now. I'm sorry that the darkness of this morning will never pass, and that you will never forget to remember me, on birthdays and death days, when a motorbike passes or whenever you see a dark blue T-shirt."

And if Paul could have returned, just for a little while, to comfort John and assure him that he was not to blame—it was not their argument that had caused the crash, but an exploding tire—maybe then, John, our eldest brother, would still be with us. Time will continue to force us onwards, and days will come and go, until we get to that place—where the brothers are.

Leigh Cunningham's seventeen-year-old brother, Paul, was killed in 1979 on his motorbike. Her family imploded. Driven by the pain of loss and guilt, Leigh's eldest brother, John, embarked on a course of self-destruction and died a decade later. A lawyer by profession, Leigh wrote *The Glass Table* and its sequel *Shards* to help others who lose a sibling. She now lives in Singapore with her husband. Find more at www.opentohope.com.

# Remembering My Sister
# and My Best Friend
By Lyn Prashant, MA, CT, CMT

My beloved sister, Donna, was a gentle, loving, and caring soul. She was my trusted confidant, my witness, and my cheerleader. She died September 6, 2002, at age forty-nine.

Donna was born three-and-a-half years after me. She was there for me, I for her. We were giddy and vulnerable with each other. I remember walking down the street with her, holding her hand, and thinking about how lucky I was to have her as my very own sister. Our commitment and our sense of knowing one another were astounding. A glance into her eyes affirmed my joyous reality: she was both my sister and my best friend.

When Donna was thirty-six, she received the diagnosis of breast cancer. I had already lost my young husband to cancer, so the words sent shock waves through me again. Since the death of my husband, Mark, in 1984, I had embarked on a path of healing that involved making peace with my own grief. Stephen Levine, the respected author of *Who Dies?* states, "We can be available to others in their grief to the extent that we know our own." This was certainly a stunning way for me to assess how authentic I'd been in transforming my grief after the loss of my husband.

I remember feelings of disbelief at the sound and meaning of the doctor's words, the physical sensation of numbness and my inability to think clearly. Later, Donna looked into my eyes. "Lyn," she asked, "as my older sister, can you be my advocate? Please understand, I do not need you to be in charge of me. I need you to hear me and give me feedback."

She then added, "What I really need from you is to be responsible *to* me . . . not *for* me."

My jaw dropped. Her simple request imprinted forever in my mind and on my heart, and it has changed the way I see my own role as a friend, family member, and professional caregiver. How eloquent, how profound. "Yes Donna, I'll practice and do my best to learn to be that."

My professional work, Degriefing, is in truth an oxymoron. There is truly no way to do it! Degriefing is about normalizing and then using our grief as fuel. By engaging in verbal expression and then choosing specific activities (physical, emotional, mental, and spiritual), this work can assist each of us in making peace with our grief.

There is loss and suffering every day on this planet we call Earth. If we allow ourselves to tune into the pain of global grief, we see that loss and grief are a natural part of the human condition. We lose five minutes in traffic, we lose the sun at the end of the day, we lose our footing and, "Oops, I just lost my train of thought!"

Grief is the most available untapped emotional resource for personal transformation. I experience a sense of purpose and find meaning doing the Degriefing work in my sister Donna's honor. It keeps her alive in my heart as her love and wisdom guide me from within.

Donna, I am remembering your beautiful smile and, with deep appreciation, I thank you forever.

Your loving sister,
Lyn

---

Lyn Prashant, MA, CT, CMT, survived the loss of her sister, Donna, and her husband, Mark. She is the founder and training director of the process called Degriefing. Lyn is an internationally recognized bilingual professional grief counselor, engaging lecturer, published author, and therapeutic massage therapist/teacher specializing in transforming grief. She teaches the process at the Mayo Clinic, the University of California, and other institutions across the country. Read her articles at www.opentohope.com.

# Reminders of a Brother Who Rarely Saw the Sky

## By Elizabeth DeVita-Raeburn

A few years ago, I ended up at the American Folk Art Museum quite by accident. A friend was visiting from out of town and we'd intended to go to the newly reopened Museum of Modern Art, but the lines were insane. Next door at the AFAM, however, there were no lines at all, so we thought, what the heck? It's a great museum. But what very much caught my attention was an exhibit on prison art.

To be honest, I don't remember the details. But the idea of what these people were expressing—what it was like to live in captivity, in close quarters, without much hope of getting out—suddenly struck a nerve. My brother, in a sense, was a prisoner. He hadn't done anything wrong. His body, or rather his immune system, had. But the end result was the same: he ended up confined to a ten-foot-by-ten-foot isolation room for the rest of his life.

As a kid, I couldn't think my way into what it felt like to be Ted. And he'd been in there so long that it had become normal to me. It never occurred to me, or rarely, that it didn't necessarily feel normal to him. Plus, he was my invincible older brother, the master of every situation. The work in this exhibit revealed, painfully, that that probably was not the case. I wasn't sure I really wanted to know. It was painful.

I was reminded of it all again today, when I opened a book called *Seasons of Captivity: The Inner World of POWs*. A friend who knows I'm interested in the psychology of place recommended it. But what really struck me, even just in the introduction, was that I couldn't stop thinking about Ted. Here's one quote that did me in:

"This was the first time we got out, without our blindfolds, from the courtyard. An interesting thing happened: suddenly I discovered the horizon. Out there, on the edge of the desert, lay the infinite horizon. I felt dizzy." He loved, he said, to look up at the trees. "All these years I had seen nothing beyond the 18 meters of our room and courtyard; only the birds up in the sky."

It reminded me of the way my brother, during the few times he came out in the sterile spacesuit that allowed him to leave his hospital room, would stand and stare up at the trees. He loved, he said, to look up at the trees. Now I can appreciate better how wondrous that must have been for him. But it's a painful realization. Imagine it being a novelty, a luxury even, to look up and see the branches of a tree outlined against the sky.

---

Elizabeth DeVita-Raeburn's brother, Ted, suffered from a rare immune deficiency disorder and spent eight years in an isolation room behind a plastic curtain before he died. He was one of two boys upon whom the movie *The Boy in the Plastic Bubble* was based. Elizabeth is the author of *The Empty*

*Room: Losing a Brother or Sister at Any Age* and has published numerous articles. Find more at www.opentohope.com.

# Before and After

By Shirley Wiles-Dickinson

Have you ever noticed how when we lose a loved one, over time we measure events and time by before and after?

My son graduated from college before Dad died. My daughter graduated from college after Dad died. I often think how my life has changed, what is different now, after Dad died. Before Dad died, I talked to my mom a lot; after Dad died I talked to my mom even more. She needed me more. She always needed me, even before Dad died. It took his death to make me realize that.

Before and after are how we measure events and time.

When my sister was brutally murdered just over a year ago, the before and after took on a new role. Before my sister died, family was important to me. After she died, family is so very much more important. Before my sister died, I lived eight hundred miles away from my family. After she died, I made the decision to move back to my home state to be closer to all of them. Before my sister died, I thought I was taking measures to keep myself safe. After my sister died, I learned to take even more of those measures.

Before my sister died, I never thought about bad things happening to good people. After she died, I learned that bad things do and will continue to happen to good people. Before my sister died, I thought we had time to do everything that we had planned. After she died, I learned life can change in an instant.

The before and after with my sister's death has been so much more pronounced than with any other loss I've experienced. I don't measure when events happened by her death as much as I did when Dad died. Instead, I measure what I've learned about death and homicide.

Before her death, I thought I had experienced most of the ups and downs of life. After her death, I learned there were many experiences of life that I would rather not be forced to learn. Before my sister died, I didn't give a lot of thought to all we had shared together. After her death, I cherish those memories, I protect them, I hold onto them so tightly, knowing nothing can take those memories from me.

Like many other people, my life has become measured by before Sandy died and after Sandy died.

Would I like to return to the before? Of course, who wouldn't? However, we know we can't go back, only forward. So I continue into the after, one day at a time, sometimes one step at a time. My life has been forever changed, not before, but after.

---

Shirley Wiles-Dickinson's sister was brutally murdered in her home in 2009. As the youngest of four girls in a Midwestern family, Shirley writes about her experience following this loss. Read more of Shirley's articles at www.opentohope.com.

# Prescription Drug Addiction Leads to Brother's Death
## By Rod Colvin

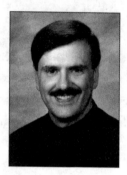

I wrapped my brother's birthday gift and left it on the kitchen table. As I headed to work, I pondered where to take Randy for dinner. The evening was to be a celebration. Not only was Randy turning thirty-five, he had just completed his college degree in business. But around noon, I got a telephone call at my office. It was a nurse from a nearby hospital, informing me that my brother had just been brought in by a rescue squad. He was in critical condition.

Terrified, I jumped in the car and sped toward the hospital. Minutes later, I was in the emergency room, frantically scanning the bays of beds looking for Randy, but I didn't see him anywhere.

Just then, a nurse approached me. "Are you Randy's brother?" she asked.

"Yes," I said.

"Let's step out into the hall," she said.

My heart sank. At that moment, I knew the worst had happened. "Is he dead?" I asked, not wanting to hear her response.

The nurse dropped her gaze and nodded.

Randy was gone.

The death of my brother—and only sibling—was one of the most profound losses of my life, but I must tell you, his early passing was not a total shock. For years, Randy had battled a prescription drug dependency that started at age twenty, when a psychiatrist first prescribed tranquilizers to help him cope with anxiety. The drugs made him feel good, so he started using them more and more. Over the years, he became very clever at obtaining Valium, Xanax, Percodan, Percocet, and other painkillers by using a common scam known as "doctor shopping."

My parents and I had long feared the toll this behavior was taking on him emotionally and physically. Repeatedly, we had pleaded with Randy to get help, but he always denied that he had a problem.

Still, at times he appeared to be leaving the drugs behind— he would be clearheaded and showed no signs of abusing drugs. He even enrolled in college. Each time we observed such positive changes, we thought he had beaten the problem.

In fact, just before he died, he had been drug-free for nearly a year. However, as I later pieced together the last hours of his life, I learned that he had relapsed. Prescription drugs mixed with alcohol, a dangerous combination, had contributed to Randy's death. He had gone into cardiac arrest at a friend's house.

My brother's long battle—and our family's agonizing battle—with prescription drug dependency was over. Sadly, we had lost. Randy died on October 19, 1988—his thirty-fifth birthday.

In the years since my brother died, I've healed from the acute pain, but I still feel the loss deeply. Left now with only memories, I'm especially grateful for an experience I had with him shortly before his death.

I'd had minor surgery, and Randy drove me home from the clinic. He fixed me a bite to eat and stayed close by while I napped. He seemed to enjoy being the caretaker, the role I was so used to playing with him. "It's so nice to have a brother," I said. He just smiled and patted me on the shoulder.

It's a memory I'll treasure always.

---

Rod Colvin's brother, Randy, died at age thirty-five as a result of his long-term addiction to prescription drugs. This experience prompted Rod to write *Overcoming Prescription Drug Addiction*, now in its third edition. In 2005, he served on an advisory panel for the National Center on Addiction and Substance Abuse (CASA), which conducted the nation's first landmark study on prescription drug abuse in America. Find more at www.opentohope.com.

# Losing Your Spouse

## Wife's Sudden Death Sends Man on a Faith Journey
### By Kyle Shelton

I've been living without my wife for seven months now. I've had to adjust to a great many things, but the most trying has been my struggle with my faith over that time. I've been angry with God, which has consumed me at times. I've been angry with Kathy for dying, and I've been angry with myself for being pathetic.

At first I was consumed by what I perceived as God's punishment of me. Why would he take the love of my life from me? Why did he not take me instead? Those questions made me doubt everything I'd ever been taught about God. I began to comb books on philosophy, theology, Jesus, even

*The Tibetan Book of the Dead.* I wanted answers and I wanted them now.

I wanted to know why, on December 3, 2009, my wife and I had had a wonderful day that ended in typical fashion. We lay in bed watching some TV to unwind. We talked about the play that would open the next day starring her eighth-grade drama students. She was so excited, and I was excited for her. I had built sets—the word "built" here is used as loosely as possible—for the production. I had helped at a rehearsal earlier in the evening. We had driven home joking and laughing and holding hands.

"I've got a big day tomorrow," she said. "I'm going to sleep now. I love you."

"I love you, too," I said. She patted my hand and rolled over to go to sleep.

A few minutes later I got up to go to the restroom and noticed something didn't look right about the way she was laying. Because I'm sometimes a little crazy, I took her pulse. It was wild and thin. She was not breathing.

I called 911. I started CPR. The next day she died without ever having regained consciousness.

In the days that followed, I felt betrayed by God. The emergency room doctor told me that Kathy had accidentally overdosed on a combination of prescription medications and a small amount of wine. The combination had caused her to stop breathing and also resulted in sudden liver failure.

While she told me these things, I wondered what I had done to deserve God's wrath. I also wondered how a merciful God could allow such pain and suffering. I wondered so much that I read *A Grief Observed* by C. S. Lewis almost immediately. I became obsessed with reading about faith and reading the

Bible, afraid that I would never see Kathy again if I couldn't make myself believe in God again.

What I found in all those hours of researching grief, God, and religions from across the world and from torturing myself with fear was a simple message: Everybody struggles with faith. Everybody has doubt. Everybody eventually loses someone they love.

With all those things decided, I looked at myself in the mirror. I allowed myself to be human and have flaws and accepted that I have the best kind of faith in God that there is. I have the kind of faith that keeps me seeking God almost every day.

From these months of searching I have also found something I wanted to share with those who read these words:

First, you have permission to be angry with God or the god of your understanding. You also have permission to be angry at the world. It is OK to question God, the person you've lost, even yourself. But at the end of it all, leave a little room for forgiveness.

Finally, I can say that I do believe in God, I am gaining acceptance of Kathy's death, and I'm not pathetic at all. I'm just grieving.

---

Kyle Shelton writes and teaches seventh grade in Pell City, Alabama. He was married to the late Kathy Shelton, a drama and literature teacher. He began his journalism career in 1994 as a sports stringer for *The Anniston Star* and a reporter for *The Birmingham Times*. He has two daughters, Gillian, twenty-nine, and Whitney, twenty-five, and two grandsons, Austin, twelve, and Gavin, nine. Read his articles at www.opentohope.com.

# I Miss My Reflection in His Eyes
## By Christine Thiele

Today I was driving, and the thought of someone I used to work with came to my mind. I couldn't think of his name. Who was that kid with glasses? Was it Dex or Dax?

Then, I thought: My husband would know. Yes, Dave would know. We worked together and have so many shared memories and experiences. That's what folks do when they fall in love and decide to spend their lives together. They share almost everything with each other. That's what we did.

Fifteen years together . . . same friends, same shared favorite places, music, etc., etc., etc.

I drove, I thought, then I cried. I miss Dave. I miss his goofy looks at me from across the room. I miss him laughing at my dumb jokes. I miss his smell. I miss his smile. I miss the me I saw through him. That's one of the things that comes to me as I think about building experiences, growing together, and sharing lives. I miss my reflection in his eyes. I miss the me that he saw and loved.

In that reflection was a knowing. Knowing that he was there to store and keep those memories—our own vault, so to speak. Now, I alone am the vault keeper. I hold the memories of our life together. I share the stories with the kids. There is still something so essential that's missing, though—being able to reflect, remember, and share that with someone who was there, with him.

Today, I not only grieve losing him, but I grieve losing a part of my life that I can never have back. We are all who we are because of what we've lived and whom we've loved. There's a big blank in my life, a big space that I can't share with anyone, because it was ours. That makes me sad, it makes me angry, and it makes me . . . well, it makes me, me.

So I guess I won't remember that kid's name from such a long time ago. I will, however, continue to remember that all those experiences with Dave made me the woman I am today. Maybe I won't have someone to laugh with about it, but I will still remember that time when the reflection I saw through another's eyes and heart made me feel loved, wanted, and alive.

---

Christine Thiele is a freelance writer. She has written for *The Journal of Student Ministries, Youth Worker Journal,* and *Grief Digest.* Since her husband's death, her writing is focused on grief and healing issues. Her blog, *Memoirs from Widow Island: A Journey toward Healing,* chronicles her life as a widow striving toward healing and hope. Along with her writing, Christine is raising two young sons. Read more at www.opentohope.com.

# "He Loved Those Slippers":
# Dealing with His Belongings
## By Beverly Chantalle McManus

The closet full of his shirts, ties, jackets, and slacks. His well-worn slippers next to his side of the bed. His wallet and eyeglasses. His razor and toothbrush. The tool chest in the garage. His harmonica collection and guitars. His treasured complete set of vintage Beatles imports on vinyl. All those science fiction books that fill half of our bookcases.

What do we do with all the "stuff" that belonged to our spouse who has died?

So many people stand ready to quickly offer glib advice: "Donate it all to charity." "Find a good home for each thing." "Just clear it away as soon as you can and move on." "Don't do anything with it for one year."

Just as the grief for each loss has its own pathway and timeline, so too does the answer to the question, "What am I going to do with his or her belongings?"

Dealing with Steve's belongings was really hard for me.

Immediately after his death, perhaps the most pressing for me was dealing with all of his "durable medical goods," including the hospital bed, the oxygen apparatus, the walker, the feeding tube, and all of the related items. These were dismal reminders that he was gone and not coming back, that all the treatments he so bravely underwent didn't work. Hospice had so kindly arranged to have all the stuff delivered, and it truly was a lifesaver during Steve's final days. However, after he died, it was left to me to figure out how to get it back. It took days of calling to get the supplier to pick them up, which they did. Except for the bed.

A week after he died, it was so depressing to see the hospital bed still in the den, despite all my calls to the supplier for pickup—so much so that my daughters and I hoisted it through the patio door and put it on our garden lawn. I then called the supplier and said, "I think it's supposed to rain tonight . . . you might want to arrange to get the bed picked up this afternoon." One hour later they were there.

Steve had been on heavy-duty medications, and we'd just received a full month's delivery shortly before he died. Some cost close to $600 per dose. I called the pharmacy to see if they wanted the unopened packages back, and they said they couldn't accept them. I was reluctant to throw away medications that might possibly be of use to someone else, and called several free medical clinics. Nobody was interested, and in the end, I tossed them.

The rest of Steve's things remained where they had been left for several months. The slippers sat next to the bed. His toothbrush nestled next to mine. I loved seeing his ties, so precisely arranged, in his closet. I think it all gave me hope: Maybe this was a bad dream, from which I'd soon awaken and find all right with the world again!

On a more pragmatic level, I honestly didn't have a clue

what to do with all his stuff. I felt guilty that I had let so much time lapse without even touching it. I just couldn't. One of my bereavement facilitators from the grief workshop I attended advised me that I'd know when to deal with it. "How?" I asked. Her answer was simple: "When you are ready, you'll be able to deal with it!"

She was right. About six months after Steve died, I realized I was beginning to be ready, but I still could not do it all at once. Every item seemed to be emotionally charged, like a ticking time bomb, just waiting to make me shatter into a long crying jag. One of my friends told me to try drinking a glass of wine prior to dealing with it, to relax. This wasn't my style. Instead my daughters blended me a frosty and potent strawberry daiquiri. Liquid courage? You bet! I needed all the help I could get!

I started with just his socks. I never realized one guy could own so many! He literally had three big drawers of socks, all organized according to color and type. I filled up a large Hefty bag and took them to the local thrift shop.

This was a big step for me. One thing that had been holding me back was the idea that I had to find the "perfect home" for each of Steve's belongings. I'd think, "Oh, my brother Ernest would love that jacket." "Bud would fit these pants." But given that train of thought, I just couldn't seem to part with anything.

Fortunately, an inspiration flashed into my mind: I didn't have to find the perfect owners; the new owners could find his stuff themselves, at the local thrift shop. This may seem pretty basic, but for those who are dealing with the broken heart of spouse loss, even basic decisions like these can be challenging!

After the socks, it became a little easier with each category I dealt with. I did the underwear next. Then his golf shirts. (I kept all his vintage rock & roll T-shirts from the concerts he'd attended, because our daughters wanted them as keepsakes.) One friend actually had her husband's golf shirts made into a patchwork quilt. Another found a person who transforms golf shirts into teddy bears and had one made for each of their children.

For some reason, I got highly emotional dealing with Steve's shoes—remembering his characteristic gait, how he'd dance, him running all over the tennis court, hiking in Yosemite, his wingtips running up the escalator to the train platform. Each time I tried to sort through all the shoes brought a downpour of tears, so I decided to save these until the end.

I've also kept his top left drawer, where he'd always stored his wallet and pocket stuff, intact. It's still nice to poke through the contents occasionally, savoring the feeling of his well-worn leather wallet, listening to the ticking of his wristwatch, trying on his eyeglasses. I also couldn't let go of his shaving kit. I loved the smell of his aftershave.

Now, years later, there are still many of Steve's belongings throughout the house. His vinyl record collection stands, intact, in the corner of the den. His tennis racket hangs on its peg in the garage, ready for friends who are making up a foursome. The tools have migrated from where he carefully stored them to their new homes, scattered around the house, as we've used them and neglected to follow his strict rules about rapidly returning them to their rightful place. (We chuckle, knowing he'd be flipping out now about this, were he here!) We've adopted his guitars and even took lessons so we could learn to play them! And Steve's hundreds of books still fill the bookcases, even though I doubt that I or our daughters will ever read most of them. Maybe someday I'll be able to deal with them.

How will I know when? When I can!

Beverly Chantalle McManus's forty-three-year-old husband, Steve, died in 2003 of esophageal cancer, and since then, she has been a bereavement facilitator and a frequent speaker and writer on the topic of loss and grief. She is a board member of the Open to Hope Foundation and lives in the San Francisco Bay Area with her two daughters. Read her articles at www. opentohope.com.

# Loss of Husband Makes
# Life Doubly Hard
By Christine Thiele

When you're a couple in a family, there are things that are no-brainers. Who will run to the grocery store, who will pick up the kids, who will help with the kids' outings and clubs? There are two of you. Together, you can divide and conquer.

When one of the two is dying, you can prepare for many things. But you can't prepare for the small stuff, the little daily things that together you handled, handled even joyfully: those little no-brainers.

There have been many days that would have been a no-brainer before my husband's death.

Just an example: Sam's Cub Scout den is having a bike ride on the local biking paths through the city parks. It will serve as a fulfillment for one of his little badges. It's a lovely day. It is a great day for a bike ride. For me, though, it is a stressful day. The bike path the den mothers chose is a good distance from my house. I cannot ride the distance on my bike and then complete the ride.

So all week, I thought about how I will get the bikes in my car. All week, I planned to try to fit the puzzle of bikes and boys into my wagon. All week, I avoided it. All week, I shoveled it to the back of my head.

Finally, today, I try to put the bikes in the car. They don't fit. No bike ride with the Cubbies. Disappointment is felt all around the house. Sam can't go. I've let him down again. We all just fester in our own pain.

If Dave were still alive, it would be a no-brainer. We'd throw the bikes in his truck (no Dave, no company truck anymore) and drive to the park, or we'd have two cars to drive; one for bikes, one for people. Or, even better, Dave would throw the bikes in his truck and take off with the boys while I'd get an afternoon of solitude!

Those days are gone. Sometimes, I just wish people could understand how huge this is. I never saw it before Dave died. No-brainers become failures and days that I am just so disappointed in myself. I get so mad that my spouse is gone, I can hardly see straight.

I'm sure there are thousands of other ways I could have handled this day. The fact still remains that on most days, my husband's death is still like an open wound.

I miss the magic of the way we worked together. I miss the ebb and flow, the give and take, the differences between us that made us such a good team. I miss the no-brainers.

---

Christine Thiele is a freelance writer. She has written for *The Journal of Student Ministries*, *Youth Worker Journal*, and *Grief Digest*. Since her husband's death, her writing is focused on grief and healing issues. Her blog, *Memoirs from Widow Island: A Journey toward Healing*, chronicles her life as a widow striving toward healing and hope. Along with her writing, Christine is raising two young sons. Read more at www.opentohope.com.

# My Life, Seven Years
# after Her Suicide
## By Abel Keogh

November 10 is a day that creeps up on me now.
It wasn't always this way.

In past years it was a day heavy with memories, emotions, and unanswered questions.

Now it's a day just like any other.

This year, it wasn't until after lunch that I looked at the calendar in my office and noted the date. Suddenly I realized what day it was. I pushed my laptop to the side and looked out the window at the green grass and sunshine. In seconds, the memory of hearing a gunshot from our bedroom and finding my late wife's lifeless body flashed through my mind, followed by a tinge of the raw terror that flowed through my body that afternoon.

But it lasted only a moment.

Then, just as fast, my mind flashed through the seven years of my life since that afternoon: Marrying Marathon Girl. The birth of two sons and a daughter. Buying a house. Having my first book published.

And I found myself smiling.

Smiling at the choices I made that put me on the path to a new life. Smiling at the thought that with this tragedy came a chance to become a better and stronger person. Smiling that I conquered grief, misery, and depression.

With happy thoughts in my mind, I returned to work.

After work, there were no side trips to the cemetery or participation in any kind of commemoration of my late wife's death. Instead I went home and ate dinner with the family, played with my kids, then helped put them to bed. I fixed a bathroom sink for Marathon Girl and wrote a chapter for my next novel before going to bed.

It was a busy day full of all the people and things that make up my new, happy life. I wouldn't have spent it any other way.

---

Abel Keogh's first wife died from suicide while expecting their first child. The story about her death and how he rebuilt his life is told in his memoir, *Room for Two*. He is also the author of the novel *The Third*. Abel works as a copywriter and has created marketing collateral for numerous organizations. He and his second wife, Julianna, are the parents of four children. Read more at www.opentohope.com.

# Can You Talk about Grief Too Much?

By Elaine Williams

Whitehen does talking about the loss of someone get to be too much? Is it still grief, or is it descending into depression?

Talking and writing about grief for me has been a catharsis, a way to heal my thoughts, emotions, and fears. It is a slow, sometimes excruciating process. Not linear, and sometimes unexpected.

At times there seems to be a fine line that can be crossed. I met a woman who had been widowed after six years of marriage. Nine years later, she still does not sleep in the bedroom she shared with her husband, nor can she bring herself to open a birthday gift she found after he passed away. She feels stuck in place but sees no way out.

We all have to be gentle and considerate of ourselves or others who are traveling through grief. But I have seen in my own grieving that sometimes we run the risk of being stuck in place. I met another widow who spoke incessantly about her husband. She refused to even consider the idea of going through his clothes or personal items, even after five years. She was adamant she would never date again, even though she also admitted her marriage had not been a happy one. Again, it is all about our personal choices. Our lives have formed how we handle stressful situations and circumstances.

The way we handle our grief and emotional outcomes is, of course, a personal choice, but I feel that some people allow their grief process to make them bitter. I know sometimes I've fallen into this myself. I consider it a trap to allow the hurts in my life to weigh me down. Well on my way to healing, I refuse to be consumed by anger and regret.

Grief is never easy or quick. It can be hard, painful, and unpredictable. If we stay rooted emotionally in the same place over many years, we're doing ourselves an injustice. Why not answer the door when opportunity for growth knocks?

There were many days in my grief process where I felt at a really low point, and sometimes, in my mind, I made my marriage out to be something more than what it was. I had a good marriage, but like any other relationship, it had its problems, too. After twenty years, not everything is rosy, and yet many times in the early days I viewed my marriage through rose-colored glasses. I glorified the good times and glossed over the days I wanted to pull my hair out with frustration.

My husband and I were two people who had grown through the years. I learned for my own benefit that I had to remain honest about my memories. Nothing is perfect. No one deserves or wants to be on a pedestal. By staying grounded in reality, I decided I would not be stuck in place. I firmly believe this thought process made my grief journey a little easier. I also knew my husband would never want me to stay perpetually unhappy. I have grown enough to know I deserve a full life once again, in whatever way I manifest. But I choose happiness over living in a past that cannot be changed.

---

Elaine Williams lost her husband, Joe, to cancer after twenty years of marriage, leaving her with three sons to raise. She has since been examining the effects of spouse loss and wrote about it in her book, *A Journey Well Taken: Life After Loss*. In addition to writing numerous fiction and poetry books, she is an entrepreneur and has launched several successful businesses and a publishing company, On Wings Press. Learn more at www.opentohope.com.

# Moving to the Middle of the Bed
## By Sandra Pesmen

Last night, I slept in the middle of our king-size bed. It took me two years to do that. For fifty-five years, I shared that bed with my husband.

He never walked on water. Sometimes we broke that cardinal rule and went to sleep angry. But far more often, we embraced that bed and each other with tremendous joy, grateful we'd found mates who showed love, kindness, consideration, and selflessness on an almost daily basis. How unusual is that?

So often people reach out their hands when they hear I'm a widow and say, "I'm so sorry for your loss."

"Thank you," I answer, "but I only had two years of loss. I had fifty-five years of gain."

I know that not everyone has my resiliency. I lead a widows' website, as well as several widows' clubs at local senior centers, and I give motivational talks to help people learn to "strive and thrive alone."

Too often, these people are so grief-stricken they find it hard to concentrate on anything except their sorrow. Their sadness has become the focus of their lives, and everything and everyone else is on the periphery.

I try and help them understand that life is not a dress rehearsal. We don't get to have a "do-over." Whatever time we do have left is meant to be spent enjoying, loving, helping, and caring for ourselves as well as others.

No one can hurry your grief or mine. No one can tell anyone else when it's time to pick up living and begin placing those loved ones who died into a beloved memory space. All day, every day, I think about my husband, silently telling him funny incidents and asking myself what he would decide when a problem arises. His photos are on his desk in the den, on our bedroom dresser, and in the living room. When I talk to our grown children and grandchildren, one of them usually says, "Oh, that's just what Dad (or Papa) would say."

He is with me always, and last night, after two years spent sleeping on my side of the bed, my husband's memory finally joined me in the middle.

---

Sandra Pesmen is a longtime journalist and a widow. She hosts a website for widows and also writes the weekly syndicated DR. JOB column for newspapers and the Internet. A member of The Chicago Journalism Hall of Fame and The University of Illinois Media Alumni Hall of Fame, she also is author of *DR. JOB's Complete Career Guide* and *Writing for the Media: Public Relations and the Press*. Find her articles at www.opentohope.com.

# Losing Your Parents

## The Last Bag of Clothes
### By Mary Bart

Mom died one year ago. When she died, we sorted through all her clothes and divided them into two categories. The first category was the clothes that I wanted to keep, either because I was going to wear them or because they had a special meaning for me.

The second group was the clothes that we planned to give away to people who needed them. My family members dropped off two of these bags at the secondhand clothing store. I promised that I would take the final bag and drop it off ... soon.

My plans changed. I could not part with the last bag of clothes. For the whole year, I kept that bag in my car trunk. There was no room for anything else. Every time I started to put something in the trunk I remembered the bag of clothes was still there. I needed to have those clothes close to me while I was on the road. It gave me comfort to know that her things were with me. I never felt guilty or silly for keeping them. It just seemed right.

Recently, I decided that one year was long enough. On the first anniversary of her death, I dropped off the bag of clothes, except for one item. I kept her terrycloth robe for use in my car. It keeps the sun off my legs while I drive and the seat cool when I am not in the car. I have found a way to move toward a less cluttered, less encumbered car and life. Keeping one piece of her clothing is enough. It is both practical and comforting.

Mom was a very practical person. Growing up through the Depression, she did not waste anything. I think that she would be pleased to know that other people are wearing her clothes now. I think she would also be pleased to know that I am learning and able to move on.

The lesson of my story is simple. Listen to your own heart about how to deal with grief, loss, and moving on. The only schedule that matters is the one that you discover for yourself. Don't let others tell you or make you feel guilty about when it is the right time to let go. Only you will know that, and when you do, everything will be fine.

As her parents' principal caregiver for ten years, Mary Bart has firsthand experience in helping aging parents, dealing with family dynamics, and working with public and private organizations. Her father died of cancer in 2005 and her mother died of Alzheimer's in 2008. Mary also chairs Losing Our

Parents, a registered Internet-based charity offering education and support to people who are coping with the declining health or death of a parent. Learn more at www.opentohope.com.

# Hearing the Voice of My Father
## By Sheena Matos

When I was fifteen years old, my daddy passed away of a massive heart attack. I was at school and got called to the office to hear the most horrifying news of my life on the telephone. The voice on the other end was his coworker; she told me he had collapsed while at work.

After falling to my knees, I broke into tears. I soon collected myself enough to call my momma and give her the news. Arriving at the hospital and seeing him on life support felt as if I were in a dream. How could this be reality? Shortly after we arrived and family began to gather, he died.

The part that hurts me the most is that I never got to say good-bye to him. The last memory I will ever have is getting into a stupid fight with him over not getting my way. Such silly teenage nonsense, thinking I knew it all.

At first I was a zombie; people would hug me and I felt nothing. I could not tell you whom I talked to, who came to visit, or what I ate. It was like I died along with him. Everything I saw, touched, or smelled reminded me of him. Finally, my mom decided it was time to move. For me, I had lost my heart, my soul, my world!

No matter where we went, it could not bring my daddy back to me. So many months passed, and I felt nothing. I was a shell, a living, breathing zombie. I had not cried since that day on the phone; I just existed.

After moving into a new house, the day finally came when I broke down. I could not possibly function anymore—the tears burst out of me and I ran into the woods to be alone. I was screaming. I suddenly stopped because the pain was so unbearable. Curled up in the fetal position, laying on dirt and leaves, surrounded by trees and sky, I gave up. I did not want to go on just existing anymore. I wanted to be with him.

It was at that moment, with my eyes closed, wet and full of tears, that I heard his voice. That single moment brought me back to life. I felt him right there with me. I heard his voice in my head. From that moment on, I knew I would be all right.

He said to me, "I am not dead. I am more alive now than I ever was in the flesh. I have not left you, my darling; I can be with you more now than I ever could before. So get up."

I jumped up, and my heart was beating wildly. Did I just hear my daddy's voice? I got down on my knees and prayed for the first time since it had happened. I prayed for forgiveness, to feel happiness again, to feel anything again. I prayed and prayed until the light began to fade.

The Lord gave me peace that day, and from that moment on, I was able to cope, I was able to think, I was slowly becoming myself again. After that day, it felt like a weight had been lifted. I could breathe easier and did not feel so depressed.

Nine years have gone by since that horrific day when I was called to the school office. I can proudly say I am happier now than I have ever been. I have a wonderful husband now and a beautiful two-year-old daughter who puts a smile on my face each day.

I'm not going to lie and say I am completely over losing my father because, the truth is, I miss him every day. When the anniversary of his death comes around each year, I become that fifteen-year-old girl again. That moment stays with me, and the pain I felt comes right back. I cannot let it go no matter how hard I try.

God has truly helped me deal with everyday life. I can sometimes go months without thinking of that day, but he is always on my mind. Any time my daughter does something that makes me smile, I wish my daddy could see it. Any time my husband buys me flowers or holds the door for me, I wish my daddy could say he was proud of the man I chose.

I wanted him to walk me down the aisle at my wedding, to hold his granddaughter the day she was born. Those are the times I miss him the most. But anytime I want to hold his hand again, I can just close my eyes, and he is always there.

---

Sheena Matos is a freelance writer who has been through a lot of pain and loss. Her father died when he was forty-six, and she had a miscarriage when she was eleven weeks pregnant. She is happily married and the mother of two beautiful daughters. She considers herself a "woman with a wounded heart who can help others know that they are not alone." Find more at www. opentohope.com.

# Turning the Corner on Mother's Death

By Gemini Adams, MNFSH

It took me a very long time to integrate the loss of my mother. Perhaps this was because she died so prematurely, at just forty-eight years old. She was still a young person in the eyes of many. As for me, at twenty-one, I was even younger. We had only just learned how to become friends, having battled through the highs and lows of my teenage years.

Just as we had come to see each other as allies, as women sharing similar challenges and interests, she was snatched away. It wasn't unexpected. Mom died from cancer, and her death was a long, drawn-out affair that took two-and-a-half years, despite the fact that when she was diagnosed, she was given only three months to live.

After her death, the journey through grief was difficult. There were plenty of misty days, thunderstorms, and moments when the car slid down the road, revealing a sheer cliff-face that had me frozen in a state of fear. But after a couple of years, the bad weather cleared, blue skies burst through the monotonous gray, and there were occasional interludes of sunbeams: small, but nonetheless brilliant. Here are a few of the poignant ones:

- When I realized I had heard the word "Mom" without my chest being flooded with searing pain and sickness.

- The first year that I noticed I was actually excited about Christmas, rather than totally depressed.

- When I was able to talk about Mom as if she were in the room, without fearing I would melt down into a blithering mess.

- The day I went to Bhakti yoga and the tears *didn't* roll down my face for the entire one-and-a-half-hour class.

Slowly, the void that had replaced the warm place of my loving heart gradually filled with new experiences, as well as faith that things would improve and new relationships would arrive, even if none of them could ever replace what I had lost. None of this happened overnight. It took three, four, five, even ten years for some of the coins to drop.

Yet it began when I made a decision. Somewhere along the way, I'd had enough. Grief had come into my life uninvited. Until it showed up, I'd been a happy-go-lucky person. I was sure this negative state didn't fit my personality profile very well. So I remember waking up one day and thinking, "Enough! This isn't who I am. I don't have to feel this way anymore. I'm choosing this, and I can make another choice."

Now, by this time, I was pretty good at doing grief. Prior to losing Mom, I'd also been good at joy, hope, trust, and laughter. So I wrote my mom a note, telling her that it was time for me to remember her with love, but I was in need of a new beginning.

I attached the letter to a beautiful red helium balloon, which I released at her graveside.

As it floated heavenward against the clear blue sky, I drifted, too, into a new place of possibility, infused with healing, hope, and happiness.

---

Gemini Adams, MNSHF, lost her mom to cancer at a young age and gained firsthand experience of the pain that is bereavement. An award-winning grief expert and author, she helps individuals, organizations, and families to overcome and prepare for the challenges of loss. She wrote *Your Legacy of Love: Realize the Gift in Goodbye* to help others discover how to leave continuing bonds for loved ones. Read her articles at www.opentohope.com.

# Can You Prepare for the Death of Your Dad?
By Neil Chethik

Sigmund Freud called it "the most poignant loss" of his life. Sean Connery termed it "a shattering blow." Norman Mailer likened it to "having a hole in your tooth. It's a pain that can never be filled." Each year, millions of American boys and men lose their fathers to death. And like the three men mentioned above, most are unprepared.

But preparation is possible. Recently, in writing a book about father-loss, I asked seventy men what they did—or wish they'd done—to ready themselves for the deaths of their dads. Here's their best advice for sons whose fathers are alive:

## Make Peace with Your Dad
This was by far the most common suggestion. Sons put it in a variety of ways: "Say what you have to say before it's too late." "As quickly as you can, resolve those old issues." "If you have any conflicts, clear them up."

The reason for peacemaking: sons who are estranged from, angry with, or otherwise unresolved with their dads have the hardest time recovering from a father's death. In addition to their sadness over the loss, these sons often wrestle for years with regrets, resentments, and might-have-beens.

On the other hand, sons who are at peace with their fathers tend to mourn intensely in the short-term but rebound more quickly.

How can a son make peace with his father? Some feel a need to clear the air, to express lingering disappointment or anger. Others need only to thank their dads. One man told me that at the age of thirty-seven, he spontaneously hugged his dad. "And then there was just this melting. I don't recall ever resenting him again."

## Care for Your Father When He Is Ill

Many sons told me they were never closer to their dads than during the weeks leading up to their father's death. They often felt free to comfort him, to care for him—to father him.

One son, who'd sat by his father's bedside swabbing the older man's forehead and lips, during the days before his death, said: "It was hard. But I wouldn't have traded it for anything. . . . He took care of me; I'm taking care of him. There was that mutual, coming-full-circle aspect of it."

Another son took his widowed dad into his home for the last two years of his father's life. After the death, this son relished the memory of that time together: "It was an important period because I'd kind of lost fellowship with my father. He was more of a stranger than a father. . . . It was a time for me and my dad to get to know each other again."

## Talk with Your Father about His Death

This may seem morbid or just plain rude. But most of the men who did this told me their fathers were glad to talk. Sons, it turns out, are often more afraid of a father's death than the father himself is.

Still, finesse is important. One son handled the conversation deftly, approaching his eighty-seven-year-old father with these words: "I'd like to be able to carry out your wishes after your death. To do that, I need to know what your wishes are." The result was a conversation in which the son learned what kind of medical treatment his father wanted in late life, what kind of funeral he wanted, and what he wanted done with his prized personal possessions.

The son also got a bonus: He saw that his father, who'd had a stroke, was not resisting death. Knowing this helped the son accept the death as well.

## Expose Yourself to Death

For most sons, the loss of a father is the first death in their immediate family. They haven't ever watched the dying process up close, and they don't know what to expect from themselves or family members during the crisis. In that case, it may help to acquaint oneself with death before it occurs in one's own family.

One man did this by volunteering at a hospice, keeping company with people in the last days and hours of their lives. "Death is something we tend to avoid . . . until it's thrust upon us," he told me. "Doing something like [hospice], a familiarity comes. I got accustomed to death."

Reading about death also can help, whether it's biblical scripture, poetry, even self-help books. One Christian man told me that as his father was dying, he read *The Tibetan Book of Living and Dying* to get a Buddhist view on the life-death cycle. It helped him enormously. "If you see [death] as a natural thing," he said, "it takes a lot of the sting out of it."

Of course, no matter how thoroughly you prepare for a father's death, you cannot fully mourn it in advance. And you can't predict how you will respond. Some sons told me they expected to be crestfallen at the loss, but felt only relief. Others knew the death was coming, but still were shocked at the finality that it brought.

Nonetheless, consciously preparing has value. By removing some of the surprise of the loss, and by intentionally bringing closure to the relationship with the dying person, it can take the hard edge off the mourning to come.

---

Neil Chethik is an author, speaker, and expert specializing in men's lives and family issues. He is the author of two acclaimed books: *VoiceMale: What Husbands Really Think about Their Marriages, Their Wives, Sex, Housework, and Commitment,* and *FatherLoss: How Sons of All Ages Come to Terms with the Deaths of Their Dads.* Neil is the executive editor for www.opentohope.com, where you can find more of his articles.

# Preparing to Say Good-bye and Other Challenges of the Heart
## By John Pete

I found out this week that my father's several-years-long battle with cancer has moved to a terminal stage. And while the news is not completely unexpected, it is a frightening jolt to be faced with his mortality in terms of months, all the same. My father has quietly admitted that he is afraid and not yet ready to die—heartbreaking words from someone whose emotions are usually very reserved.

My dad would likely be surprised to know that I have always seen him as one of the strongest men I have ever known, despite the fact that there have been many differences between us. He has not lived a perfect life by any means, and he has certainly made his share of mistakes. But I have always admired the strength of character he has displayed throughout his life.

My parents divorced when I was very young, and I have often reflected with sadness that my father and I have not been very close through the years. While many in our family believe it is because of our differences, the truth is, it is more because we are so much alike in many ways. And no matter how many disagreements there have been, or how much time we spent apart throughout our lives, I have never ever wavered in my love for my father. Deep in my heart I will always be that little boy excitedly waiting to see his "daddy" on weekend visits and holidays; and he will always be the father I have been so proud of and quick to defend to others.

A little over a year ago, my dad lost his mother to congenital heart failure in hospice. I watched intently as he sat by Grandma's bedside day after day, holding her hand, wetting her dry lips with a damp cloth, and gently stroking her hair. And I watched his quiet tears when she took her last breaths and eventually passed. It was a very touching side of my father that I have very rarely witnessed.

Then just a few weeks ago we lost our much beloved dog, Tucker, and I was very surprised to receive a call from Dad, saying he was sorry to hear about her passing. I was not surprised because I believe he lacks compassion, but because I have so rarely seen him express his feelings in this way. We talked about how much people love their pets and how they insert themselves into our lives as cherished family members.

Later, it occurred to me how much we both have changed over the years; how we have finally allowed each other to see our vulnerabilities and to respect our differences without judging each other so harshly. And more importantly, we have opened ourselves up to expressing ourselves to one another in new ways, such as by saying "I love you" whenever we see each other or talk on the phone—quite an accomplishment for us.

So now, as the precious commodity of time diminishes into the frightening inevitability of what lies ahead, I ask myself how I can comfort my father in his final days, and how I will ever be able to say good-bye. And the unexpected answer is, I will do it by being my father's son. By summoning the compassion, courage, and strength in myself that I have found in him, beneath his tough, reserved exterior. He's the man whom I have discovered on a long and complex journey, which has led us both to more personal and spiritual growth than either of us could have imagined.

---

John Pete is a certified grief counselor and founder of a website he started in 2006 in response to a need for an online community promoting peer support for coping and healing following loss. He is currently developing a series of grief-related workshops and frequently blogs about grief, spirituality, and healing. Read his articles and find out more at www.opentohope.com.

# The First Mother's Day
# Without Mine

By Connie Vasquez

I've always been adept at compartmentalization or, as it's less euphemistically known, *denial*.

I've read some wonderful books about the grieving process and its non-linear stages, most notably Elisabeth Kübler-Ross and David Kessler's *On Grief and Grieving*. While those books were comforting, I confess that being an only child and a New Yorker make me disdainful of generalizations.

Sometimes, though, there's just no escape. Try as we might, the heart feels what the mind and senses seem to ignore. In April, the lilacs begin to bloom. That first year after my mother's death, I pushed back the familiar thoughts that they had always been "Mother's Day flowers" to me, but my heart recognized the magnificent scent that always reminded me to pick up a bunch on my way to visit Mom. The fragrance found its way to the places I was trying to protect. That year, the beauty of lilacs was acutely bittersweet.

I returned to my apartment after another lovely jaunt among the now-in-full-bloom lilacs and turned on the television for some respite from missing Mom. *Not so fast!* Though I'd overlooked the approach of Mother's Day, apparently everyone else on the planet had not, because card and flower companies issued reminders every fifteen minutes on all 1,914 channels available on cable.

After a couple of weeks of this, Mother's Day started to feel like it was coming at me like a freight train. I kept trying to slap a "happy face" on my feelings by thinking of all the friends and family I love who are moms and the one who's been a second mom to me (thanks, Ginnymom!).

Still, all I wanted to do was sleep through the lilacs and commercials, and wake up the day after Mother's Day.

Ultimately, my self-created geyser made its way to the surface, and I began weeping—for no apparent reason—while on the A train. The tears just streamed down my face. The grief was as fresh and consuming as it was in the weeks after my mother's death.

I managed to contain my yawps and gasps only until I'd made it inside my apartment door. I was stunned by how huge and raw the grief still felt, but remembered that someone told me the amount of sorrow is a reflection of the amount of love. As an homage to my mom, I sat on the floor in my foyer, allowed myself to feel the pain and the love, and wept.

Not a day goes by when I don't think of her. This year for Mother's Day, I have planned a quiet weekend of nurturing myself and remembering her . . . with love . . . and lilacs.

---

Connie Vasquez is an only child who recently lost her mother after years with Alzheimer's. Through that experience, she learned about compassion, love, forgiveness, and grace. Her sense of humor also saw her through. A practicing attorney, cardiac yoga teacher, and life coach, Connie lives in New York City. Find her articles at www.opentohope.com.

# How Men Grieve

---

## Healing a Broken Brain, Mending a Broken Heart
### By Eric Hipple

W hat comes to mind when you hear the word "quarterback"? Maybe you remember Joe Montana's cool or Joe Namath's swagger or Bart Starr's grit. Or maybe you think back to your high school or college days. The quarterback is always the Big Man on Campus, the guy in charge, the leader.

It's a tough job, but a glamorous one. And I loved it. The ten years that I played professional football were the best years of my life.

On the field, the buck stopped with me. I was in control—twenty-one other big, tough men responded to what I was doing. Tens of thousands of people in the stadium, and millions more watching on television, had their eyes fixed on me. Every game was in the spotlight.

Off the field, people looked up to me. They assumed that because I was the quarterback I must be full of self-confidence; that I was completely in control, not only of the game, but also of my entire life. But that image was far out of sync with reality.

During the off-season I would just lie on the couch for days or even weeks at a time or get into moods so black that no one wanted to be around me, or I would try to relieve the pain inside with alcohol and, later, with drugs. I didn't see these problems for what they were: the warning signs of chronic depression.

My playing career ended abruptly at age thirty-two. That's prime time for many quarterbacks, but I was done. Actually I was done in a lot of ways, which became apparent within a frighteningly short amount of time.

My first marriage ended in divorce.

I went bankrupt.

I threw myself out of a moving car at seventy miles per hour in a bungled suicide attempt.

And my only son, Jeff, actually did what his father did not do. He died from suicide at age fifteen.

Spiraling even further downhill from there, I went from Monday Night Football to Monday night in jail, arrested and convicted of drunk driving.

It took all those shocks for me to realize that I had what I call a "broken brain." And my son had one, too. If you don't do something about it, a broken brain can become a string of broken lives.

Jeff was a happy, funny, outgoing kid. He did well in school, enjoyed sports, and seemed to enjoy life. But once he reached high school, he hit a wall. He took his mother's second divorce very hard, especially since he was really attached to his stepfather. My personal and financial problems at the time certainly didn't help.

He began having trouble sleeping and suffered a loss of appetite, energy, and pleasure. He started cutting school, and his grades dropped. He was also cutting himself with a knife to, ironically, dull the pain.

I took him to doctors who said there was no physical problem, but he and his body were trying to tell us something. I learned later that Jeff had been writing letters about his problems to a friend, saying things like "I can't take it much longer." Plainly, he was asking for help, but, unfortunately, he wasn't asking the right people.

On April 9, 2000, I kissed Jeff good-bye and went off on a business trip. It never occurred to me that it would be the last time I would see him alive.

After Jeff's death, I became the world's greatest Monday-morning quarterback. The benefit of perfect hindsight showed me that Jeff had been clinically depressed and calling out for help. But I didn't see the signs. How could I, when I couldn't see them in myself?

The rage, shame, and guilt that I felt began to overwhelm me. I pushed the pain aside with more and more alcohol—until finally, on the way home from a bar one night, I was busted for drunk driving and sent to jail.

Although I certainly don't recommend it to anyone else, my time in jail was therapeutic. My fifty-eight-day sentence included a mandatory detox program, so I got off the alcohol and medications I had been using to blot out reality.

I was able to think clearly for the first time in years. I realized that I'd been playing defense most of my life. And even with the best defense in the world, you can't win. I needed a better offense.

I soon found the right doctor, and we talked about all my symptoms and what they meant. Together we found the right combination of antidepressants. I also began Cognitive Behavioral Therapy, or CBT, so I could understand how the brain's chemistry works.

Is life perfect for me now? Hardly. But the black clouds of depression that used to envelop me have parted. The air smells sweeter. Colors seem more vivid, and everything seems brighter.

On most days, I can look at a picture or video of Jeff and remember the good times we had together. For a long time after he died, I couldn't do that. But even now, years later, his birthday and the anniversary of his death are very tough days for me. That's OK. I know what's wrong and I know how to deal with it.

And yes, I cry. Real men, I've come to learn late in life, do cry.

In the first years after Jeff's passing, I cried so hard that sometimes people would give me "The Madman's Berth"—that wide walk around someone you just can't console.

Now, when I need to weep, I weep. When I need to laugh, I laugh.

It's a lot more authentic. My image and my inner self are finally at peace.

Depression remains one of the most treatable diseases in the world and also one of the most under-diagnosed. Learn the warning signs. Remember that serious depression is, in reality, a broken brain. It's not a sign of character weakness, just as a broken arm isn't a sign of character weakness.

If you have deep sadness or feelings of worthlessness and lethargy for two weeks or more, take a leap of faith and seek help.

But just as important as learning the signs of depression

in yourself is learning to look for these signs in someone you love—your son, your daughter, your spouse, or your best friend. One in five teens has serious thoughts of suicide.

I know how easy it is to get caught up in the day-to-day stuff and rationalize the behavior of someone you live with every day. It's easy to convince yourself that everything is OK.

Step back. Don't miss the proverbial forest for the trees. Think, "Wait a minute, real life is happening here."

It isn't easy, as I am the first to admit. I couldn't do it when it counted. But I think one reason we have tragedy in the world is that it serves to snap us back to reality.

If my writing about depression can spare one family from going through what my family and I went through, then this will be priceless and your actions going forward will be well worth your best efforts.

---

Eric Hipple lost his fifteen-year-old son, Jeff, to a self-inflicted gunshot wound in 2000. Eric was a quarterback for the Detroit Lions from 1980–1989. He is an outreach coordinator for the University of Michigan's Depression Center and is the author of the award-winning book *Real Men Do Cry*, his inspiring story of tackling depression and surviving suicide loss. He speaks from personal experience, spreading the dual message of depression warning signs and suicide prevention. Read more at www.opentohope.com.

# Surrounded by Love,
# Blinded by Pride
## By Ron Villano, MS, LMHC, ASAC

*I couldn't care less.* That's how I felt in the months and years after I lost my seventeen-year-old son, Michael. I felt like the life was taken out of me. I was stripped down on the outside, torn apart on the inside, and utterly vulnerable to the world.

In short, my very essence, my power to be the strong, tough, and secure man, was gone in an instant. I had no identity. I had no point of reference to reach out to, because from a very young age, men are taught to be the ever-strong and solid provider. It's that double-edged combination of nature and society telling men to just, in short, suck it up and deal with it on your own.

I'm a licensed psychotherapist, and most of my patients are not men because of this type of thinking. And for those men like me, who are faced with grieving, it seems like there's nowhere to turn. Men do not reach out and look for the help they need as often as women do. Men are also not as sensitive to each other's needs. So when they reach that breaking point, it often becomes something they feel that they need to do on their own. Their grief is a lonely grief.

The healing process, the stages of grieving, take a lot more time for most men because, quite simply, they haven't had experience working with those deep-down emotions. Women share the ups and downs of life with each other on a regular basis, so they are used to reaching out. When dealing with a man, more sensitivity is required, because men don't want to show any hurt in the first place. Relationships (e.g., marriage) go through enormous stress, so even more patience is necessary to work it through.

For women, it means a more gentle touch, because the emotions are so hard-packed and deep down. Men often shut themselves out from even the simplest enjoyments. There is a desperate unwillingness to even talk about this ultimate life-changing experience. Women endure life's challenges with each other's help. Men often suffer in silence.

Avoiding breakdown is a step-by-step process. Fathers need to allow that body armor to come off. It doesn't mean that they are weaker. In fact, there is a great strength and energy that comes from standing up and saying, "I am broken down now. But with good help and faith, I will make my life stronger than it has ever been." The flood of emotion is powerful.

Let it happen, because once these emotions are out there, you will have made room in your mind to allow for some much-needed forward momentum.

---

Ron Villano, MS, LMHC, ASAC, is a leading expert of change. As a bereaved father, he speaks from the heart. As a licensed psychotherapist, he counsels others on working through difficult times. As a nationally recognized speaker and author, Ron appears before sold-out audiences across the country. His fun, captivating, and approachable style creates the powerful, life-changing moments you have been looking for. Read his articles at www.opentohope.com.

# Grooming and Crying: Man Mourns His Brother While Watching TV
### By Scott Mastley

My first- and second-grade daughters, Margo and Molly, were surprised to see their daddy blinking back tears while watching a dog grooming show on TV. They were successfully avoiding bedtime by snuggling with me on the couch, so I found a show that we could watch together, and even though I had no interest in the Groomer of the Year, it was age-appropriate for them.

Then, something happened that instantly and emotionally connected me to the outcome of the show. One of the two finalists mentioned that he had buried his brother six months earlier and hoped to earn a life-changing win for his business and his family.

This television competitor was in my club, a club that neither of us had wanted to join, one that requires a harsh initiation. We had to endure the loss of our only siblings, and each of us lost our brother. That was enough to put me in his cheering section. Knowing that he had suffered the absence of his brother made me hope for his victory. I knew how badly he needed the force of something positive in his life.

When the winner was announced and my guy won, he fell to one knee and covered his face with his hands. He talked through tears about losing his brother to a violent lifestyle and described the transformative power that this honor would bring to his life. He would move his wife and child out of their dangerous neighborhood and begin a new legacy, get a fresh start. I was saddened by his loss, endeared to him by his vulnerability, and uplifted by his ability to go after and attain a new life for himself and his family. I cried a little, and my girls saw me.

I cry now. That's just the way it is. When Artist, the newly crowned Groomer of the Year, drove off in his mobile pet-grooming studio holding a check for $50,000, I was proud of him. Sometimes a smile and a tear share a moment, and it was nice to share that one with my daughters. Go, Artist!

---

Scott Mastley's brother died in a car accident. To learn how to heal from his grief, he joined the Compassionate Friends and attended, and later led, the monthly sibling group meetings. He eventually was asked to be the Sibling Representative for metro Atlanta, which led to television appearances and his decision to write the book *Surviving a Sibling* to raise awareness about sibling loss. Read more at www.opentohope.com.

# Bereaved Father Discovers
# He's Not Alone
By Patrick T. Malone

A few weeks after my son Lance was killed, my wife, Kathy, received some information about the Compassionate Friends. She told me it was a support group for bereaved parents and wanted to go to a meeting.

My reaction was that I didn't need a support group. All my life, I was the one person who people turned to in crisis. I was the cool head under fire. I was the fixer. I surely didn't need a support group, but Kathy was in no shape to drive, so I went with her. I went into this sharing group and when it came time for me to talk, I cried. I could barely get out Lance's name.

I left the meeting knowing that I wouldn't put myself through this again. The next month came and Kathy was still not able to drive, so we went back to the group together. Again, I cried so hard that I could get out only the bare essentials of Lance's accident.

At this point I was convinced that I was going crazy. I have had all of these weird thoughts. I thought I was having a bad dream and would wake up and everything would be OK. I thought I was a failure as a father because I couldn't protect my children. Every kid on a motorcycle or street corner looked like Lance but wasn't. My wife was a wreck, and I couldn't make her better. I was angry at the truck driver who killed Lance, at God for letting it happen, even at Lance for not going a little faster or a little slower and avoiding the accident. I was guilty because I bought the boys their first dirt bike and Lance's first street bike, and I let him buy the sport bike that he got killed on.

And now I'm weeping in front of strangers. Someone told me you need to go to three meetings before you decide if a support group will help.

So here I am in my third meeting. I'm in a group with another father, John Dubose, whose daughter was killed in a bus accident a year before Lance died. John starts to talk about how he thought he was going crazy in those first few months after Autumn died. He relates how he thought it was a bad dream from which he would awaken. He talks about his guilt at letting her go to Oxford in England for the summer and not being able to protect her. He talks about driving to work and seeing Autumn on the corner and actually turning around only to discover it isn't her.

It's like he's inside my head, because he's saying exactly what I'm feeling. All of a sudden I'm relaxed, and when it's my turn to talk, there are still tears, but I can talk about what I'm feeling. For the very first time I don't feel alone. I remember thinking I still may be going crazy, but at least I'm not going alone.

I believe the lesson here is to find someone with whom you feel comfortable sharing your most intimate thoughts and feelings. It may be a support group like the Compassionate Friends. It may be a grief specialist or therapist. It may be a member of the clergy or a close friend who is willing and able to help you with this burden. It could be someone you meet through the Open to Hope website.

Just knowing you are not the only person having this grief experience, and that what might seem crazy to outsiders is really your new normal, will go a long way to helping you manage your grief process.

---

Patrick T. Malone's twenty-five-year-old son, Lance, died in 1995 in a motorcycle accident. Earlier, his children Scott and Erin died as infants. Patrick is a senior partner with The PAR Group, with more than thirty-five years of experience in operations, customer service, and sales management. Patrick speaks extensively on the topic of surviving loss and has served in leadership positions on the National Board of the Compassionate Friends. Find his articles at www.opentohope.com.

# Grieving Dad Defines "Courage"
## By Kelly Farley

Courage. It's a word that paints many different images in our minds. Each one of us has a different picture of what courage looks and feels like. This may change for us based on events we have experienced throughout our life. I want to tell you a little bit about my recent experience and how I, a bereaved dad, view courage.

I was recently a guest workshop presenter at the national conference for the Bereaved Parents of the USA. This was my first presentation on the subject of child loss and how it impacts dads. Although I am not a professional speaker or a professional grief counselor, I believe I am an expert on the subject, because I lost two children during an eighteen-month period.

I admit I was a little nervous before the start of my workshop. However, all of those nervous feelings went away when I observed the dads entering the room. I knew the look on many of their faces and could see the burdens they were carrying.

Their body language said it all: heads hanging a little low, not making much eye contact, nervous energy and sadness in their eyes, slightly hesitant about what they were about to get themselves into. However, many of them also had the look that said, "Somebody, please help me." I know that look, because I wore it before I searched for help.

Not all the dads who showed up had the look of despair; in fact, many of them showed signs of healing. They offered smiles and handshakes to the other dads who sat near them. Although the loss of a child is a wound that will never completely heal, they were finding ways to smile and laugh again without the guilt. They were showing a lot of courage by reaching out to the dads who were still stuck and stricken with grief.

All the guys who attended this workshop appeared to be searching for some sign or semblance of what they themselves were feeling and experiencing, trying to find some "normalcy" in a not-so-normal situation.

There is comfort in knowing that others are experiencing many of the same emotions and life struggles brought on by the unfortunate circumstance of losing a child. It's confirmation that you're not alone or losing your mind, that everything you're feeling is normal—even the stuff you are afraid to tell others.

I witnessed a large group of dads opening up and telling stories about their loss, their child, their pain. What I witnessed was courage.

+ Courage to get out of bed that day: some of these guys were newly bereaved (under a year), and although this may sound weird to someone who hasn't lost a child, there are many guys who don't want to get up and face another day without their son or daughter. They don't want to go out of the house and try to blend back into society.

+ Courage to be at this event: to walk into a room of

strangers dealing with child loss makes it hard to contain your own emotions. You know the pain the others are feeling. Seeing them is another reminder of what you yourself are dealing with. Although it's comforting to be around other bereaved parents, it still takes courage.

+ Courage to comfort another guy: to be able to reach out and put your hand on another dad's shoulder or offer him a tissue to wipe away his tears takes a lot of courage for men. Most of us become very uncomfortable when others, especially men, become emotionally distraught. What changes this is having someone reach out to you in these moments and provide compassion. Once you are the recipient of such compassion, you understand the power of a touch or someone who just listens.

+ Courage to share their story and experiences: it takes a lot of courage for a man to open up in front of a room full of other men. However, that's exactly what I witnessed from these dads at the workshop. A lot of sharing and a lot of courage.

+ Courage to show their tears and all other emotions: We all know that "big boys don't cry," right? This is what we are taught as young boys, "to be strong." One thing they forgot to tell us is this shouldn't hold true for everything. There is a time and place to be "strong;" the loss of a child is not one of those times. Thank you to the guys for having the courage to reject the notion that men always have to be strong. This is an impossible feat, especially while you are dealing with the loss of a child.

+ Courage to search for others who are traveling on this journey: there is an old adage that says, "Misery loves company." After experiencing the loss of my second child, I knew I couldn't survive it on my own. I needed to be around others who were on this journey, because they "get it." However, I believe whoever created this adage had it wrong. It should read, "Misery *needs* company." There is no reason we have to go through this alone. To see these guys searching out other grieving dads is courageous. Not only are they helping others, they are also helping themselves.

I am honored by all the dads who had the courage to show up to this workshop and share their stories. Thank you to the dads who told me that what I was doing is making a difference. They inspire me to continue my work with my web-based Grieving Dads project. My main objective is to bring awareness to what dads deal with after the loss of a child and to offer some sort of healing to other grieving dads along the way.

---

Kelly Farley is a bereaved father who experienced the loss of his two children over an eighteen-month span. He lost his daughter, Katie, in 2004 and his son, Noah, in 2006. During that time he realized that there is a lack of support services available to fathers suffering such a loss. As a result, he is working on his first book as a resource for grieving dads. He also created and maintains a website for this project. Read his articles at www.opentohope.com.

# Men in Pain: Stay or Walk Away?
## By Bob Baugher, PhD

You've heard the comments: "Men can't handle pain." "Men think they're so tough. They could never go through the pain of childbirth." "My husband was in pain for weeks before he finally told me. What do you expect? He's a man."

In my work with hundreds of bereaved people, it has become clear to me that a huge part of the bereavement process is the management of pain. Let me ask you some questions about the emotional pain you've been feeling related to the death (or deaths) in your life:

1. How much pain are you in right now?

2. Where is it located?

3. Does it move from one part of your body to another?

4. Is it dull or sharp?

5. Is it concentrated in one area or is it widespread?

6. What causes it to become greater or less?

7. How do you decrease it?

What did you discover about yourself? What do you realize about the intensity and description of your pain? Most importantly, is there anything that you can do about it?

Much research has been conducted on physical pain. However, it is difficult to conduct real-life studies, because most ethics boards rightly prevent researchers from delivering painful stimuli directly to a person's body (even if they volunteer). What we do know is that the report of pain is a combination of objective and subjective data.

We know that we can ask several hundred volunteers to plunge their hands into ice water and keep them there for ninety seconds, and the self-reports of pain vary widely from person to person. When it comes to emotional pain, such as what accompanies the death of someone we love, researchers have a difficult time conducting meaningful studies.

Has this ever happened to you? You are having a heated discussion on a difficult issue with a person you care for deeply and the person leaves, disappears! If you are the person left standing, it is likely that you become even more ticked (a nice word for boiling *mad*). Why would someone do this to you? Or if you are the fleeing person, why are you taking off in the middle of a sentence?

A beginning answer to these questions has been the subject of fascinating research from the lab of psychologist John Gottman. Dr. Gottman has been investigating the way couples handle conflict in their marriage. He invites couples into his lab and hooks them up with wires attached to machines that measure their heart rate, blood pressure, breathing, and so on. He then asks the couple to discuss an area of disagreement in their relationship while he videotapes them.

Amazingly, after a few minutes the couple has acclimated to

their new environment and they're bickering away. As a result, for the first time in history, we are able to have a close look at exactly what happens to a person's body in the midst of an argument.

Gottman found some obvious results: the more sensitive the topic, the higher the level of physiological arousal. His most intriguing finding, however, was evidence from the physiological data that one of the partners often displays consistently higher levels of arousal. Furthermore, the arousal levels are often so painful that the partner finds it necessary to get up and leave the room. And who is the partner most likely to do this? Have you guessed it yet? That's right: *men*.

When I give workshops on anger and grief and I get to the point of revealing who it is that most often leaves during an argument, I pause for a moment, and when I say "men," the room explodes in laughter. And the laughter is not, I believe, intended to put down men; but for those who live with a man, especially a bereaved man, the laughter appears to be a release that finally validates what both parties have known all along.

If what you are reading makes sense to you, I want to end with a few suggestions:

1. Show this article to the person(s) in your life who might benefit from reading it.

2. Sit down and decide on a signal that you both could use that indicates your need to leave the scene. For example, it could be a hand signal, such as making the letter "T" for time out.

3. In your discussion of the signal, make an agreement that whoever uses the signal is responsible for bringing

up the (obviously difficult) topic of discussion as soon as his or her physiological arousal level has returned to normal.

4.  If you are the partner who more often stays, understand that it may take your partner several minutes or several hours to return to normal. It some rare cases, you may have to wait until the next day.

5.  To repeat: it is critical that you return to the topic of discussion as soon as both partners are ready. Do not use this technique as a way to avoid discussing difficult issues.

6.  On the other hand, there may be a few issues that are just too difficult to discuss at all.

For example, a year after their teenage daughter was murdered by her boyfriend, a couple had several intense arguments over forgiveness. The husband had reached a point where he had forgiven the murderer, and the wife vehemently disagreed. After more than a year of several screaming arguments, the couple went to counseling and eventually hammered out an agreement that any discussion of forgiveness was off limits. Although neither partner relished the idea of closing off certain areas of communication, they both agreed that, in this case, it was the best solution.

Physical pain is tough. Emotional pain is often tougher, especially when it is in response to the death of someone we love. For reasons that experts are still sorting out, it appears that many men and some women have a predisposition to experience high levels of physiological arousal in the context of discussing emotionally charged issues. In our increasing understanding of the grieving process, this fact can help us as we interact with the important people in our life.

---

B ob Baugher, PhD, an instructor at Highline Community College in Des Moines, Washington, teaches courses in psychology and death education. As a trainer for LivingWorks, he has trained more than a thousand people in suicide intervention. Bob has given more than five hundred workshops and has written seven books on grief and loss. He is a Fellow in Thanatology from the Association for Death Education and Counseling. Read more at www.opentohope.com.

# PART III

Rebuilding Your Lives

# Getting Through
# the Holidays

## First Thanksgiving after a
## Death Is Challenging
By Anne Hatcher Berenberg, PhD

One night in April, my two sons, then four and nine, were tucked into their beds by their loving young father, Richard. That was the last time they saw him. The next morning, they woke up to learn that he was dead from a heart attack. Our world had shattered overnight. The boys cried in pain and bewilderment, and so did I.

Over the next months, I struggled to find what pieces of our lives could stay the same, what could be there in altered form, what could now only be held in memory, and what new pieces had to be created. Each option mingled the greatest sorrow I had ever known along with resolve to keep going for the boys.

Before long, it was time for Thanksgiving, our first major holiday without Richard.

Thanksgiving had always been the holiday associated with Richard's family. Every year of the boys' lives, we had traveled to Boston for a big reunion of his extended family. Aunts and uncles, first cousins, first cousins once removed, second cousins, and more, all came together from all over the country to be together with the grandparents.

In the early years, it had taken me some time to get used to the crowds. It wasn't anything like the quiet Christmases we spent with my parents and my brother's family. Once, when our older son was about seven, he commented thoughtfully that he knew Thanksgiving was a Jewish holiday because he always spent it with the Jewish side of his family.

The boys and I were tense as we got ready to make the plane trip from Chicago. I felt lonely preparing to make the journey as the only adult. The older boy was anxious and the younger one was cranky as we packed. Yet I knew that it was crucial for them to have this continuity. Not all of life as they knew it had stopped with their father's death. So we went.

Fortunately, some wonderful friends offered to drive us to the airport. Their calm, caring presence helped us feel we could do this.

When Richard's parents met us at the Boston airport, the boys fell into their arms. All through the weekend, they were reminded that they were loved, that they belonged, that they would be held by bonds that had lasted and would continue to last through generations—and I was, too.

Losing their father didn't mean they lost his family. That year and every year, family members told stories about Richard to his sons and shared pictures and mementos, as well as making an effort to know and value each of the boys as a unique individual.

Now the boys are young men preparing to go to Boston with their wives for Thanksgiving. My new husband and I will join them there. None of us would dream of missing it.

---

Anne Hatcher Berenberg, PhD, was widowed when her children were young. She is a clinical psychologist in Northfield, Illinois, specializing in work with children, adolescents, and their parents. With her new husband, Jack Cain, she is the coauthor of *Now: Overcoming Crushing Grief by Living in the Present*. Her new book is *10 Steps for Parenting Your Grieving Children* (coauthored with Vicki Scalzitti and Jack Cain). For more, visit www.opentohope.com.

# Years after Son's Suicide, Mother Lives in Peace and Joy

By Pamela Prime

Sean died in the month of August. He was sixteen years old, and he took his own life. He shot himself with his father's hunting rifle. I never saw his body but, in retrospect, I now know that it was for the best. I did not feel that way at the time. I begged to see him. My heart ached with an intense longing to touch him . . . just one last time.

Those first months were a nightmare. Hell could not be worse! I do not recall our first Thanksgiving. As many memories as there are in my heart and mind, that first Thanksgiving is not one of them. How could it have been? How could I find my way to gratitude in such a short time? Even if I ate turkey and pumpkin pie, I am sure I was just barely in my body and smiling only because it served the others at the table, if I smiled at all.

But I do remember the first Christmas. I remember trying to decorate the Christmas tree. I think I cried tears on every ornament as I painstakingly hung them, not caring where they fell or how the tree looked! I remember wandering through the stores in a daze trying to buy presents for my other children.

But I did decorate the tree, and I did buy presents because I willed myself to do so.

That first year, I willed myself to get out of bed in the morning and smile, even if I did not feel like smiling. Every day I made a choice to live, and by live, I mean enter into life as best I could without judging myself, without thinking I "should" do better. I just did my best. Each night, just before going to bed, I reflected on the day and gave thanks to God for whatever I could accomplish—however little. I also gave thanks for whatever help I received that day—however little!

There were many things that helped me to heal, to smile, to will myself to live. My family and friends were a great blessing. I learned quickly who to be with and when to leave. Some folks just cannot bear another's pain, mostly because they refuse to bear their own. Bury your pain, and you will do your best to help another do the same.

I believe that the best thing I did, the thing that helped the most, was to pray. It is what helped me every day to choose to live. I would take time as often as I could to sit in the quiet of my room and pray, sometimes only for a few minutes, but it was always healing. It was not what we often call prayer, not formal prayer. I was not capable of that. I would just be with what I call God, what you might call Divine Mystery or Universal Consciousness or Love, and I would allow myself to be and feel—to feel my anger or my fear, to feel guilty or despairing, or simply to cry my heart out.

I did this in the presence of God's love. Most often, I could not feel that love, but my faith is deep and, even in the midst of grieving my son's suicide, I believed it was there.

Today, twenty-eight years later, I live with a smile on my face that comes naturally and often. I am more free than I have ever been, more at peace, more in love, and more joyful.

I believe this is so because I have been willing to feel the depths of my suffering—the pain, the anger, the fear, the guilt, and whatever else arose. I have been faithful to myself as I refused to bury that which I am. The love of God has given me that gift—the safety to feel as deeply as possible into the hell that lies within. As I was faithful to my feelings, I healed, and each holiday became easier to enjoy.

It isn't that time heals all wounds, but rather that fully feeling the pain heals all wounds. There is hope, and those of us who have walked the walk are living proof!

That said, I must add that not a holiday or birthday or death day goes by that I don't feel a need to sit quietly with God and feel the loss. I never know when something will invite tears, but now I welcome them. They are my connection to a child who I dearly love. When it is my time, I will die knowing that I will see my son, and I will find great joy in that moment.

---

Pamela Prime's four-month-old daughter died of sudden infant death syndrome, and her son, at the age of sixteen, died of suicide. Pamela is a spiritual director, an educator, and a writer. Her first book is *When the Moon Is Dark We Can See the Stars*. Pamela is a mother and grandmother, and lives in California. To read more of her articles, visit www.opentohope.com.

# Choose Positive Memories During this Season of Hope

By Patrick T. Malone

We would have traded places with our child without a second thought, but we weren't given that choice. When that enormous pain of grief rolled into and totally disrupted our nice, neat, little life, we didn't have a choice. Even now, months or years later, when a residual wave of grief chooses to crash along our shoreline, we aren't given a choice. It just shows up.

None of us aspired to be part of the Compassionate Friends. In fact, it ranks last in organizations that parents and families wish to join. We didn't choose this, but here we are.

So it is easy to allow this journey through our grief to make us its victim. Before long, I started treating every event in my life as if I didn't have a choice, and I became my worst nightmare. I became a victim.

Then, if we're lucky, something penetrates the fog of grief and depression and causes us to re-examine the manner in which we are working through our pain. For me, first, it was an article by my future friend, Rich Edler, which was published in *We Need Not Walk Alone* magazine. The specific line in the article was, "Grief is mandatory, misery is optional."

Second, it was the following poem by Howard Thurman, which appeared in a grief newsletter distributed by Dinah Taylor in Kentucky.

## I Will Light Candles for Christmas

I will light candles this Christmas:
Candles of joy despite all the sadness,
Candles of hope where despair keeps watch,
Candles of courage for fears ever present,

Candles of peace for tempest tossed days,
Candles of grace to ease heavy burdens,
Candles of love to inspire all my living,
Candles that will burn all the year long.

The message is that we do have a choice. We cannot change the facts of what happened to our child, children, or grandchild. That is the past. We think we can plan for the future, but those plans may or may not have any effect on the actual future course of events. But we can do something about the here and now—the present.

So, as we prepare to light these candles in the memory of our children, let us choose, to the degree each of us is able, to create a positive memory of our child if only for the briefest of moments.

+ Remember that vacation at the Magic Kingdom that she loved so much.

+ Remember how he loved the Braves way before they started winning.

+ Remember that soccer match and how proud you were—not because he won, but because of the way he played.

+ Remember how the dream came true when he made Drum Major of the band, but mostly remember he was part of finding the cure and that "ain't for nothing."

+ Remember how she loved Christmas and the light in her eyes whether she was giving or receiving.

+ Remember how much he loved to cook and the joy of making it his profession.

+ Remember her first day of school and how excited she was.

+ Remember all those scouting badges and how proud you were of all his efforts.

+ Remember how many of his college friends told you how much he had helped them.

+ Remember how hard she worked in school to make you a proud dad.

+ Remember his first smile, her first word, and their first steps.

+ Remember the warm days, bright sun, and flashing skis as she sailed effortlessly across the water.

+ Remember that slick, mischievous grin he flashed before he flipped down his visor and roared away on that purple motorcycle.

Some day, we will all see our children again, and when we do, they are going to ask what we did with the rest of our lives. I believe Scott, Erin, and Lance would be disappointed if I told them I spent the rest of my life grieving their deaths. That isn't how they want to be remembered.

However, I think they would be pleased if we are able to tell them that we lived the rest of our lives inspired by the positive memories of their lives.

So for the briefest of moments during the Christmas season, set down your burden. Refresh yourself so that you can continue your grief journey buoyed by positive memories of a significant life, regardless of how long or short. A significant life lived well.

You have a choice. Choose well.

---

Patrick T. Malone's twenty-five-year-old son, Lance, died in 1995 in a motorcycle accident. Earlier, his children Scott and Erin died as infants. Patrick is a senior partner with The PAR Group, with more than thirty-five years of experience in operations, customer service, and sales management. Patrick speaks extensively on the topic of surviving loss and has served in leadership positions and on the National Board of the Compassionate Friends. Find his articles at www.opentohope.com.

# Carrying Old Memories into a New Year
### By Alice J. Wisler

Christmas has ended, and the living room still has that unwrapped look. With the festivities now part of future memories, I anticipate the next hurdle: the start of a new year. TV commercials romanticize champagne toasts illuminated by glowing candles. People make resolutions, hopeful that this brand-new unblemished year will be the one that fuels their successes.

For the parent who has lost a child to death, a new year can be daunting. The first New Year's Day after my son Daniel's death was scary. I wanted to hold onto 1997. Although it was the year he'd lost his battle with cancer and died, it was also the year he'd lived. I knew that 1998 would mark the first calendar year without him.

For some reason, the image of an old-fashioned wooden bucket came to me. With this item, I heard the word "carry." That's it, my newly bereaved mind said. The key with a new year is to carry the old into it.

So here we are, on the brink of another year, with fresh

hopes and dreams. It's a clean slate. There are many things about the previous year I wish to forgive and forget, but I don't want to ever forget my son.

Each year marks a year further from when I last held him, heard his voice, and saw his smile. I yearn to hug him, tell him how much he's grown, and ask him what he'd like for dinner. My heart feels that distinct hollowness and sorrow that belongs to a mother without her child.

But the bucket I have isn't empty. It is brimming with memories and fondness, warmed with love and laughter; I hold it tightly.

Just as I carried memories of my four-year-old into 1998, thirteen years later I will continue to carry them. And I will do more than just hold them. I'll let them trickle out, forming their own glow, as I share this special boy with my world. "Wasn't it funny when Daniel called adults 'redults'? Do you remember how he gave stickers away in the hospital, and once when he was bored he made a collage out of baby lotion and glitter?"

Daniel lived, he loved, and I believe he continues to live in Heaven.

So get yourself a sturdy bucket and boldly carry the memories into the New Year. Along the way, give yourself permission to forgive. Let the memories you recall be the brightest ones.

There is nothing to fear. Listen. Your child's voice can be heard in your heart.

---

Alice J. Wisler's four-year-old son, Daniel, died from cancer treatments in 1997. She is the founder of a grief-support organization, Daniel's House Publications, and the author of four inspirational novels and two cookbooks. Her writing focus has been on how to help others in grief. She facilitates Writing the Heartache workshops across the country. Alice and her family live in Durham, North Carolina. For more of Alice's articles, visit www.opentohope.com.

# Creating a New Life in
the New Year
## By Tom Zuba

The death of someone we love transforms us. It has to. Over time, we decide whether we are going to consciously participate in that transformation or if the transformation is going to be unconscious. It's a decision we make daily. As we count down to the New Year and talk of resolutions, it's the perfect time to create a plan to consciously participate in our transformation, to consciously create our new life.

Some concrete steps to consider include:

Commit to active mourning. Make the effort to find a therapist, a support group, or a "grief buddy." Healing occurs when you find a safe place where you can excavate, explore, and express your grief in the presence of others. Being stoic, pretending, repressing, rejecting, or ignoring all that wells up inside of you is not a path to healing.

Commit to going outside and walking in nature every day, even if it's only for five minutes and you have to force yourself to do it. Build up to ten minutes, then fifteen or twenty. Lose yourself in nature. Over time, notice the change of seasons.

Spring always follows winter. The days get brighter. What appeared to be dead brings forth new life.

Commit to finding ways to release the heavy, burdensome energy stored in your body. A massage therapist cannot only help you physically relax, but he/she can help your body release stored energy and even memory that no longer serves you. Consider working with a Reiki master or a craniosacral therapist. At the very least, the physical touch will be healing.

Commit to spending quiet time with yourself every day to simply be with yourself and your new life. Again, even if you have to force yourself to be quiet and alone for five minutes, do it. Over time, five minutes becomes ten, then fifteen and then twenty. If you keep running from yourself and your new life, how can you live it? How can you consciously participate in it? Pray. Meditate. Ask. Listen. Be. Receive. Allow. Surrender. Feel.

Commit to writing in a gratitude journal every day. Do this first thing in the morning or last thing at night. Buy a journal. Put it by your bed. Write five things you are grateful for every day. At first, you may simply be glad another day is over. You may be thankful for the soft pillow, the comfortable bed, the warm blankets. And then you may remember that the first cup of coffee actually tasted good, and you're grateful for that. And one day you notice the sun in the sky.

Commit to being gentle with yourself. Be really gentle. Trusting life enough so that you are willing to create new dreams takes time—lots of time. As the saying goes, we often take one step forward and two steps back. Healing is a process. It's a journey. Be gentle.

As this New Year unfolds, set the intention to heal. Set the intention to consciously participate in your own transformation. A New Year. A New Life.

Tom Zuba is a grief guide, author, and inspirational speaker. His eighteen-month-old daughter, Erin, died suddenly in 1990. His forty-three-year-old wife, Trici, died equally as suddenly on New Year's Day 1999, and his thirteen-year-old son, Rory, died from brain cancer in 2005. Tom and his son Sean are learning to live a full, joy-filled life, one day at a time. Tom has appeared on The Oprah Winfrey Show. For more, visit www.opentohope.com.

# Parenting after Loss

## Helping Your Child with Loss and Grief
By Lauren Littauer Briggs

How can we help our children deal with deaths of loved ones? Here are some ways:

+ Prepare your children for what will come. The more open you can be about what is ahead, the less uncomfortable your children will be. Explain what the funeral will be like, what they will see, and what feelings they may experience. I tell children and adults alike that we hurt so much because we love so much.

+ Encourage your children to ask questions, and answer them clearly and accurately. Tell them, "Any time you have a question or don't understand what is happening, please ask me. I will tell you anything you want to know." Children have a great need to talk about what has happened, but they will only do so when the environment and time is right, and they are ready.

+ Spend one-on-one time with each child. Sit on the floor or ground so that you are on his level. Play or color with him. Then, when the timing is right, ask questions about his feelings, memories, and understanding. "Have you had any dreams about _____?" "Do you feel sad some of the time?" "Would you tell me what you've been feeling?" "Could we draw a picture of _____?" You will probably be amazed by how easily the conversation flows when your child knows you are available and want to be a part of his or her feelings.

+ Don't over-spiritualize the death with comments like, "Grandma is in heaven now." "Jesus came to take your sister to heaven." "God is in control." "God just needed another angel in heaven." Be careful about using references to God or Jesus when explaining death to a child. They may believe that death is God's fault and develop a sense of anger toward God.

+ Don't put timetables on the emotional reactions. Grief work is individual and truly unending. We will never be "over it" or "our old selves again." Expect life to be different following the death of a loved one. Once our life has been touched by tragedy, we will never be the same again.

+ Share your own feelings of loss with your child. Let her know that you are sad, you miss the loved one, you think about her often. It is OK for your child to see you cry. That lets your child know that it is all right to cry, as well.

+ Don't minimize your child's feelings with comments like, "You're a big girl, you can handle this." "You don't need to feel that way." "Boys need to be strong." Instead, validate their feelings by saying, "This is a very sad time for you." "I know this is very difficult." Or "I love you and will be here for you." Comments like these let your child know that you are aware of his pain and it's OK for him to feel that way.

+ After a death, children need to be reassured of your love and your presence. They may feel abandoned or think the death was somehow their fault. Reassure children that the death isn't their fault. Say "I love you" often and provide as stable an environment as possible.

+ When it comes to feelings, don't use the words "should" or "shouldn't," such as, "You shouldn't feel that way" or "You should be doing better by now." That indicates that there is a right or a wrong way to feel. Feelings aren't right or wrong. They just are. The more open you are to their feelings, the more willing they will be to share them.

+ Children feel that adults are at the funeral services for the other adults. Kids have a need to grieve, too. When it is age appropriate, I encourage children to attend the funeral. My son had a friend in kindergarten who was killed in a tragic accident. Almost the entire class went to the funeral. They couldn't fully grasp the magnitude of his death, but they knew it was very sad and they would not see Chris again. It was so touching to see child after child pass the coffin and leave a small toy "for Chris." Children shouldn't be isolated from their friends and childhood activities during the period of mourning.

+ A question children often ask is, "Is _____ still in our family?" We want to assure them the deceased are a part of our family and always will be. I love what Maria Shriver wrote about her grandmother in *What's Heaven?* "Everything she ever taught me is alive in me. She taught me that it is really important to love my family, to treat others with respect, and to be able to laugh a lot. Most important, she taught me to believe in myself."[1] Our loved ones do live on in us if we remember what they taught us and meant to us. Encourage your child to keep his loved one alive by remembering what she taught and how she lived, and by letting it show up in his life.

+ Keep an open dialogue with your children about the loved one and the feelings connected to the loss. You don't ever want them to think that talking about the loved one will hurt you too much, that it is better left alone, or that time marches on.

---

Lauren Littauer Briggs experienced grief and loss through the deaths of two brothers when she was a young child. She has been helping hurting hearts for more than twenty-five years through peer support groups, medical seminars, and

---

1. *What's Heaven?*, by Maria Shriver, New York: Golden Books, 1999.

the Compassionate Friends organization. The keys to offering support can be found in her book, *The Art of Helping—What to Say and Do When Someone Is Hurting*. To find more, visit www.opentohope.com.

# Help Grieving Children Know They Are Not Alone

By Howard Winokuer, PhD, LPC, NCC, FT,
and Heidi Horsley, PsyD, LMSW, MS

*"What we have once enjoyed we can never lose.
All that we love deeply becomes a part of us."*
**—Helen Keller**

The death of a child is traumatic. It often turns our lives upside down and puts everything we ever believed into question. Regardless of the way a child dies, we are never prepared to lose them. As parents, we do not expect to outlive our children, and as siblings, we just assume we will travel through life and grow old together. Not only are parents dealing with their own grief after a loss, but they worry about their surviving children and want to make sure that they are doing what's best for them.

Talking about death with adults is difficult, but talking to your children about death may be even harder. Although it may not always look like your children are grieving, it is critical to understand that they also grieve. They experience their grief differently, but nonetheless, they do grieve.

As parents, you may be asking questions such as: What will we say? What will we do? How do we best help our child after the death of his or her sibling? Where do we learn the answers to these questions? What can be said? What can be done?

First and foremost, children need to be made aware that they still live in a safe and predictable world after a sibling's death. Being reassuring and behaving in ways that communicate to your children that you are there for them and that you will be able to take care of them, even though you are grieving, is key. Further, it is very comforting for them to know that they are not alone in their grief and that as a family you will all get through this difficult time together.

Even though parents often have the best intentions in mind, what we do or say may not always be helpful and can sometimes even be harmful. It is important to be aware that children oftentimes take things very literally. When you tell a child that someone died because he was sick, your child may be afraid every time he or she gets a cold. Kids often have difficulty differentiating between being sick with a cold or the flu versus being sick from cancer or some other terminal illness.

Do not tell a child that someone just went away, because every time there is a departure, the child will perceive that as "going away." Kids will worry that when you leave to go to work or even go to the grocery store, you may never be coming back. Also, guard against saying that someone just went to sleep or that death is just like sleep. Once again, remember that kids take things literally, and they may develop sleep difficulties because of fears that if they fall asleep, they will not wake up again.

There are things that can be said and done that will help children explore their grief and express their feelings:

+ Allow expressions of feelings—there are a wide range of feelings associated with the grief process. Feelings aren't right or wrong, they just are. Reassuring your child that it's normal to experience feelings such as anger, sadness, or anxiety will let your child know that what he or she is going through is not unusual.

+ Create an open and supportive environment—provide honest answers and age-appropriate information. Some children may be more comfortable drawing, writing stories, or acting out their emotions in a play, rather than talking.

+ Communicate through touch—touch can often express thoughts and feelings that words cannot. For example, putting an arm around the child, sitting close to him, holding him on your lap, or even holding his hand lets him know that you are there and he is not alone.

+ Talk about worries and concerns—children often express a lot of worries after loss. They may begin to act younger and become clingy and whiney. Regression is a common reaction and usually doesn't last too long. Be supportive and don't criticize regressive behavior. You may need to spend extra time with your child during transitions—for example, when dropping him off at daycare. Your child may also need to sleep with a nightlight, stuffed toy, and/or favorite blanket.

+ Encourage your child to ask questions—don't be afraid to answer your child's questions openly and honestly in an age-appropriate way. The truth is always easier for a child to deal with rather than the often-frightening fantasy that he might create in his mind, if not given information.

Other tips that you might find very helpful include:

+ Be gentle but truthful in telling your child about the death.

+ Have as many pictures and reminders around your home of your surviving child as you have of your deceased child.

+ Let your surviving child know that, although you are devastated over the loss, life is still worth living, and remind her how grateful you are to have her in your life.

+ Recognize normal child reactions to grief.

+ Give your child your assurance of love and support.

+ Assure your child that nothing he did or thought caused the death.

+ Encourage your child to talk about how he feels.

+ Encourage your child to cry, but don't put too much pressure on her.

+ Cry or grieve with your child in a way that is not scary and conveys to her that although you are upset, you will still be able to care for her.

Talking to your child about death can be one of the most significant life events that you will participate in. Children are very resilient, and although a sibling loss may define your child's life, it will in no way destroy his life. Your child will forever miss his sibling, but in time he will find new ways to incorporate him or her into his life through continuing bonds. It is important to honor the grief that your child experiences and validate that grief through your care and presence. By doing this, you can make a significant difference in his life. Remember that your openness may help decrease your child's fear and that being there for your child is the most important thing that you can do.

---

Howard R. Winokuer, PhD, LPC, NCC, FT, is the cofounder of TO LIFE, a not-for-profit educational and counseling organization that specializes in issues dealing with grief and loss. He has worked with thousands of people suffering from grief. He has conducted workshops and seminars throughout the United States, as well as in nine foreign countries. He has written and published extensively. For more, visit www.opentohope.com.

Heidi Horsley, PsyD, LMSW, MS, is the executive director and cofounder of the Open to Hope Foundation. She is an internationally known grief expert and author. Her seventeen-year-old brother Scott and cousin Matthew died together in a car accident, and she has experienced two miscarriages. A licensed psychologist and social worker, she cohosts the syndicated Internet radio show "The Open to Hope Show" and frequently presents at conferences across the country. She is an adjunct professor at Columbia University and has a private practice in Manhattan. With her mother Dr. Gloria Horsley, she coauthored *Teen Grief Relief.* Find more at www.opentohope.com.

# Helping Kids with Traumatic Death
By Linda Goldman

Ordinary fears are a normal part of a child's developmental growth, and children create internal and external mechanisms to cope with these fears. But a child's ordinary fears can be transformed into very real survival fears in the face of severe trauma. After children experience the traumatic death of a parent, they often feel alone and different. Frightened because their once comfortable world now seems unpredictable and unsafe, they may react in ways that we as adults truly cannot judge, understand, or anticipate.

As a therapist working with military and non-military children experiencing traumatic death, I have seen common symptoms of trauma emerge. The impact of a dad's or mom's traumatic death can be so disturbing that the terror involved with the death and the way the parent died may override a child's ability to grieve in a natural way and share sadness and frustration.

These events can cause panic, stress, and extreme anxiety in kids' lives, and feelings can be heightened or triggered by sounds

241

and images. Danny's father was shot and killed by a gunman during a robbery. Six months later Danny went to a friend's birthday party. When a balloon burst, he thought it was a gun and ran out of the room screaming and crying. He didn't expect to be hit with a "grief bullet" that day.

The terror that grips our children in these circumstances emerges from situations that suddenly overwhelm them and leave them feeling helpless, hopeless, and unable to cope. Trauma is defined by the Encarta World English Dictionary as "an extremely distressing experience that causes severe emotional shock and may have long-lasting psychological effects." This unexpected and shocking event destroys a child's ability to cope and function in a normal way.

Children can suffer from a state of trauma that can develop into post-traumatic stress disorder, in which present events trigger memories of trauma resulting in panic, anxiety, disorientation, fear, and all the psychophysical feelings associated with the traumatic memory.

## Signs of Traumatized Children

- After seven-year-old Joey's dad was killed in a drive-by shooting, he constantly questioned Mom. "Tell me exactly what happened. Did my dad suffer?" Joey had nightmares and regressed to bedwetting.

- A stray bullet killed Tyler's dad during military combat. His father had always told him, "Nothing can stop me from coming home." Tyler constantly worried about where the bullet hit his dad, did it hurt him, was he unprotected, and did he die instantly. He began having stomachaches and panic attacks, worrying that his mom could get killed, too.

+ Jonathan's dad was killed in a firefight in Iraq. Instead of being honored as the son of a military hero, he was often victimized on the playground by a school bully. Jonathan kicked him, and both boys were punished. His grades dropped from straight A's to F's after his dad died.

Many young people may experience physical, emotional, cognitive, and behavioral symptoms. These signals range from stomachaches and nightmares to poor grades, isolation, depression, regression, and hostility.

Traumatized children tend to recreate their trauma, often experiencing bad dreams, waking fears, and recurring flashbacks. Young children have a very hard time putting these behaviors into any context of safety. Many withdraw and isolate themselves, regress and appear anxious, and develop sleeping and eating disorders as a mask for the deep interpretations of their trauma. Young children engage in post-traumatic play by compulsively repeating some aspect of the trauma.

The most common identifying indicators that children are re-experiencing the event are play reenactment, nightmares, waking memories, and disturbing thoughts and feelings about the event. Sometimes kids avoid reminders of the traumatic event or show little conscious interest.

Developmentally, young children live in an egocentric world filled with the notion that they have caused and are responsible for everything. George's dad was killed in the Twin Towers on 9/11. Over and over George explained to his teacher, "It's my fault my dad died. I should have made him stay home from work that day. He hated his job. I should have made him quit." Some kids may also feel survival guilt. They may think, "Why am I living when so many others have died?" A parent or teacher can help a child reframe the guilt and magical thinking from "What could I have done?" to "What can I do now?"

Caring adults need to recognize the signs of grieving and trauma in children, and be aware of the techniques and resources available that help bring safety and protection back to the child's inner and outer world. For example, listening to children's thoughts and feelings, as well as providing a safe means of expression, helps teachers, parents, and educators reinforce their ability to ensure a safe and protected environment.

When parents, educators, and other professionals can identify traumatized children, they can develop ways kids can express their feelings and emotions. They can also model, present, and support comfortable ways to bring safety and protection back into kids' lives.

## At-Risk Behaviors

Children may begin to exhibit at-risk behaviors after a traumatic event. The frequency, intensity, and duration of these behaviors are important factors to consider. Children may experience post-traumatic stress, revisiting the traumatic event through outside stimulus such as photos, music, and the media, or by reliving the sights and sounds of the tragedy in their minds. Expect children to re-experience a degree of their original trauma on the anniversary of their parent's death.

The following behaviors may be indicators that a child may benefit from professional help:

+ Sudden and pronounced change in behavior

+ Threat of suicide or preoccupation with suicide,

evidenced through artwork or writing

+ Harmful acts to other children or animals

+ Extreme confusion or incoherence

+ Evidence of substance abuse (drugs, alcohol, etc.)

+ Sudden change of grades

+ Sudden, unexplained improvement in behavior or schoolwork

+ Avoidance or abandonment of friends

+ Angry or tearful outbursts

+ Self-destructive behavior

+ Inability to eat or sleep

+ Overconcern with own health or health of a loved one

+ Giving away important possessions

+ Depression, isolation, or withdrawal

## Helping Kids Express Thoughts and Feelings

Helping children to establish a sense of order in an ever-changing and chaotic world is important. Not only do we want our kids to realize they are survivors of a difficult event, but they also need to know that their life still has continuity and meaning. Parents and educators working with traumatized children should keep to the daily routine as much as possible. This allows kids to feel a renewed sense of security.

Establishing family activities also has a reassuring effect on children. Preparing meals together, eating dinner as a family, reading stories aloud, or playing family games can help to reestablish a sense of normalcy to kids' lives. It is also important to initiate safe places for kids to express their ideas. This can be done by finding quiet times at home, in the car, or on a peaceful walk. Being with children without distractions can produce a comfortable climate to begin dialogue. Bedtime should be a reassuring time, too. Often, this is the moment when children choose to talk about their worries. Parents can consider an increase in transition time, storytelling, and book reading to create a peaceful, uninterrupted nighttime environment.

## Hope for the Future

The sudden and traumatic death of a mom or dad can shatter a child's emotional and physical equilibrium and stability. Too many boys and girls experience fear, isolation, and loneliness after a parent's traumatic death, as well as a myriad of secondary losses ranging from moving, change of school, upset of daily routine, loss of skills and abilities, reduced income level, and public mourning. Many children are left in a world in which they see no future and no protection.

A primary goal of trauma work with children is to restore security and protection to their world. Young people who have experienced the traumatic loss of a parent may need time, patience, and space in order to regain their sense of safety and well-being. Another goal is to provide parents and youth workers with the information, understanding, and skills related to the issues creating trauma. With these tools, we can help our children become less fearful and more compassionate human beings, thereby increasing their chances of living in a future world of increased inner and outer peace.

Linda Goldman is a Fellow in Thanatology: Death, Dying, and Bereavement (FT). She has a private grief therapy practice in Chevy Chase, Maryland. She works with children, teenagers, and families with prenatal loss, as well as grieving adults. Linda has written many articles and shares workshops, courses, and trainings on children and grief and trauma, as well as working with LGBT youth. She currently teaches as adjunct faculty at Johns Hopkins University. She is the author of *Life and Loss, Children Also Grieve,* and *Great Answers to Difficult Questions about Death.* Learn more at www.opentohope.com.

# Children React to a Divorce Much Like They Do to a Death
By Suzy Yehl Marta

*Note: After my husband and I divorced, I was so overwhelmed with my grief that I didn't notice that my three boys were hurting, too. I learned that kids aren't resilient, as so many people say, and I knew I had to look for ways to help them. Following is an excerpt from my book,* Healing the Hurt, Restoring the Hope. *I founded Rainbows for All Children more than twenty-six years ago to help youth all over the world who are suffering and grieving from the death of a parent or divorce.*

## My Journey

"Don't worry about the children. They're resilient. They'll bounce back." These reassuring words were salve to my wounds. My husband, Jim, and I had recently divorced. At the time, my children were young—five, six, and seven—too young, I hoped, to comprehend and be seriously affected by the enormous changes that had taken over our lives. Despite my own deep emotional pain, I clung to the belief that my sons would move through the upheaval in their lives relatively unscathed. "They'll be fine," I told myself.

After the divorce, everything in our household changed. For a while, I held down three jobs just to make ends meet. My time for parenting was drastically reduced. The little touches of family were no longer there—time to cuddle, watch television together, or play in the park. Most days, I felt like a machine that was running on drained batteries. Every task was a struggle. I just didn't seem to have enough time or strength to organize the house, feed the children, and get them to and from school on time. But the kids seemed to be just fine. Doing better than I was, actually.

As it turns out, I was naïve and dead wrong.

My sons were not just fine. They were grieving terribly, but I was in such pain that I wasn't even aware of their distress. In addition, everyone—my friends, family, doctor, counselor, and even parish priest—assured me that my boys would handle the situation and move on. "Kids bounce back," they said. In the midst of my own agony, I took comfort in their words. In retrospect I find the very notion absurd.

Children are not rubber bands that can be stretched out of shape and then expected to snap back into position. They are living beings with their own feelings. Like adults, they are deeply affected by loss.

I remained in an emotional daze for nearly a year after my husband moved out, numbed by my own pain and oblivious to my sons' grief. Then one day, for the first time in many months, I sat down and took a long, hard look at my children. The unmistakable pain in their eyes shocked me. I felt a searing ache in my heart. How could I have missed this?

In the past, the boys had been active in their school functions, participated in park district sports, and had lots of neighborhood friends. This last year had been different. They'd become withdrawn, sullen, and angry. They fought constantly. They were cruel to each other—punching and shoving one another so much that I lost track of the number of trips we'd made to the hospital emergency room for stitches. Occasionally, they were verbally nasty to me, as well.

Even worse, Michael had started to shoplift candy from the local convenience store. Tom was getting into scrapes at school with his closest friends. And Tim had started spending all his free time watching television or curled up in bed asleep.

Academically, they were struggling too. Their grades were spiraling downward. In class, the boys daydreamed; they weren't "applying" themselves to their work, their teachers said.

My children—the most precious beings on the earth to me—had been hurting all this time, and no one, not one single adult, had made the connection between the divorce, their behavior, and their emotional pain. Even today, I cannot imagine how they must have felt, torn by unfamiliar emotions and yet completely ignored. Divorce was the most significant event that had occurred in their lives, and no one—not me, their dad, their grandparents, their teachers, or their pediatrician—had asked them how they felt about it.

That night, I vowed that I would *talk to them* about the divorce.

Knowing that children chatter best around food, I made a big bowl of popcorn and sat us all down around it on the living room rug. As the boys munched their snack, I fired questions at them.

"How do you feel now that your father isn't living with us?" Michael shrugged his shoulders.

"Do you mind going to your dad's on the weekend?" Tom stared at the floor.

"Does it bother you that I'm working so much?" Tim avoided my gaze and snatched a handful of popcorn.

I didn't know what to do. I'd been advised to always appear strong in front of my children. I was counseled to be brave, allow no tears, voice no fears, and never complain. My strength would inspire the children to be strong, as well. Sitting with the boys that evening, I realized that I had been living a lie.

So I decided (or was inspired) to *share with them* what was going on inside me. I started with what was most important: I told them how much I loved them. I apologized for not talking to them openly and honestly about what had happened to our family. I admitted that this new status of divorced single parent was embarrassing and awkward for me.

I went on to say that I often wasn't sure how my friends would treat me or how the neighbors would act around me. I even told them that I was still concerned about my family's reaction. Finally, I told them that I was scared because I didn't know how to be a single parent.

Along the way, I've learned:

+ Adults often don't recognize when children are grieving.

+ Children don't know how to grieve, and the consequences of this can be devastating.

+ Children don't distinguish between the pain of loss that results from death and divorce, separation, or abandonment.

+ Children can be healed from loss.

Suzy Yehl Marta is the founder and president of Rainbows for All Children, a charity dedicated to giving children and teens the guidance to grieve and grow after a loss. Since 1983, Rainbows has had more than 2.5 million children participate. Suzy's book, *Healing the Hurt, Restoring the Hope*, was published for caregivers to help guide children and teens through times of divorce, death, or crisis with the Rainbows approach. Find more at www.opentohope.com.

# How to Help a Young Adult with the Loss of a Parent
By Emily McManus

 My father died nearly six years ago of esophageal cancer when I was eighteen and in my first year of college. Looking back on that time, I feel as though it happened both yesterday and decades ago. Death acts as a supernova to memories; seconds stand crystal clear illumined, while whole weeks are a blur. I'm so grateful that I am blessed with my mom and sister in my life. While we have all traveled our own individual grief journeys, I think that we have been invaluable fellow travelers, meeting on the road and warning about rocky passages ahead or sharing in warmth. Honoring the individuality of each of our relationships with my dad has allowed us to share in the commonalities of losing someone we all loved dearly.

Children and teenagers deal with their grief and emotions differently than adults. This may seem odiously obvious when thinking of how teens confront contemporary issues—obsessing over objects of affection, hysteria over clothes, the desire to listen to the same song ten million times on family car trips—but it's easy to forget when experiencing a child's reaction to the death of a parent. Seemingly dismissive or facetious attitudes often conceal a deep well of emotion.

I know that during the time my father was ill and after he died, I compartmentalized my feelings a great deal as a coping strategy. A teenager's head and heart are not always connected, and although I received straight A's that first semester in college, I found it nearly impossible to cry in front of people. If I hadn't possessed a cool exterior, it would have been impossible to carry on, to say good-bye to my daddy after a weekend visit from college without ignoring the possibility this would be the last time I saw him. Perhaps because I seemed "fine" on the surface, extended family members were less inclined to offer the emotional support I so desperately needed, but didn't know how to ask for.

An agreement to honor individual feelings is pivotal to weathering this difficult time. Family members cannot judge each other on who seems to be the saddest. Grief isn't a contest, the only prize on the other side of the fog is survival, and any "new normal" will never exist if failure to thrive proves who loves the deceased the most. Offer support to bereaved family members as if they were actually coping far less well than they seem to be, because in private they probably are worse than you can imagine.

For those supporting grieving children, I think that the worst thing a surviving parent can do is invoking the deceased parent's name to control the child. "If your mother was alive . . . " or "Your father would never allow . . ." Besides being manipulative, these words alter the relationship of the child with the parent who is gone and can't speak for him or herself.

Children are already missing one parent at every moment. If a parent can't be present for every occasion, joyous and miserable, why only bring his memory into already fretful conversations? However, on the other side of the coin, I'm always appreciative when people bring up my father in a positive way. At my younger sister's college graduation, I was touched when family members said how proud my dad would have been of her, because it affirmed all of the wonderful ways he was a tremendous gift and influence on our lives, rather than solely focusing on his absence.

I've often heard that after a huge loss, those grieving should try to not make any big decisions or changes in their lives for at least a year. This is wonderful advice for adults, to not sell the house or run off to Vegas, but virtually impossible for teens or young adults. In the year following my father's death I moved twice, stopped speaking to virtually all of my longtime best friends, and decided to transfer to a college across the country. While many of these changes were a natural part of becoming an adult, I wish that I had understood then how much I was not really myself during that period.

People grieving should be given small business cards to act as an in-person answering machine that reads, "I'm sorry, I'm not here right now. Please come back in a year, and I'll try to be more pleasant." It's more to remind oneself than to make excuses to other people. As normal as melodrama in relationships is to younger people, the deep, enduring sadness that is grieving is beyond even the most well-meaning friends' comprehension.

After receiving insensitive comments from the most mature adults, we all know that no one really understands until he or she has experienced a loss. But it would be tremendously helpful for a teacher, coach, or close family friend to explain to friends and classmates of a grieving child what has happened, and what a gift time and patience are.

Most importantly, remind the grieving child to be patient with him or herself, and allow time to remember and time to continue growing, following a staggering loss. "Bereaved" originally meant "to be deprived," and while we who have experienced a loss will always be deprived of our loved one, eventually the sense of being deprived of oneself will depart if we can first be compassionate with ourselves.

---

Emily McManus's father died of esophageal cancer when she was eighteen years old. Emily earned her undergraduate degree from New York University. She has written and published original fiction and nonfiction, has edited numerous articles, journals, and books, and is an accomplished artist. While in college, she was an intern at *McSweeney's* and is currently attending graduate school. To read more, visit www.opentohope.com.

# What Parents Need to Know about Grieving Teens

By Gloria Horsley, PhD, MFT, RN,
and Heidi Horsley, PsyD, LMSW, MS

*I* *hate you! Leave me alone! I'm not going to some dumb support* *group! You can't make me! I don't want to talk about it! You're* *so unfair! It's none of your business if I'm drinking! So what if my* *grades have dropped! The only people who really care about me are* *my friends!*

If you have been living with a grieving teenager, you have no doubt heard some of these comments and more. Parents who are bereaved themselves seldom feel that they are coping well with their own feelings, let alone supporting their teens. It is important to also realize that despite your best intentions, it is easy to make mistakes, so be compassionate with yourself and hold fast to the idea that you are doing the best you can under the most difficult circumstances.

The death of a loved one is one of the most painful events anyone can experience. It turns a teen's world upside down and puts everything into question. As you well know, adolescence is a time of transition and change, which makes it particularly difficult to deal with a loss. We hope to give you a feeling for what your bereaved teens may be going through, as well as give you some suggestions on how you might help.

## Five Reasons Why Bereaved Teens Suffer

1. **Pressed to talk.** Parents often tell us they are concerned because their teen does not talk about the loss. Teens tell us that they are talking about the death with their friends, but they do not want to burden or cause more pain to their parents, who are also grieving. It is difficult for teens to see their parents in so much pain. They also do not want to run the risk of breaking down and regressing in front of their parents. Crying can make teens feel like children at a time when they are trying to behave like adults.

   **Suggestion:** Because teens have more difficulty than adults compartmentalizing, they can become easily overwhelmed with feelings about the loss. Therefore, discussion with teens regarding loss should take place in short time segments and at times when they do not need to concentrate. Although teens like their parents to mention the person who died and talk about memories, they do not like to be pressured to respond.

   Teens want parents to know that even if they are not talking to them about their loss, they are grieving. It is important for parents to model healthy grieving, such as setting aside a special time for mourning, journaling, walking, or exercising, as well as talking about their own feelings of loss.

2. **Developmental issues.** During the teenage years, the developmental task is to explore and test limits, to begin to separate from the family, and to become more autonomous. It is a time for progression, not regression. Teens are also developing independence by learning new skills such as driving a car. After a death, bereaved teens often tell us that their parents become more anxious and overprotective about their safety and want to know where they are on a minute-by-minute basis. Teens tell us that the cell phone can be both a blessing and a curse.

**Suggestion:** Even though it is easier said than done, try not to worry so much. The developmental task of teens during these years is to pull away. You may fear for their safety, but try to hold on with open hands. Remember their loss happened just at the time when teens crave more freedom. It is not personal; it is biological. Compromise. Teens want parents to know that they need age-appropriate freedom.

3. **Feeling different.** Teens can feel isolated because they seldom receive recognition of their loss from the community. While adults often receive dozens of condolence cards, teens often do not receive any personal notes. The focus is usually on the adults' grief, and statements like "your parents are going through a lot right now" and "be strong for your parents" are common.

Other teenagers can be sympathetic up to a point, but if they have not suffered a similar loss, they seldom recognize the intensity of the experience. While teens want others to know that they have suffered a significant loss as well, they do not want to be different or pitied. Most teachers are also sympathetic up to a point, but often do not have the knowledge of grief and loss required to support a bereaved teen who is emotional, acting out, or unable to concentrate.

**Suggestion:** Acknowledge the uniqueness of the loss for teens. Let them know that you are there if they want to talk. If it is a death of a sibling, tell them that you have lost a child but that you do not know what it is like to lose a sibling. Support them in taking breaks from their grief by planning fun activities together. You might also want to give their teachers an article or two on the impact of loss in the teenage years.

4. **Life must go on.** Grief takes an incredible amount of psychological, emotional, and physical energy. Teens only have a certain amount of control over their lives. For the most part, they cannot drop out of school for a semester or cut back on their team practices or after-school activities. Some teens who have experienced profound loss feel driven to over-achieve to make life seem meaningful. But in doing so, they do not allow themselves the time or energy required for grieving and healing.

**Suggestion:** Although adults may want teens to remain active after a loss, it may be realistic to encourage them to scale back in some areas—for example, taking part in fewer extracurricular activities. It is also helpful if you meet with schoolteachers and administrators to alert them to any anniversary dates that might be difficult for your child. It has been our experience that the school personnel may be willing to reduce the homework load during these times and will be more aware if your teen shows problem behavior.

5. **Numbing the pain.** Drugs, alcohol, and high-risk behaviors are always a concern when considering teenagers. However, for bereaved teens it may be more than just adolescent experimentation. Drugs and alcohol may be used to numb the pain of loss.

**Suggestion:** It is important for teenagers to experience their losses and not numb their feelings by using substances. Teenagers are going through important developmental milestones, and substance abuse can have long-lasting effects. Bereaved teens do tell us that there is a certain loss of innocence when someone they know dies, and that they do not feel that others understand what they are going through. Sometimes this drives them to reckless behaviors and a "live for the moment" attitude. It is important for all family members to be aware that grief continues to happen, even if numbed. The substances simply delay the healing.

## Tips for Grieving Teens

Teens who have experienced the death of someone they love have been through a lot. Although teens might not look like they are grieving, internally they are often on an emotional roller coaster. They need to find healthy ways to cope with their loss. It is important to keep communication open. Making statements such as, "I'm here if you want to talk" or "It must be very difficult for you right now; I will always be here for you," can be very validating to grieving teens.

While teens might not be willing or able in the moment to talk about their loss, they will know from these statements that you are there for them. Certainly make sure that there is not easy access to alcohol, medications, or other substances within your own home, and as an adult, be aware of how you may be using substances to deal with the loss.

## Conclusion

The death of someone we love is a sad and painful experience. As a parent it is heartbreaking to see your teen suffer as he or she copes with the profound sadness of loss. It takes time to heal. Our teens are going through important developmental years, plus carrying the extra burden of grief. Remember, that burden will forever change them but will not destroy them.

With your help and support, they will go through life remembering their loved one and incorporating them into their lives in new ways. Try not to be too hard on yourself or your teens. They will smile again, laugh again, and find joy again.

---

Dr. Gloria Horsley and Dr. Heidi Horsley are a mother/daughter team and internationally recognized grief experts. They are the founders of the Open to Hope Foundation and the hosts of the "Open to Hope" Internet radio show. In addition, Dr. Gloria is a board member for the Compassionate Friends and Dr. Heidi is an adjunct professor at Columbia University, with a private practice in Manhattan. They have coauthored *Teen Grief Relief,* among other books. Find more at www.opentohope.com.

# Saving Your Marriage or Dating Again

## How to Maintain Your Marriage after Child Loss
### By Sandy Fox

Many couples who have experienced the death of their child may also experience a crisis in their marriage as a result. But this can be an opportunity for growth, bringing them closer together.

The belief that bereaved couples are doomed to divorce has been blown way out of proportion. In fact, a Compassionate Friends survey indicates that only 4 percent of couples who divorce do so because of their child's death—something else was wrong in the relationship before the loss occurred. If a couple has always had a good marriage, typically their marriage will grow stronger, not collapse.

Making your relationship a priority during this difficult time should be your goal. One way to do this is to talk about your child. Remember the good times and funny incidents. Laugh at something silly that he or she did, as well as remember any awards, honors, and graduations that made you so proud. Don't dwell on how your child died. That is not going to bring him back. If you feel guilty about something, talk about it. If you are angry about something, talk about that also. Couples have a bond with their child that no one else can match, and by talking about those bonds and your feelings, you may realize how very similar you feel or at least respect how you differ.

The chance that both of you will grieve in the same way is unlikely. Partners should allow each other space to grieve at their own rate and in their own way. Personality, previous experiences, and your style of grieving contribute to that respect of grieving space. If one partner wants to cry, that doesn't mean the other one has to cry. If one partner doesn't feel like going out, she shouldn't feel obligated to do so. If you can't decide what to make for breakfast, don't worry about it. Your child died; you need time to adjust, and you eventually will.

A few other suggestions: Talk to friends about your relationship with your spouse to ease the stress buildup. Perhaps they have a good resource for any problems you're experiencing. You may also need to express feelings about your loss that you are not ready to discuss with your spouse to friends. Sometimes, going off on your own for a few hours or a day may give you a new perspective.

Don't bring your spouse down or make him or her suffer by making sarcastic comments or harmful accusations simply because you feel miserable. Look for ways you can please your spouse to ease the pain. Do some activity with your partner that you don't usually do but know he would like. Make a special meal that he enjoys. Or do something related to your child that up until now you have not been able to do.

At the end of the day, coming together is important. Review with your spouse what has happened that day, how you are feeling, and what you are thinking. You will more than likely learn a lot more about your partner during this period of your life than at any other moment in your relationship.

Time is also a great healer. As time passes, you will discover a sense of acceptance of what has happened to you and your spouse and will hopefully have the willingness to find new ways of living your life together, without your child.

---

Sandy Fox's only daughter, Marcy, died in an auto-mobile accident in 1994. Her new book, *Creating a New Normal . . . After the Death of a Child*, has more than eighty coping articles on surviving loss and many inspirational stories. Her first grief book is *I Have No Intention of Saying Good-bye*. Sandy has headed two national bereavement conferences for childless parents and speaks around the country. Read more of Sandy's articles at www.opentohope.com.

# Transcending the Loss of a Spouse to New Love

By Gloria Lintermans

The unimaginable has happened—you are a widow or widower. Mourning your loss has been the focus of your life for the past year or two. Finally, as you begin to surface from your profound grief, with a deep breath and a lot or a little trepidation, you find yourself falling in love again. Is this new relationship fraught with landmines? You bet! Here are important stepping-stones to help keep you afloat along the way—Do's and Don'ts, as it were, for widows/widowers beginning a new, loving relationship.

Perhaps you joined a bereavement support group, progressed through the stages of loss, and are doing pretty well. And then, surprise, you find yourself attracted to someone of the opposite sex. Not just someone to hear your grief, but someone who makes your heart quicken. What to do? What feels right? You are still grieving, but you're attracted and you want to date. You're also lonely and crave company. And yet, you feel guilty, disloyal to your late spouse.

+ **Do** take your time starting a new relationship; it's not unusual to feel like an awkward teenager again.

+ **Don't** rush into romance; start with friendship.

How do I let my grown kids know that I want to date? How can I help them to react in a positive way? I don't want to hurt them while they grieve their mother or father, but I also want to go on with my own life. How do I talk to them about my needs and be respectful of theirs? I know that they grieve on a different timetable.

+ **Do** be sensitive to the feelings of your children; encourage them to "speak their truth," while moving on with your life in a positive way.

+ **Don't** flaunt your dating or sexuality in front of your children.

I met someone I can see having a future with. She/he has furniture; I have furniture; how do we blend that? What do we do with family pictures?

+ **Do** be respectful in valuing the treasures of your partner.

+ **Don't** discard family pictures; find a way to blend what is important to both of you.

How do I financially protect my new partner and myself? Do we do a prenuptial agreement? What is fair? I want to leave money for my children and I also want to protect her/him, how do I do that? It's distasteful to seek the counsel of an attorney, but I feel I should do that. I have a townhouse, she has a townhouse; which townhouse do we live in? What do we do with our extra stuff, how much do we give away?

+ **Do** talk about your personal values, what is fair, and what is important to you.

- **Don't** rush into legal agreements until you have explored your feelings together.

- **Do** listen to your partner, even if his/her ideas are different from yours.

All of these questions are common and very real. You might be asking yourself: Do we like each other enough to resolve these questions? Can we come out of our own chaos and have a mutual life?

- **Do** realize that you have two "containers" in your chest, one for your old life and one for the new. You're adding, not subtracting. It is a tribute to your late spouse that you want another loving partner.

- **Don't** compare your new love to your late spouse.

- **Do** accept that your new partner has different interests that will enable you to explore new areas of growth.

- **Do** accept that it can be an interesting and rewarding challenge to meet each other's friends and children. For instance, his friends knew him as part of a couple, and it may take patience until they learn to see you as a new partner, but one who is not trying to replace his late spouse in their eyes.

A new partner and a shared life is indeed a positive challenge. Many widows/widowers take on the growth and welcome new love, wanting to heal and move forward to a renewed life with eagerness, joy, and expectation.

Gloria Lintermans wrote *The Secrets to Stepfamily Success: Revolutionary Tools to Create a Blended Family of Support and Respect* and *The Healing Power of Love: Transcending the Loss of a Spouse to New Love* (coauthored with Dr. Stolzman) following the death of her husband, Rick. She is a former internationally syndicated columnist and has appeared on radio and television across the country. To read more articles by Gloria, visit www.opentohope.com.

# Ten Dating Tips for Widows and Widowers
## By Abel Keogh

Dating again after the death of a spouse can be an awkward experience. It can bring out feelings of guilt and betrayal for you and feelings of confusion and concern from friends, family, and those who were close to the deceased spouse.

If you've lost a spouse and are looking to date again, here are ten tips to make sure you're able to navigate the dating waters successfully.

## 1. When you decide to date again is up to you.
There's no specific time period that one should wait before dating again. Grieving and the process of moving on is something that's unique to each person. Some people take years, others weeks, and then there are those who choose never to date again. Whatever you do, don't let others tell you you're moving too fast or waiting too long. Make sure it's something you're really ready to try before taking that step.

I started dating five months after my late wife died. Too soon? There were some friends and family who thought so. But five months was when I felt ready to at least test the waters. And though it took a few dates to get the hang of things, I have no regrets about dating that soon.

## 2. Make sure you're dating for the right reasons.

Take some time to understand why you want to date again. It's not wrong to date because you're lonely or desire some company. Single people date for those reasons, too. But if you're dating because you think it is going to fill the void somehow or heal the pain that comes from losing a spouse, it's not going to happen. However, dating does give you the opportunity to open your heart to another person and a chance to experience the unique and exquisite joy of falling in love again.

## 3. Feeling guilty is natural at first.

The first time I went to dinner with another woman, I felt like I was cheating on my late wife. As we entered the restaurant, I was filled with feelings of guilt and betrayal. Throughout our date I kept looking around to see if there was anyone in the restaurant I knew. I thought that if someone saw me out with another woman, the first thing he'd do was run and tell my dead wife what I was up to. It sounds silly, but I couldn't shake that feeling the entire evening. A week later, I went out with someone else. The guilt was still there but less intense. It took about five dates before I could actually enjoy the company of a woman without feeling guilty.

Those feelings should subside over time, especially when you find that special someone you might want to spend the rest of your life with. If the guilt's not subsiding, you might not be ready to date again. Take a break and try again when you might be more up to the task.

## 4. It's OK to talk about your deceased spouse, just don't overdo it.

Unless you're good friends or have known your date previously, he or she is going to be naturally curious about your spouse and your marriage. And it's OK to talk about your spouse when you're first dating someone. Answer questions he or she may have about your marriage, but don't spend all your time talking about the deceased or how happy you were. After all, your date is the one who's here now. And who knows, he or she might make you incredibly happy for years to come.

Constantly talking about the past may make it seem like you're not ready to move on and start a new relationship. Showing that you care enough to get to know your date can help reassure her that you're ready to start a new life with someone else.

## 5. Your date is not a therapist.

Would you like going out with someone who constantly talks about his issues? A date isn't a therapy session. It's an opportunity to spend time with someone and enjoy her company. If you find yourself dating just to talk about the pain in your heart, how much you miss your spouse, or the tough times you're going through, seek professional help. Spending $60 an hour on a therapist will benefit you much more than spending $60 for dinner and a movie. Besides, your date will have a more memorable night if it's about her, rather than about everything you're going through.

## 6. It's OK to make mistakes while you're finding your dating legs.

When I started dating again, it had been seven years since I had gone out with anyone other than my wife. Because I had a certain comfort level with my first wife, I often found myself forgetting proper dating etiquette, such as opening the car door or walking a date to her door at the end of the evening. If you find yourself forgetting simple dating etiquette, don't worry about it. Most dates would probably understand if they knew how long it's been. But don't make the same mistakes over and over. Learn from them and continue moving forward. You'll be surprised how fast your dating legs return.

## 7. Defend your date.

You may discover that once your family and friends learn you're dating again, they may not treat this new person in your life very well. It may come in the form of a cold shoulder at family activities or constantly talking about the deceased wife in front of your date. The offending parties need to be told privately, but in a loving manner, that this behavior is not acceptable. If you wouldn't let family or friends treat your spouse that way, why would you tolerate that behavior toward someone else, especially when your date could become your future spouse? Don't be afraid to defend your date. If you can't do that, then you have no business dating again.

## 8. Realize that not everyone will understand why you're dating again.

There will always be someone who will not understand why you've chosen to date again. They may give you a hard time or have some silly romantic notion that widows and widowers shouldn't fall in love again. Their opinions do not matter. All that matters is that you're ready. You don't need to justify your actions to them or anyone else.

## 9. Take things slowly.

The death of a spouse means losing the most intimate physical contact. After a while we miss the kisses, having someone's head resting on our shoulder, or the warm body next to us in bed. This lack of physical and emotional intimacy is enough to drive a lot of people into the dating scene. Don't feel bad if you find yourself missing these things. It's completely normal.

But in the dating world, wanting something that was part of our lives for years can become a ticking time bomb. It can force us into a serious relationship before we're ready. The result: lots of broken hearts and emotional baggage.

Don't be afraid to take things slowly. This isn't always easy. Sometimes it's hard not to throw ourselves at the other person, because we want to be close to someone again. We want that warm body next to ours and the words "I love you" whispered in our ears. But it can save you both a lot of emotional heartache if you wait to make sure what you're doing is because you love the person, and not because you miss the intimacy that you had with your late husband or wife.

## 10. Make your date feel like the center of the universe.

It's a basic dating rule, but widows and widowers often forget it. Because we already have someone special in our lives, we may forget sometimes to make our date feel special, too. She shouldn't have to compete against a ghost, even if you only have one date with her. As long as you're out together, she should be the center of your universe.

Even though dating can be awkward and difficult at times, it can also be a lot of fun. There's no reason being a widow or widower should hold you back from enjoying a night out. Part of the reason we're here is to *live* and enjoy life. And dating is a great way to start living again.

---

Abel Keogh's first wife died from suicide while expecting their first child. The story about her death and how he rebuilt his life is told in his memoir, *Room for Two*. He is also the author of the novel *The Third*. Abel works as a copywriter and has created marketing collateral for numerous organizations. He and his second wife, Julianna, are the parents of four children. Read more at www.opentohope.com.

# Widows: Let Love Win Out over Fear

By Michele Neff Hernandez

Five years ago when my husband died in a cycling accident, the last thing on my mind was finding a new man to love. Horrified by the unexpected jump from wife to widow, I struggled to regain both my sense of self and my will to live.

When I first was able to entertain the thought of marrying again, I thought I would be rendered mute when asked to utter the phrase "till death do us part." Those five words mean something completely different to me now that I know what *parting* actually feels like.

As my heart slowly recovered and love did again enter my life, I subdued a sense of dread about making another lifelong pledge. When I finally said "yes" to a wonderful man and faced the fact that I would be expected to make this promise out loud, I braced myself for the moment in our wedding ceremony when I would be asked if I would love him until death took him from my side.

But when the time arrived, I found myself overcome with joy that Michael and I made it to that moment. Together we allowed grief to coexist with love, though the concept may not make sense to many people. He didn't require me to walk away from my widowhood in order to become his wife.

With the assurance that my love for my first husband, Phil, was safe, my love for Michael found room to grow. This new love includes my kids, my family, my friends both old and new, and my widowed community. Finding someone who could embrace every part of my life is a blessing I experience with awe, and instead of crying all I could do was smile.

On our wedding day, the tears did fall when Michael and I finally laid down at the end of a wonderful evening full of love, laughter, and friendship. I cried and cried. When he asked me what was wrong, I said, "I don't think I believed until right this minute that this day would actually come." I explained to him that it was as if I'd held my breath for the two years we dated, waiting for the other shoe to drop. But love won out over fear, and so did I.

I write this article today being able to very clearly recall saying the words, "No one will ever measure up to Phil." The journey that has led me to the place I am today has been equal parts terrifying and amazing. I am not implying that being married again will wipe away all the pain of past loss, nor do I believe that finding a new life partner is somehow mandatory as proof of healing. I just wanted to share with you my reality, which is that I don't have to trade in one love for another . . . I can have both.

---

Michele Neff Hernandez's husband died in 2005. Since then, she has reached out to other widowed people as the founder and executive director of the Soaring Spirits Loss Foundation, which provides peer-based grief support programming worldwide. Michele is the creator of the Camp Widow program, a motivational speaker, a freelance writer, and the proud mom to three amazing kids. Read her articles at www.opentohope.com.

# More Valuable Tools and Advice

## The Value of Music for Resolving Grief

By Tony Falzano

It's no secret that many therapists, clergy, and medical professionals believe one of the best things we can do while grieving a loss is to have contact with loving, supportive people who will keep us active and provide company.

But in the times when we either want to—or need to—be alone, there is something that can give us privacy and yet take the empty stillness out of a room. This element is music, and it can be a quiet, supportive companion as we travel the road with grief.

Using music to keep us company is nothing new. Throughout our lives we have played our favorite songs for companionship when we were alone. We have counted on music to make our surroundings lighter, brighter, and more hopeful.

When you turn on music, it is like a friend or relative has stopped by to pay a visit. It fills the room with sound and activity. And while it plays, you are not entirely alone. You can talk to it, cry with it, and even shout at it. Having music play in this situation feels comfortable, like putting on a warm sweater on a cold day. You feel better when you are around music. While it plays you can do what you want.

And it will stay with you as long as you wish. However, unlike with a friend or family member, you don't have to worry about its feelings when you don't want to visit any longer. You can just shut it off and move onto something else with no explanations.

I'm not suggesting that music is all you need or that it should ever take the place of human interaction when you are upset, under stress, unsure, and feeling alone. What I am saying is that music can be an important ally as you integrate it in your total care and well-being.

Music can be a strong presence as we grieve. Music is like water that seeps into the soil of our souls so our emotions can come to the surface. What usually follows is crying, even sobbing. This should be welcomed. It's therapeutic to cry. It's one of the best things we can do. We release stress and toxins when we release tears. We also let go of pain, which helps us return to a calm state. That is why many of us feel better after a good cry.

We don't need music to cry. But just as a movie's soundtrack can augment the action or drama on the screen, music has a way of enhancing the emotions we are feeling from loss. There is something about it that heightens what we are experiencing.

Listening to songs is one way to keep us company when we are alone. But there are other ways that music can embrace, stabilize, and support us.

I realized this several years ago after my dad passed away. I was responsible for settling my parents' affairs. I knew going through their last possessions was going to be the most difficult, so I procrastinated for months. Then one day on the spur of the moment, I put on some music and proceeded to go through the many boxes still left.

I realized that I could only keep a few special tokens and most things would need to be discarded. Consequently, I held in my hands old photographs, letters, and memorabilia for the last time. These objects were not only part of my mother and father's lives, they also represented earlier periods of my own life.

It was an emotionally charged afternoon. But though I was physically alone, I did not feel alone. Those songs filled the silence with beautiful sounds. The best way I can describe it is that the music was like a friend working quietly on the other side of the room, helping me with the difficult task at hand.

Notice I said music and not the television or radio. Many television programs that enter our homes are loud and contain violent graphics that come to us at a rapid-fire rate. The radio is more subtle, but still can have people shouting to draw attention to their product. If you think about it, you probably would not want anyone to come over to your house and scream at you to buy something. Consequently, music is the better choice in these situations.

Many people believe music is the highest art form. It's hard to argue the point when we see all that it can do for us, including offering us health benefits, distracting us from our troubles while extending companionship to us. Music is an aural thrill.

It is an incredible gift and one we can count on to surround us with warm, tender, comforting sounds.

Along with family and friends, think of music as another partner on your journey through grief. The songs you listen to are true, reliable friends. And they prove what the Beatles sang to us all those years ago; we do get by, *with a little help from our friends.*

---

Tony Falzano writes about the healing power of music. His articles can be found in many major grief publications. Tony also writes music that is listened to by individuals grieving loss. His albums, *Just a Touch Away* and *In Abba's Arms,* contain beautifully orchestrated, instrumental music designed to be a companion to those searching for healing and hope. Find more on www.opentohope.com.

# The Role of Ritual Following a Major Loss
### By Stephanie Frogge

Several years ago, I was watching news coverage following the crash of a passenger plane that killed all on board. The plane actually crashed into the ocean, so over the next few days, survivor families gathered at the shore near where the plane had gone down to get information, comfort one another, and engage in memorial rituals.

Some family members chartered helicopters to fly over the actual crash site; many participated in impromptu candlelight vigils; literally hundreds joined together for a more formal ceremony that culminated in throwing wreaths of flowers onto the water at sunset. One broadcast journalist covering this particular event was overheard saying, "What's wrong with these people? Why don't they just go home and get on with their lives?"

For those of us who are bereaved, what we wouldn't give for it to be that simple.

Acknowledging the reality of our loved one's death takes both headwork and heart work. Our heads know, but our hearts take so much more convincing. That is one of the important roles of ritual—to help us re-experience the reality of our loved one's death in a structured environment. Those rituals may be public (such as a funeral) or private (as when you spend time in your loved one's bedroom with your nose buried in his T-shirts). They may be planned or spontaneous.

They all say the same thing: "Yes, this really happened."

For some, the notion of ritual either feels like something primitive and strange, or like something dry and boring, devoid of meaning. Our rituals need not be either. Ritual can be as contemporary as a marathon and as meaningful as creating a special design for our loved one's headstone. Ritual only loses its value when it becomes disconnected from the love we feel for the person who died.

Thanatologists—those who study death and dying—note that the rituals surrounding death serve a variety of important functions. One is to provide a behavioral expression of something that cannot be adequately expressed in other ways. "When words are inadequate, have a ritual," says Alan Wolfelt, Phd, CT, the founder of the Center for Loss. Indeed, words are wholly inadequate when it comes to articulating the significance of our loss, but meaningful acts may serve as additional expressions of our feelings.

Beth is a quilter. Following the death of her husband, she has begun creating a memory quilt. She plans to hang it over the bed they shared for thirty-six years. Selecting which items of her husband's clothing will go into the quilt, designing a pattern that is meaningful, even making a special place in her home where she can work on the quilt are all part of Beth's quilting ritual.

As Beth says: "I've cried countless tears as I've worked on it, but each stitch literally represents the love I have for Bob. I am creating this for my family and me, but I feel like I'm doing it for him and with him, too. I feel closer to Bob when I quilt, and it's the last thing I can do for him."

Familiar rituals, such as birthdays and graduation ceremonies, offer opportunities for marking our loved one's passage from physical presence to memory.

For Marci and her family, Christmas brings a new ritual honoring the life of her oldest son, Sean, who was killed in a motorcycle accident. "The kids and I just went through the motions that first Christmas after Sean was killed, but agreed when the next one approached that we would have to do something to include him. My younger son came up with the idea of a special Christmas tree for Sean, and now it's something we look forward to. We have a three-foot tree and we decorate it with things that were his and things that remind us of him. We eat gummy bears while we decorate his tree since that was Sean's favorite candy. Of course, we laugh and cry while doing it, but it's like Sean is still a part of our family and part of our holidays.

"I knew we were doing the right thing when my daughter had a friend over and took her to see the tree and said, 'This is my brother, and this is the bow tie he wore to his senior prom.' Now her friend knows about Sean and we don't have to pretend that he never lived."

A third role ritual plays is connecting us to the larger community at a time when the support of others may be comforting. After Kyle was killed in Iraq, his parents, Kyle, Sr., and Bev, thought often of how much Kyle loved hiking and camping while growing up, having learned about the outdoors from his father and grandfather. From those memories, the idea of a special outdoor event designed to give other children an experience that Kyle loved so much was born. Some two hundred children participated the first year, and dozens of Kyle's friends were on hand to help with the festivities. "Seeing Kyle's friends meant so much to us," recalls Bev. "Knowing that they remember and miss Kyle helps us cope with our own loss."

Another role of ritual is simply to mark something as being out of the ordinary; to give something special meaning. Acknowledging an anniversary is this type of ritual. For Sumer, it's simply taking a day of vacation on April 2, the anniversary of the day her mother was murdered, and doing something special in her memory.

"I've never been one for public rituals, but I have her pictures all over my apartment and I enjoy wearing her jewelry. When my brother and I were growing up, my mom would really sacrifice to get us something that we wanted; she loved buying things for us. So I do that for one of my cousins who lives in another country. His dad, my mom's brother, is disabled and can't work, and I know if my mom were alive, she would be buying things for him like she did for my brother and me. My cousin says he's the only kid in school wearing clothes from America! I know my mom would love that."

Even neurobiologists are discovering scientific evidence of the value of ritual. It appears as though some ritual actually provides a point of "unity" between our brain's left and right hemispheres—an intersection at which logic (left brain) and the ability to self-soothe (right brain) come together.

But for Lois, the mechanics of ritual aren't as important as the feelings they generate. "I just know that when I go to church and light a candle in honor of my dad, I feel at peace. I can watch the flickering candles and think about what a wonderful father he was, and I know that I can keep on living because he still lives inside of me."

Stephanie Frogge is a professional crime victim services consultant with more than twenty-five years of experience with programs that address social justice issues and assist victims of crime and the bereaved. She is the former national director of Victim Services for Mothers Against Drunk Driving (MADD) and also was the director of Peer Support Services for TAPS (Tragedy Assistance Program for Survivors), helping those whose loved ones died while in the military. Find more at www.opentohope.com.

# Healing Ink: Writing into Your Grief

## By Alice J. Wisler

A weeping willow tree, one flowery journal, two pens (in case one ran out of ink), and a box of tissues stayed close beside me. In my early confusion over the loss of my son, these items never ignored my grief or told me to "get over it."

When it grew too dark to see underneath the stringy weeping willow, I carried my pen and journal inside a house that seemed too empty and wrote some more. At night I woke to grapple with turmoil, with the noises in my head, the flashbacks of the cancer ward, the cries of my son. I wrote the ugly words "why?" and "how come?" before I could sleep again.

I scribbled through myths and clichés. I unleashed resentment and longing. I addressed prayers to God.

And, surprisingly, I discovered. Some of the confusion slid away, some of the guilt abandoned me. There was nothing I could have done to save my four-year-old's life. Even my love had not been strong enough to destroy the infection that flared inside his tiny body. I was human and really not as in control as I wanted to believe. I would have to live with that. I began to understand the new me. She was a tower of strength and compassion; she was tender and vulnerable; realistic, with just the right touch of cynicism. She needed protection from too many plastic smiles; she could not go long without a hug or sharing a story about a blue-eyed boy with an infectious laugh.

My written words healed me, and I jumped at the opportunity to tell others. I'd found comfort and clarity. I smiled at my husband and three young children and, at last, I didn't want to run my van over the cliff. I wanted to smell the peonies and taste the salt from the ocean on my skin.

The beauty about grief writing is that no one has to read it. You don't have to worry about a teacher correcting your spelling or grammar. There's no grade, no pass or fail. No one cares if your letters are sloppy. It's written by you and for you. And, yes, it works.

- Find a secluded place to write where you can think clearly without distraction.

- Write, at first, for your eyes only. It doesn't have to be shared with anyone.

- Write to chart progress for you to read years down the road.

- Write with the feeling, "I will survive this."

- Write to identify your emotions and feelings.

- Write to help solve some of the new situations you must now face.

- Think of your journal as a friend who never judges and who can never hurt you.

+ Write your spiritual struggles.

+ Write to rebuild your self-esteem and your self-confidence.

(From *Down the Cereal Aisle: A Basket of Recipes and Remembrances* by Alice J. Wisler)

---

Alice J. Wisler's four-year-old son, Daniel, died from cancer treatments in 1997. She is the founder of a grief-support organization, Daniel's House Publications, and the author of four inspirational novels and two cookbooks. Her writing focus has been on how to help others in grief. She facilitates Writing the Heartache workshops across the country. Alice and her family live in Durham, North Carolina. For more of Alice's articles, visit www.opentohope.com.

# The Healing Power of Dreams
# for the Bereaved
By Carla Blowey

Have you ever had a dream that made you question your sanity, your morals, your desires, or your fears? Dreams of being chased, going back to school, falling off a cliff, or driving a car without brakes can be quite unsettling, and we quickly credit a wild imagination for such scenarios. For the bereaved, these universal themes merge with memories and images of our deceased loved one, creating strange symbols and bizarre landscapes that fuel the fires of grief.

Carl Jung, the early twentieth century psychoanalyst, philosopher, and spiritual seeker, believed that our dreams were a spontaneous and symbolic depiction of what was happening in our life at that moment. He believed that the dream self taps into a personal warehouse of our thoughts, feelings, behaviors, and experiences to communicate its need for healing the wounded and broken parts of our being. In an effort to express itself more fully, the dream self will search for archetypal images and themes in the universal warehouse of humankind's collective experiences to convey its message.

For the bereaved, this inner warehouse becomes crowded as memories of our deceased loved one surface, competing with personal conflicts and spiritual issues that need attention and resolution. Our dreams then will reflect the status of our grief journey and uncover the issues and hidden agendas that block the path to acceptance and reconciliation. In the privacy of our inner world, we can act out behaviors or express emotions deemed unacceptable to us or to others.

Our fear of being overwhelmed by the "bad" dreams forces us to escape the situation by waking up, leaving the dream message incomplete. For the unaware dreamer, nightmares and recurring dreams seem to cause more pain and stress because the dreamer dismisses the very thing intended to bring understanding and healing.

We can begin to understand and interpret our dreams using metaphor, personal associations, universal symbols, myth, folklore, and scripture. If we are open, trusting, and receptive to this process, we can discover the gift of the dream in whatever form presented.

My appreciation for dream work began in 1991 with a precognitive and prophetic dream predicting the death of my five-year-old son, Kevin. Fear and doubt pushed the images aside that day, and I chalked it up to another one of those weird dreams.

Less than twelve hours later, my son lay unconscious, bleeding to death on the snow-packed street at the foot of our neighbor's driveway. While I had been in the kitchen making dinner, the nightmare flashed before me. Fearful, I rushed out the door to meet him on the sidewalk. To my horror, Kevin had been struck down and driven over by a truck as he rode his bike on the sidewalk past our neighbor's home.

In the days that followed, frightening images from the nightmare attacked my sanity and held me captive whether I was asleep or awake. Consumed by guilt, I believed I had lost my chance to heed its warning and save Kevin. Everything I believed to be true was tested, and my belief system crumbled around me. I had entered the dark night of the soul, a place where every bereaved parent has lived in the wake of his or her child's death.

Strangely, though, within days of Kevin's death, I was not just dreaming about Kevin, I was dreaming Kevin! He was whole and holy! That wonderful feeling of being with Kevin in my dreams felt the same as if he were alive.

Initially, I recorded my dreams to preserve my "new" memories of Kevin. The disappointment of waking up and not having dreamed of him at all was sheer agony. Meanwhile, a pattern emerged of other dreams that mirrored the pain of our separation and reflected my chaotic life. Each night my fears, desires, and memories appeared on my dream screen, fueling the persistent themes of guilt, suffering, and separation. I soon learned that my dreams contained guidance and wisdom for healing my tortured soul.

Ultimately, my soul's desire was to heal itself, and God's response was to send some amazing companions to love and support me. The key was recognizing that I had a choice in the way I perceived my dreams and my grief. I could choose to allow the nightmare and my grief dreams to possess me and fuel more fear and guilt, or I could choose to expose them to the light and see them differently. When I viewed the dream using my intuitive eyes, suspending all the criticisms and judgments of the mind to allow the images, feelings, memories, and emotions to surface and tell their truth, I discovered that Kevin had simply transitioned from matter to spirit, and that his love for our family and me was stronger than ever.

The message of the dream was not a warning to save Kevin. I could not save him from his destiny. Rather, the dream was intended to prepare me for the dramatic spiritual transition that would enable me to see differently and to love more consciously. The nightmare was actually a blessing in disguise designed to heal my soul and empower my life.

---

Carla Blowey is a bereaved mother and author of *Dreaming Kevin: The Path to Healing*. She is a former editor and columnist for *Living With Loss* magazine. A Certified Dreamwork Facilitator through the Marin Institute of Projective Dreamwork, Carla is an exceptional speaker, presenting customized programs and workshops on using dreams as a tool for healing loss and grief to local and national bereavement groups, retreats, and conferences. Learn more at www.opentohope.com.

# Scrapbooks Memorialize
# Loved Ones
### By Diana Gardner-Williams

Your pain is a reflection of your love for those who have made the journey to another place. It may feel as though part of you has left with them. We never want to part with the memories; we hold them close in many different ways. That's where creating a scrapbook can help.

Some memories are captured on film or video, in writing found in journals, cookbooks or calendars, and in personal clothing, hair, or jewelry. When a loved one passes away, family members usually gather favorite pictures of the deceased to display at the funeral or wake. Sometimes pictures are pasted to large poster boards in a collage and placed on an easel for all the guests to view. This activity is a form of scrapbooking.

This craft is an increasingly popular activity today; however, it has been practiced for a very long time. Scrapbooking allows people to select favorite pictures, tell a story by journaling, and embellish pages with memorabilia significant to the deceased and to the person creating the scrapbook. Memorabilia may include poems, recipes, plane tickets, or anything that conveys the message of your scrapbook page.

The word "scrapbooking" may intimidate some who think of it as an elite craft for creative-minded people. *Remembering* is a simpler word to describe scrapbooking. Ask yourself: What do I want to remember? What do I want those in the future to know about the deceased? There are certain events that only you and the loved one have had the pleasure of experiencing together. This is your opportunity to document it in a unique and special way.

You can pour yourself into your pages so that when people view this tribute, they also feel as though you are telling a story. Your personality, your handwriting, and your favorite pictures placed in a certain way will make your scrapbook dedication unique. It is not just the pictures themselves, but also the presentation and perspective of the person telling the story. You are memorializing your love and, in turn, another person will interpret your love in the future.

After spending some time scrapbooking at your own leisure, you will develop your own style—whether it is organic and free-flowing, or more structured and organized. There are no rules, of course. The only concern is using products that are lignin and acid-free to preserve your pages for a longer period of time.

As you prepare your scrapbook, you will be able to explore your emotions in depth. If you never truly had the chance to vocalize your feelings in person, take this time to reconnect with those thoughts. It is never too late to express love and gratitude. Keep a journal close by to jot down anything that comes to mind. We need to continue living, and we need to find a way to heal from our losses. Scrapbooking gives us that outlet by allowing us to preserve our loved one's legacy in a positive and productive manner, without having their physical bodies present.

---

Diana Gardner-Williams is the mother of four children and has sadly experienced two early pregnancy losses and one stillbirth. This inspired her to create Just a Cloud Away, Inc. to help families grieving the loss of an infant create specialty remembrance kits, memory garden tutorials, scrapbooks, and keepsake crafts. She also speaks on topics of pregnancy and infant loss. Read more of her work at www.opentohope.com.

# Bereaved Mom Saved by Looking Outward, Helping Others
By Genesse Gentry

After the death of our daughter, Lori, I was completely devastated. Everything I believed about life was tossed out the window, and I was filled with despair. It felt as if grief would destroy me.

Much of that time is now a blur, too painful to remember. But I do recall clearly my feeling of disconnection from most of the world of the living. My life had been ruined, and I had no idea what to do. The friends with whom I'd surrounded myself before Lori's death had no way of knowing how to befriend me in this, and I had no idea how to ask for the help I needed. So hurt and loneliness were added to my overwhelming grief, because friends who didn't know what to do or say often opted to do and say nothing.

Then my husband and I found the monthly meetings of the Compassionate Friends, a support group for families who have experienced the death of a child. I won't say it was immediately a perfect fit for me, because it wasn't, or that I felt comfortable at the meetings, because I didn't. I was a very private person; I had no experience crying on anyone's shoulder. My tears had always been in solitude. I'd never learned to express my feelings in words.

So when someone asked me how I was feeling, I'd almost panic. How *did* I feel? And after listening to the others in the circle, by the time my turn came, I was often overwhelmed with feelings. Like many others, I can't cry and talk at the same time, which caused people to have to wait as I tried to get the words out. I hated all the eyes on me while I tried to gain enough control to speak.

Why did I keep going? At the beginning it was because my husband, Bill, wanted to go, and it was there that I learned more about how he was feeling. I was also learning ways of coping with my loss from the more seasoned grievers. All too soon I learned that the Compassionate Friends provided a sanctuary, the rare place where I could try to explain my feelings or talk about Lori and her death without people trying to change the subject because they were being made uncomfortable by my words.

And it was such a relief to find out that not only was it OK to voice my darkest thoughts and feelings, but others often felt the same way, too. They understood! Some months, I had to overcome my lethargy to get into the car and drive the half hour to get to the meetings, but every time I went I was thankful that I had. Looking back now, I realize that the meetings, and the friends I made at the meetings, probably saved my life.

By the spring before the second anniversary of Lori's death, we were no longer attending every meeting. I regularly spoke with the Compassionate Friends, but didn't feel I needed to go every month. I had come to the point, as so many do, where I felt I'd received most of the help I would get from the group. I might soon have stopped going altogether.

Now I can't even imagine who I would have become if that had happened. Instead, I was given a gift, a reason to keep attending. Our facilitator was moving out of the area, and I was asked to facilitate the local meetings. I said yes and found there was a whole new world of healing when I stopped going only for myself and began to attend meetings to help others. I can't overemphasize the importance of this turning point in my life.

From then on, every month I had to look outside myself into the hearts and minds of others and try to give them hope. I found the intensity of my own raw pain began to take a backseat to that of others more newly bereaved than I. Because I needed to find words for *them*, to try to help ease *their* pain, a floodgate was gradually opened in me and words, amazing words, began to fill my life.

Feelings, with the words to describe them, began to well up from my innermost being—feelings from the past, from those first months after Lori's death, and feelings in the present. The words came in the form of poetry—poems to help me understand myself and poems to help others. Truly, I believe this would not have happened if I hadn't opened my heart to my newly bereaved compassionate friends.

I believe there is the potential for something like this to happen to all who become actively involved in the "helping" aspect of the Compassionate Friends. I don't mean that everyone begins writing poetry. But I do believe that the greatest healing derived from the group is this outward movement, this growth away from the self-centeredness, the self-absorption of grief toward the openhearted hope of helping others.

It occurs to me that parenthood itself does something like this. From our self-centered, self-directed lives before our children are born, we learn the awesome responsibility of another person's life when we first gaze upon them. Our lives change focus, and their survival and growth become our highest purpose; our hearts become larger because our children are in them. When our children die, we not only hurt because the most important, most loved people of our lives are gone, but that intense focus is also gone along with our sense of great purpose. We wander in a wasteland, searching for what has been lost.

When Lori died, we still had our fifteen-year-old daughter Megan at home, but I felt so crippled as a mother. How thankful I am that Megan was somehow able to get through those early years with a mother so distracted by grief—and emotionally distanced by fear. I was half a mother in more ways than one.

Now, because of the Compassionate Friends, I began to find a new focus for my maternal instincts and a new way to grow back into the loving mother I'd been before Lori died. As I tried to grow to the task of helping those more newly bereaved than I, just as I'd had to grow to the task of being Lori and Megan's mother, I was benefiting threefold. First, my "mother" energy, which is a huge part of me, was again flowing outward. Second, as I was learning ways to help others heal, I was learning them for myself. And third, once again, I began to feel that I was doing something important with my life, that my life mattered, that my life had purpose.

And just as important to me, the Compassionate Friends have allowed me to keep Lori more visibly in my life. Wherever I go, whatever I do for the group, Lori's name is mentioned; Lori is not forgotten. All I do for the Compassionate Friends, I do in her name, and because what I do for the organization matters, Lori's life continues to matter, all these years after she left this earth. Through this organization Lori remains in the forefront of all I do, the guiding star in the direction of my life. I could not have found a more loving or fitting way to honor her than I have through the Compassionate Friends. My grief and the Compassionate Friends have forced me to grow in ways I had never dreamed. And Lori has been with me every step of the way.

From *Catching the Light—Coming Back to Life after the Death of a Child.* A version of this was previously published in the Compassionate Friends' quarterly magazine, *We Need Not Walk Alone.*

---

G enesse Gentry's daughter, Lori, died in a car accident in 1991. Genesse is the author of two books of poetry, *Stars in the Deepest Night* and *Catching the Light.* She is active in the Compassionate Friends, currently serving on the steering committee of the Compassionate Friends Marin, as well as regional coordinator for northern California. She presents writing workshops at national and local Compassionate Friends conferences. Read more at www.opentohope.com.

# Helping Others Helps You
## By Ariane de Bonvoisin

Taking time to put your situation to the side and focus on somebody else is a powerful way to get back in touch with who you are and what you can give. When you stop obsessing about your own pain and problems and instead direct your energy to helping somebody else, you will find that you also have the strength to move through your grief.

I know a woman who recently became a single mother. During this period she decided to help an elderly woman who lived across the street with grocery shopping, meals, and general organizing. Even though her whole life required major reorganization now that her husband had walked out and she had very little free time, she found that the most calming action she could take was to help someone else.

She felt important and necessary. If she didn't show up, this older woman would be stuck. She got back in touch with what really matters: being kind, being loving, and helping someone out during the day.

You don't have to help a stranger. Make a list of your friends and loved ones, even your colleagues, and ask yourself: What can I do for this person that would help? What does he or she need? Your help can be as simple as sending a card, making a phone call, mailing a clipping of an interesting magazine article, or finally taking the time to share a meal.

When her brother committed suicide, Rachel found that helping others was the best method of moving through her own pain. During the first, and hardest, day after her brother's death, she nurtured her family in the most basic yet essential way. "They hadn't eaten all day, and I focused on feeding them. It was the only thing I knew how to do," she says. "Being there for others has always helped me get out of my own way."

To move through change, it's essential to burst through the illusion that you are the only one experiencing pain or suffering. It is the gift of perspective. Yes, your job, health, or finances may be changing, but you also have a responsibility to show up in the world for your friends, family, and community. Be bigger than just your change. Someone else needs you.

I love this Chinese parable about helping others:

> *If you want happiness for an hour—take a nap.*
> *If you want happiness for a day—go fishing.*
> *If you want happiness for a month—get married.*
> *If you want happiness for a year—inherit money.*
> *If you want happiness for a lifetime—help others.*

Adapted from *The First 30 Days: Your Guide to Any Change* by Ariane de Bonvoisin

---

Ariane de Bonvoisin is the founder and CEO of The First 30 Days, a start-up media company focused on helping people through a major life change, event, or decision. Her book is entitled *The First 30 Days: Your Guide to Making Any Change Easier.* She is also a TV and radio personality, a mentor, and "Chief Change Optimist." Please visit www.opentohope.com to find more about Ariane and The First 30 Days.

# When the Crying Won't Stop
By Gloria Arenson, MFT, DCEP

I recently met a woman I'll call Anna, who lost her spouse in a terrible accident ten years ago. Although time has passed, for her it is as if it happened yesterday. Whenever she remembers, as she does every day, she can't help but weep.

Anna wanted to tell me her story, and as she started to speak, she was so overwhelmed by her pain that she could only sob. I knew that reliving the moment over and over keeps the wound open, and this is harmful physically, emotionally, and spiritually. Therefore, I showed Anna a simple technique for lessening the pain. It is called EFT (Emotional Freedom Technique).

EFT is a rapid way to eradicate negative emotions. You can perform EFT any time and anywhere when you feel out of control. When you are feeling upset, and especially if you are crying, the body tightens and you may experience a knot in your stomach, neck, or shoulders. This results in restricted breathing.

Begin by taking a deep breath to rate how distressed you are from 1 to 10. The deepest, most satisfying breath you are capable of is rated 10. Anything below an 8 indicates that you need this quick grief reduction treatment.

1. Take a deep breath. Rate the depth and pleasure of your breath from 1 to 10.

2. If your rating is 8 or less, rub or tap along the outer edge of your hand below the little finger and say this three times: "Even though my breath is constricted, I am releasing grief and tension now."

3. Using your index and middle finger, gently tap or touch the following power points for only three seconds while you say or think, "I'm releasing this sadness."
   + The inner edge of the eyebrow near the nose
   + The outside edge of the eye socket
   + Under the lower lid of the eye
   + Under the nose
   + Under the lower lip
   + Under the collarbone
   + On the side of the body about four inches under the armpit

4. Take a deep breath and rate how satisfying it feels again.

Keep doing steps two and three until you are breathing deeply and pleasurably. You will notice that as your breathing deepens you will also feel calmer.

Since Anna could not stop crying at first, I asked her to start tapping the energy points as she told me what had happened. As she talked and tapped each point she gradually stopped crying and was able to talk clearly. By the end of her tale, she was calm although still very sad. Overall, she felt great relief.

Do this exercise one or more times a day to calm yourself any time you feel as if your despair is too much to bear.

Gloria Arenson, a licensed marriage and family therapist and diplomat in comprehensive energy psychology, is passionate about helping people using EFT (Emotional Freedom Techniques) to heal negative emotions and behaviors. Gloria is the author of the award-winning book *Five Simple Steps to Emotional Healing*, as well as other books and articles. She is in private practice in southern California. Read more of Gloria's articles at www.opentohope.com.

# PART IV

Let Hope Blossom

# Continuing Your Bonds

---

## Tell the Positive Story of Your Child's Life

By Sandy Fox

I have a suggestion for all bereaved parents to call up positive memories of your child:

First, you need to find a quiet place in your home with no distractions. Sit in a comfortable chair and, with pen and paper or on your computer, jot down a few phrases of every good memory you can think of related to your child. Make the memory phrases just long enough so it is clear in your mind. You may end up with twenty-five, fifty, or even more than a hundred.

They can be in any order or age. You can rearrange later. Make sure they are labeled. They can be labeled by year, by events, by honors, by family gatherings, by humor, or by whatever you'd like.

At first, it may be difficult to think of many things because you are consumed by your child's death, but as time moves forward, many memories will return as your mind begins to focus once again.

Go back over these memories and select ten. For each of these ten, write as much as you can remember about the memory. In other words, tell a story. Use these ten memories when appropriate. For instance, you can tell a few stories to friends or family members who may live out of town and were not an everyday presence in your child's life. One of the best places to talk about these memories is at family dinners or holiday events where others may reminisce as well about their children.

When you have gone through these ten memories with everyone suitable to hear them, put them aside and start on another ten. Repeat these stories to others and so on, so that you always have stories and reasons to talk about your child. You can always come back to many of them, depending on the situation.

For example, a story I remember about my daughter I like to tell happened when she was in a beauty contest at age four and was finally called to the stage to be interviewed. Her personality really shined. She had the whole audience in hysterics as she demonstrated, very dramatically with stories and expressions, what it was like waiting backstage for hours.

Typically, people will be afraid to bring up your child's name for fear it will hurt you and make you sad. I think just the opposite happens for me. When someone brings up my child's name and asks a question, I am so happy to talk about her, and in turn, that shows others they do not have to be afraid that I will be upset. What makes me upset is when others ignore the fact that I even had a child!

Keep these memories in a file so you don't lose them. However, don't dwell on them or focus exclusively on them and ignore the present. That is not healthy. These memories will always be fun to look back on years later when the pain is less severe and the memories begin to fade. These are the types of memories you always want to reinforce in your heart and mind, because we will never, nor do we want to, forget our children.

---

Sandy Fox's only daughter, Marcy, died in an automobile accident in 1994. Her new book, *Creating a New Normal . . . After the Death of a Child,* has more than eighty coping articles on surviving loss and many inspirational stories. Her first grief book is *I Have No Intention of Saying Good-bye.* Sandy has headed two national bereavement conferences for childless parents and speaks around the country. Read more of Sandy's articles at www.opentohope.com.

# The Gifts That Keep on Giving
## By Pat Loder

As I sit here writing, it would be my father's birthday. His physical presence has been gone from my life for many years. But the memory of him—his essence, his teachings, and his love—surrounds and envelops me every moment of every day. The same thing holds true for each of the very important people whose physical presence was lost to me, within an eighteen-month period of time, almost two decades ago.

I'd like to take a few moments to tell you about each of those wonderful people and their magnificent gifts that have graced my life. Perhaps in so doing you, too, can shift your thinking from how your loved one died to how your loved one lived.

My brother, Rick, was the first to leave, dying of cancer in 1990. Rick was the firstborn in the family, ten years my senior, and, boy, did he use that to his advantage!

Rick had a quick wit. I always thought of him as a free spirit. Most of his adult life he lived from paycheck to paycheck, seldom with much money in his pocket. But if a friend needed a dollar and Rick had only fifty cents, he would give him what he had and figure out a way to help his friend get the rest of the money.

When Rick learned of his terminal cancer, it was important to him to see as many of his friends as possible—and he had many. When the pain medication made it impossible for him to drive himself, he asked me to take him to visit his friends. He wanted to say good-bye. These good-byes were not full of sadness, but were filled with reminiscing and laughter.

He taught me generosity, the importance of friendships, dignity in death, and laughter in life.

A few months after my brother's death, my two children, Stephanie and Stephen, were killed in a car accident. Oh, how I miss them, but what lessons those beautiful kids taught me.

From the moment they were placed in my arms, I was mesmerized by the wonders of human creation—the softness of their skin and the sweetness of their being.

Stephanie and Stephen taught me how fuzzy-seeded dandelions could tickle your nose and how blowing the seeds could erupt into silliness and giggles within seconds of starting our game. They showed me how much fun it was to lie in the grass on a warm summer day, looking for shapes in the clouds that reminded us of their favorite cartoon characters. They taught me how wonderful hair freshly washed with Johnson's Baby Shampoo can smell on a pajama-clad child who is cuddled in your lap, all warm and cozy on a winter's night. They taught me that even warming up a frozen meal made me a good "cooker."

They taught me how a small hand held in mine meant I was entrusted with the most important job in the world—being Stef and Steve's mom.

Stephanie and Stephen showed me that beauty surrounded my world every day. They taught me the meaning of unconditional love, trust, and sharing. Most important, they taught me that the four most beautiful words I would ever hear are, "*I love you, Mommy!*"

Thirteen months after Stef and Steve died, my dad joined them. Although not the "official" cause of death, he died from a broken heart—trying to be brave by holding in his pain after the deaths of his son and two beloved grandchildren.

Dad taught me the importance of family—to be there for each other in good times and bad. He sat silently in my hospital room after Stef and Steve died. There was nothing to be said, but it was important to him that he be with me, and equally important to me that he was there.

My dad grew up with an undeniably strong work ethic. His life was lived by the golden rule. He taught me that you had to earn people's trust and live up to your promises. On Sundays you could find him in church. He sat in the pew on the right side, fourth row from the back. I sit there now.

Dad's hands were rough and calloused from years of hard work, but he had a tenderness that could instantly calm a crying baby and a mechanical genius that could fix anything. He taught me the importance of family and God, to work hard, to always try my best and be the best I can be.

These types of gifts our loved ones have given us can't be measured by the years they lived. These gifts are measured by the love we shared with them. They are not wrapped in pretty paper and tied with a big bright ribbon and a bow. These are the gifts that define who we are and are intimately woven throughout the fabric of our lives. They are priceless, always to be treasured and appreciated.

When darkness falls and the quiet hush of night gently covers you, reflect on those special persons you miss who so greatly affected your life, and remember the unique memories and gifts with which they so blessed you. Allow their love to surround you, envelop you, and bring you inner peace.

When the morning dawn awakens you, spend a few moments reflecting on the gifts that you received. Make them "the gifts that keep on giving" by sharing them with others throughout the day . . . and throughout your life. In so doing, a part of your loved ones will always live on.

---

Patricia Loder lost her eight-year-old daughter, Stephanie, and five-year-old son, Stephen, in a tragic car accident in 1991. She founded a Compassionate Friends chapter a few months later and has been involved in leadership positions in the organization for many years, currently serving as its National Executive Director. She has written many stories regarding grief and bereavement and is a frequent workshop presenter and grief speaker. Learn more at www.opentohope.com.

# Continuing Your Connection
By Gloria C. Horsley, PhD, MFT, RN,
and Heidi Horsley, PsyD, LMSW, MS

"**S**cott is dead!"

These are the dreaded words that no parent or sibling should ever have to hear, words that irrevocably changed our lives forever. We heard these words twenty-eight years ago, when Scott Preston Horsley, our beloved son and brother, died in a fiery collision when he was a passenger in a car that hydroplaned and slammed into a bridge abutment. He was only seventeen years old. In an instant, his life was snuffed out and our lives were suddenly turned upside down, plunging us into the dark depths of grief.

As our journey of grief began, we looked to others further along in the grief process for guidance and strength. The journey was bumpy. Grief came in choppy, unpredictable waves. The seminal thinker Elisabeth Kübler-Ross wrote about moving through five stages (denial, anger, bargaining, depression, and acceptance) to deal with a loss. Acceptance is seen as the final stage and the goal to recovery. We certainly did recognize those feelings as we grieved for Scott.

But many well-meaning people told us we would eventually move on with our lives, get over it, and find closure. In the past, the bereaved have been told that moving on, cutting ties, and disengaging from deceased loved ones would help them get on with their lives. In fact, many mental health professionals saw this as an important part of the grief process.

These concepts were not comforting and did not make sense to us. We didn't want to "get over" Scott. To "get over" him felt somehow like we were erasing him from our lives. Scott is the only son and brother we will ever have. To deny our relationships with him would be to deny an important part of our family.

We realized that we wanted to continue having a relationship with him. In fact, research now shows that maintaining a connection with the deceased is actually adaptive and emotionally sustains people. In other words, we are now encouraged to maintain emotional bonds by incorporating the deceased into our lives, while simultaneously investing in new relationships and moving on in productive ways.

One of the projects we undertook in memory of Scott was to collaborate on a book, *Teen Grief Relief: Parenting with Understanding, Support and Guidance*. Also, as a mother-daughter team, we host a daily radio show called "Open to Hope," and we dedicate each show to Scott. He will always be an important part of our lives. Over the years, our connections to him have changed and evolved, but they have not lessened, nor do we want them to. Our memories bring us comfort and emotionally sustain us.

At this point you may be asking, "How do I incorporate my deceased loved one into my life and move onto new relationships?" It does take time and patience. If you are in the early stages of grief or under stress, we suggest you start by first taking care of your personal welfare. Find opportunities to tell your story and talk about your deceased loved one. Grief groups like the Compassionate Friends provide a great forum for this. Talking about your child, sibling, or other loved one allows you to begin developing those lasting memories that will sustain you and become part of the tapestry of your life.

It is our experience that as time goes on, your journey will become less painful and you will naturally begin to recognize and cherish memories or little moments that will bring you comfort and joy. In other words, the continuing bonds will become bonds of light that will help ease the fear that you will forget your loved one.

Our guests, listeners, and friends have found many creative ways to keep the connection with their loved ones:

+ Chet got an extraordinary gift from his daughter, Patti: her heart. Thanks to Patti's heart, Chet is still going strong after eleven years. He honors his daughter's name by advocating organ donation.

+ Dan, whose son died by suicide five years ago, is a golfer. He and his son played together often. Dan now carries his son's hat and favorite club cover with him whenever he plays the game.

+ Ronda's daughter loved sunflowers. It has been two years since her daughter died of a brain tumor. This year, Ronda planted sunflower seeds in little pots and gave them to her daughter's friends for graduation. Ronda also has a garden filled with sunflowers.

+ Henry and Patricia's son, and Lauren and Kerri's

brother, was a firefighter who died in the September 11 World Trade Center attacks. The family has created a picture book that they distribute to honor his memory.

+ Heidi, Rebecca, and Heather, whose brother died in an automobile accident, each wear a gold heart on a chain with an engraving of their brother's name.

+ Joyce, whose daughter died by suicide ten years ago, wears her daughter's army boots every year on her birthday.

+ Cheryl and Ben, whose son was a National Guard Volunteer and died in a roadside bomb explosion in Iraq, have established a scholarship in their son's name.

+ Sandy, whose son was killed when he grabbed a high-voltage line, keeps his watch, which stopped at the time of his death, in her purse.

+ Darrell, whose daughter was shot and killed when two teens opened fire at Columbine High School, travels the world preaching and promoting a message of love and tolerance.

+ Chad, whose big brother died in a mountain-climbing accident, wears his brother's football letterman jacket on Super Bowl Sunday.

+ The Reed family releases environmentally friendly balloons every year on their deceased baby daughter's birthday.

+ Lisa and her sister loved listening to music. When her sister died of cancer, Lisa made a tape of their favorite songs. She and her best friend listen often and have a good cry as well as a laugh.

+ Karl and Sue, with the help of their hospice nurse,

Eileen, created an online memorial through the Library of Life for their son, who died of thyroid cancer.

+ Mitch saved his twin sister's purse after she died in an automobile accident. He gave it to his sister's daughter on her sixteenth birthday.

As you can see, there are as many creative ideas as there are people. Many of these ideas take some effort, but something as simple as thinking about your loved one provides a connection. They will always be in your hearts, especially during life transitions such as graduations, birthdays, weddings, and births.

Harriet Schiff, author of *The Bereaved Parent* (1977), put it well when she said, "The reality is that we don't forget, move on, and have closure, but rather we honor, remember, and incorporate our deceased children and siblings into our lives in a new way. In fact, keeping memories of your loved one alive in your mind and heart is an important part of your healing journey."

Although they are no longer living on this earth, we will always be their parents, siblings, and loved ones. Those relationships never end. Thankfully, our deceased loved ones are a continuing presence in our lives and always will be. Remember, you don't have to walk this path alone. If you've experienced a loss, there are many groups and organizations, such as the Compassionate Friends, that can help you. Some offer education and information, and some offer guidance, friendship, support, a listening ear, and a caring heart.

We wish you peace, joy, and love on your healing journey, and may your ongoing connections with those you have loved and lost sustain you during your darkest hours.

**References:**

Horsley, H., and T. Patterson. "The Effects of a Parent Guidance Intervention on Communication among Adolescents who have Experienced the Sudden Death of a Sibling." *The Journal of American Family Therapy* 34 (2006): 119–37.

Packman, W., H. Horsley, B. Davies, and R. Kramer. "Continuing Bonds Following the Death of a Sibling." *Death Studies Journal.*

Schiff, H. S. *The Bereaved Parent.* New York: Crown Publishers, 1977.

D r. Gloria Horsley and Dr. Heidi Horsley are a mother/daughter team and internationally recognized grief experts. They are the founders of the Open to Hope Foundation and the hosts of the "Open to Hope" Internet radio show. In addition, Dr. Gloria is a board member for the Compassionate Friends and Dr. Heidi is an adjunct professor at Columbia University, with a private practice in Manhattan. Their message is that others have made it through the grief journey, and so can you; if you do not yet have hope, lean on theirs. Find more at www.opentohope.com.

# Son's Fortieth Birthday Would
# Have Been Today
By Carol Loehr

Our son, Keith, died when he was almost thirty years old. As Keith's fortieth birthday approached, I wondered what he would have accomplished during the last ten years had he lived.

Keith loved the outdoors, so I can still see him fishing, running, hiking, skating, skiing, and scuba diving. I know how much Keith loved children, so if he were not married with children of his own, he would be working with children who needed a Big Brother. I can also see Keith working with young children, teaching them to play ice hockey.

Keith would continue to be close to his sisters, Cindy and Carrie, laughing and teasing them. He would visit them and be an important part of their lives. He would be proud of Cindy's art and her writings, and he would wonder if her new home was in a safe area. Keith would be staying at all the hotels where Carrie has worked and analyzing all her new job opportunities. He would continue to call Carrie his *little sister* even though she is now in her thirties.

Keith would still be calling me on Sunday morning, when my husband was singing in the church choir. He would still want to know what was going on with his mother; I would have appreciated that concern. He would continue to tell me about what he had done during the week and the things he wanted to try.

My husband, Dick, would still be going on special fly-fishing adventures with Keith, and he would encourage his dad to perfect his fly-fishing techniques.

Keith would have made special time for his friends, calling often and going on hiking, fishing, and hunting trips.

We can think of what Keith would be doing if he were alive, but that is not reality. We cannot physically have a celebration with him present; however, we do understand that Keith will be with us for his birthday in a spiritual way. He has touched our family in such mysterious ways, but the way Keith reaches out to those we have never met amazes us!

Through my website dedicated to Keith, I receive many e-mails from people I have never met who have felt a connection with him. I was doing a web-radio show with Drs. Gloria and Heidi Horsley when a young man phoned in and explained he was suffering from depression. That morning, he had gone to my website feeling depressed and read that I was talking that same day on the show. He called to talk to me and explain the connection he had with Keith. He felt Keith guiding him as he learned ways to deal with his depression.

Keith also helped save another young man's life. A while ago, I got an e-mail from a young man who said that his life would soon be over. My husband called the police, and using the information from the e-mail, they were able to find the man in another state. The police and the local hospital were able to get him the mental health care he needed, and he is alive today.

Yes, it is always hard facing the fact that I cannot see Keith on his birthday this year or in future years. However, I can still see my son, if only in my mind and heart. He is smiling and continues to touch my life. Keith will never be forgotten; his love will continue to be felt in different and wondrous ways. Consider yourself touched by Keith as you read this article. Wish Keith a Happy Birthday!

Happy Birthday, Keith! I miss you so much, words cannot express.

Love Always, Mom

---

Carol Loehr's only son, Keith Loehr, died at the age of twenty-nine by suicide in 1999. She is the author of a children's book, *My Uncle Keith Died,* which addresses children's questions about suicide and depression. Carol is the webmaster of The Gift of Keith, a website to help comfort and educate survivors of suicide and those who support them. Find her articles at www.opentohope.com.

# Mother Remembers Son
# and His Firebird
By Anne Dionne

It was Mother's Day, 2001. The boy I cherished the most, my son, Michael, was nineteen years old and slipping out of my grasp too quickly.

Where was that little boy with the infectious laughter, the boy who brought so much life and fun into our family? Wasn't it just yesterday when I took that photograph of the excited little boy all dressed up for his first day at kindergarten?

I remember feeling a little resentful because I hadn't seen Michael smile much lately. His smile was the physical attribute that could melt my heart and make everything all right with my world. Due to our conflicting schedules—he was usually in bed when I left for work in the morning, and I was in bed before he was in for the night—we didn't see much of each other for days at a time. But on this day, Mother's Day, we would spend precious time together, just the two of us.

Michael invited me to have lunch out with him that day. I'd had lunch earlier; however, I was so happy to have the opportunity to spend a few hours with him that I never told him I'd already eaten. Michael filled the gas tank of his prized 1968 Firebird, and off we went.

I will treasure the memory of that special day for the remainder of my life. Every detail is videotaped in my mind to replay over again whenever I choose. On that day, I got to see my boy smile and laugh as we shared funny stories together.

In retrospect, I believe that Michael gave me a priceless gift that day—the gift of his presence and precious smile. Neither of us could have known that only two short days later he would be gone, killed in an automobile accident.

There is a new Mother's Day tradition in our lives. My husband takes Michael's Firebird out of storage and we go for a drive. As I climb inside the car, I feel and smell its interior. I close my eyes, and I remember. . . .

---

Anne Dionne has been actively involved with the Compassionate Friends since the death of her son, Michael, in 2001. She currently serves as coordinator of the Compassionate Friends Online Support Community and has been a workshop presenter at the organization's National Conference. She coauthored the book *Every Step of the Way: How Four Mothers Coped with Child Loss*. Anne is a registered nurse, wife, and mother. Learn more at www.opentohope.com.

# Woman Sets Out to Complete Loved One's Bucket List

### By Kim Go

My beloved partner, Brian, was a very young man when he was diagnosed with pancreatic cancer. Doctors gave him an estimate of six to twelve months to live.

As timing would have it, the movie *The Bucket List* had come out a year before. This caused much discussion among visiting friends, who suggested that Brian should make a bucket list.

Brian seemed disinterested. He made two concrete but modest requests—the purchase of a beautiful bathrobe and the commitment to keep up his grooming. Brian was a fastidious man, and I made his requests happen.

His friends talked of helping Brian attend a Burning Man event, of taking him on exotic travels and doing fantastic things. Brian's lack of engagement in these topics made me suspicious that he felt worse than he looked. I was privately a little angry that his friends talked so much about the bucket list idea because I wondered if we would have enough time.

Twenty-two days after his diagnosis, Brian was gone.

With time, it occurred to me that I wanted to do a bucket

list in remembrance of him. So I made a list of things that I imagine he would have liked to do, as a way to actively engage in activities to remember him. I have my own personal bucket list, but I really wanted one to honor Brian.

There are websites to help about creating a bucket list that offer lots of advice.

The biggest thing about a bucket list is that it takes time to write a good, thoughtful list. It helps to expose yourself to other people's bucket lists whose personalities and interests are like your beloved's. It can give you ideas and inspire your imagination of what they might have put on their list.

In doing grief work through a bucket list, it is important to find some overlap in your desires. The goals need to be resonant enough with your personality so that they will foster enough desire and drive to help you accomplish them.

For instance, Brian was always braver, in general, than I am. So many of the things on his list require more raw courage than my own. He always wanted to parasail again. I would *never* put parasailing on my list. But I can consider it and put it on my remembrance list because I might actually be able to find enough courage to do it. Desire is everything.

My world will be bigger by the act of doing his bucket list.

---

Kim Go is an artist, expressive arts coach, and writer, focusing on the theme of impermanence after her father's death in her early childhood, her own brush with mortality at age seventeen, and the death of her life partner, Brian, from pancreatic cancer in June 2008. She hopes to connect to others who are "learning to be present and alive regardless of the impermanence in their story." Read more about Kim at www.opentohope.com.

# How to Honor a Loved One Who Has Died

By Diana Doyle

Until the year 2000, my life resembled a fairy tale. I had a loving family, a husband, and an adorable two-year-old daughter. Over the next three years, what seemed impossible back then happened to me.

I lost three of the most important people in my life. My sister was killed in a car accident, leaving four little ones motherless; my mother was diagnosed and succumbed to ovarian cancer; and, most inconceivably, my previously healthy daughter, Savannah, died from a rare genetic disease.

Although each death was different, the tsunami of emotions was similar. I felt like my life had become an out-of-control freight train. Finding ways to honor the people who died helped me move forward in the grieving process.

Each relationship was different, so I honored each loved one differently. For my sister Tarnia, I planted a cherry tree that blooms with delicate blossoms around the anniversary of her death. I also wrote detailed letters to her children, describing what she loved about them, her favorite perfume, and other little tidbits that they'll be desperate for in years to come.

For my beautiful mother, Beverley, I bought a rose-covered photo frame and placed my favorite picture of her in it. The photo reminds me of her spirit, and I smile whenever I look at it. I wear something pretty for Mom on her anniversary and birthday, lighting a candle and placing a vase of roses next to her photo.

Savannah was the ultimate loss. We lost our future in many ways when she died. Our daughter was cremated, which enabled us to create a special shelf in our family room where her urn sits alongside angel figurines, a rainbow candle we light, and other presents friends have bestowed on us.

I wear a dainty, gold, heart-shaped locket designed to hold a bit of her ashes, so a small amount of what remains of Savannah's earthly self is dangling over my heart every day. I find the locket to be healing.

Every year on her birthday, we release balloons into the heavens. Letting go of them symbolizes her freedom from her painful disease. We also planted a climbing rosebush that displays an abundance of white flowers most of the year, reminding us of our beautiful little girl. We do something on those days that she would've loved, like going to a fun park or sitting in the sun reading one of her favorite books with our other daughter, Dempsey.

I still buy a birthday card for Savannah every year and write in it how I feel and what is happening in our lives. Our surviving daughter will one day be able to read them.

I have a book in progress about this journey that I hope to have published. Writing it has been a healing experience. I believe that I am honoring someone I love when I help others survive their grief.

I've read many ways people honor those who have passed out of our lives. Some make quilts from their loved ones' clothes. Some ask friends to send them a letter with a memory about the loved one. Others, like me, light candles and think of the happy memories that will always live on in our souls.

However, the most profound way to honor someone who has died is to *live*—not just exist, but to try new things like skydiving or chasing your dreams. Perhaps you simply notice the glisten of morning dew on the lawn or listen to the sound of children laughing. Take a moment to be alive, in memory of those who can't!

I know all of these things make me feel the person who's died is somehow still alive. It's something I can control and makes those difficult times seem a little bit easier.

---

Within three years Diana Doyle lost her sister, her mother, and her daughter Savannah, who was diagnosed with metachromatic leukodystrophy at the age of two and a half. She died at age four. Since then, Diana has been writing a blog in hopes of helping others. She lives in Los Angeles with her husband, Peter, and her daughter Dempsey. To read more articles by Diana, visit www.opentohope.com.

# Taking the Plunge to Honor My Son

By John French

It has been well over a year now since my life suddenly plunged into despair. Losing my son was devastating on every level, and life continues to spiral out of control. Every day, I fall a little further from the height of my elation, from those glorious days when I was on top of the world. Now, I struggle just to maintain my composure.

There are days when I feel that I am regaining some stability, and moments when I plummet into a boundless despair. Everything seems so distant and distorted. I can't look to the past or ponder the future. When my mind begins to wander, my emotions tumble out of control.

I have often heard grief described as a roller coaster. To me, that implies a series of peaks and valleys. But, from my perspective, life has been traveling in one direction—down. An experience I had over the summer is seemingly more analogous to the shocking plunge into death's bleak oblivion.

On May 24, what should have been Brandon's eighteenth birthday, we found a unique way to celebrate. We wanted to do something monumental, not only to honor our son, but also to fulfill one of his long-held plans. So that is what our family, as well as a large group of his friends, set out to do.

We all met about an hour away from our homes, in a small grassy field. On that narrow strip, we remembered Brandon's life and prepared to face our own deaths. You see, that little field serves as a runway to one of Michigan's leading skydive facilities, Midwest Freefall. Brandon always talked about jumping on his eighteenth birthday. Because he wasn't able to do it himself, we felt compelled to do it for him.

Eight of us took to the skies and made the slow climb to 14,500 feet. It takes about fifteen minutes to reach that altitude, which is plenty of time to reflect and ponder. As I looked out the window, I couldn't help but think about how fearless Brandon was. And how anxious I was becoming.

But my trepidation faded when I remembered something he used to say: "To fear is to fail." That expression calmed me completely—even when the door rolled open and I stood on the threshold looking down at the tiny squares of indistinguishable real estate.

When I leapt out, I was instantly reminded of just how powerless I am. Initially, the blast from the propeller flips you around and there is nothing you can do. As gravity takes over, you quickly regain your stability. Even though you're plummeting toward the ground at one hundred and twenty miles per hour, you begin to feel as if you're floating on the wind. Your mind goes blank and you can only think about the skydive.

It is an amazingly freeing experience. For that sixty seconds, I forgot all my pain; I was above the torment and outside of my skin. It was almost as if I was hovering between life and death.

When my chute opened and the world went silent, I hung

for a moment on heaven's horizon before descending again into the depths of my own living hell. Since that time, I have continued to live in limbo. I have now completed my skydiving training and have made a total of eight solo jumps.

But the free fall of grief does not end. As soon as my feet hit the ground, my thoughts get all twisted. And I have the dreadful realization that life isn't unfolding the way that I expected.

## The Plunge

Seen have I the world on high.
And awestruck held my breath.
I've leapt into eternal skies,
and plunged towards certain death.
I've tumbled out and peeled away.
I've been humbled by gravity; and I have seen it at play.
I've flipped around, been upside down, and
flown a seamless track.
I've fallen in perfect symmetry, with the
world beneath my back.
It is not a frantic flailing fall.
In fact, it is tranquil and sublime.
I control my fate and accelerate beyond the speed of time.
I chase a peaceful inner space,
I glide atop the wind.
I pierce the clouds and wispy shrouds
At free fall's bottom end.

---

John French's son, Brandon, died at the age of seventeen in August of 2009 from an undiagnosed heart condition.

Brandon's sudden death inspired John to share his writing with the world, in the hope that something beneficial will come from his mourning. John lives in Highland, Michigan, with his wife of twenty-one years, Michelle, and daughter, Veronica. John's articles can be read at www.opentohope.com.

# My Daughter Is
# Never Far Away
## By David J. Roberts, LMSW, CASAC

Before my daughter Jeannine died in 2003, I was never one to believe in things that I could not see. My version of reality was defined by hard evidence, not by intuition or feel. Jeannine has given me signs of her presence in a variety of different ways since her death. As a result, my new reality has been defined more by what I feel and experience than by hard facts. With that in mind, I would like to describe one of my more memorable experiences following her death.

During college spring break in March 2006, my wife, Cheri, and I flew to Phoenix to spend a week with two close friends. This was the first extended vacation that we had taken since Jeannine's death.

I was excited about the prospect of leaving upstate New York's cold weather for a much warmer climate and spending some time with my friends. However, as I was waiting to board our flight, intense sadness suddenly began to consume me as I thought about how much Jeannine would have enjoyed this trip. She was always the adventurous, live-in-the-moment type of woman who brought out that quality in anyone whose life she touched. I missed not having her with me on this trip.

We boarded our flight in Albany, New York, and flew into Baltimore, where we had to change planes. During our layover, a young woman sat across from me; she did not appear to have a care in the world. She seemed to be around twenty-one, which would have been Jeannine's age had she lived. She was attractive, with shoulder-length brown hair, similar to our daughter's.

When Cheri and I boarded the plane, I took the seat closest to the window, and Cheri took the middle seat, leaving the aisle seat empty. Much to my surprise, this same young woman asked if she could sit with us. For most of the trip, she read and listened to her iPod. I enjoyed watching her engage in routine activities similar to those that Jeannine used to do when she was alive. My pre-flight sadness was a thing of the past.

We spoke just before our flight landed. She told me that she was a college student who was studying communication at the University of Rhode Island. She explained that she was visiting some friends in Arizona during spring break. I never did find out her name, but it didn't matter. She gave me the gift of her presence, and that was enough.

I believe that Jeannine made her presence known to me and Cheri through this young woman. Jeannine was looking out for me in death as she had in life.

In July of 2007, Cheri and I went to Nashville for our first Compassionate Friends conference. As we were waiting for our flight, a little girl and her family sat next to us. The little girl was holding a Tigger doll. Jeannine's favorite Disney character was Tigger. I just smiled.

David J. Roberts's daughter, Jeannine Marie, died at the age of eighteen from a rare form of cancer in 2003. He is an adjunct professor in the psychology and psychology–child life departments at Utica College. Dave is a bereavement volunteer for Hospice and Palliative Care, has spoken at many national conferences, has written numerous articles, and has coauthored two books on loss. Learn more at www.opentohope.com.

# Love: Our Hope for the Future and Our Immortality

### By David Daniels, MD

H ope means cherishing something with the anticipation of fulfillment. Hope connotes confidence, even assurance. As each of us allows in hope, a natural unfolding takes place. It is true that the only thing that is constant in life is change. Yet when we come back to our higher essential qualities, we actually experience something that is both constant and unchanging, and underlies all else. To me, this means unconditional, enduring love. This is the ultimate hope and the ultimate assurance of our immortality!

As you read on, give yourself the time to stop and reflect on these key understandings in the loss and grief process, especially as these relate to your own life and experience.

When we live each new day freshly the best we can, we express the hope that love gives us. When we live each day with the inner knowledge that we human beings can develop and become more loving and whole, we express hope. For without the hope that love provides, there is despair, desolation, and despondency. In truth, hope means living each new day as fully as we can—even as though it would be our last day. This, I deeply believe, is also a sure path to immortality.

In my work both personally and as a therapist with those who are dying or grieving, it has become clear to me that at the heart of avoidance of, and difficulty working with, grief and loss is our splitting away from unconditional love. This occurs as the natural consequence of personality formation and seeking a satisfactory life in the world. Along with this splitting away from unconditional love, what arises is the need to forgive ourselves for not loving ourselves unconditionally and, of course, others, as we cannot truly love others without loving ourselves.

This return of unconditional love, which has always been there in the background before we went away from it, would naturally allow back in all of our higher qualities. The process involves not only befriending our judging mind and reactivity, but literally also engaging in the work of becoming our own best friend and a more whole person. This is the art of inner friendship and ultimately the friendship with life that brings us back to our soul and liberates us into loving and living life each day.

When our son, David, died in an accident at age twenty-five, we knew that he represented hope to all who knew him. There is a nature center dedicated in honor of his life. The plaque simply says, "With hope for the future of all who pass this way." David gifted us with a profound learning regarding the validity of a life lived in love and joy with an open heart.

This past fall, it had been just more than twenty years since his passing when a college friend of David's contacted us proposing a celebration of his life. He and others created this event, which more than seventy friends from around the United States attended at the nature center.

Why do this after twenty years? At the time of David's passing, these young friends were in their early twenties and just beginning the journey into adulthood. At the celebration, one after another rose to express what David's life continues to mean to them. How he inspired them to love more deeply, how he shared joy and hope, how he supported their lives at difficult times, and how he loved unconditionally.

While we, his family, couldn't keep track of all David's enduring friendships, we knew that his qualities of being were his ultimate contribution to every person in his life. David had an adventuresome, spontaneous, and fun-loving spirit; he was also determined, thoughtful, and disciplined. And what really mattered most to him were his friendships, which were imbued with love, care, delight, and helpfulness.

At this lovely celebration on a warm fall day, a woman named Tracy summed up the core of David's meaning to others in this remarkable spontaneous statement:

"I first heard about David when I met my husband, Mark, almost nineteen years ago. His passing was still very raw to Mark. So when he would talk about David, I would think, 'Wow, he really has this guy David on a pedestal. No one is that perfect or that great!' But then I met Bea, and she would talk about David in a similar manner. Then I met Denise, his sister. She too would talk of David with this sense of reverence. Then Marianne and Brian. . . .

"Over the years, it didn't matter whom I met who had known him, the story line never changed. It was always the same—he was and still is the essence of love. And it is evident by the love that is here today at the celebration of his life. It is apparent his spirit is alive and his presence, his legacy is here at this gathering to honor and remember him. It's palpable. It is real.

"What a blessing to be touched in such a way, by someone I've never met. So I thank you. I thank all of you for giving me the opportunity to know David and experience his love through all of you."

When we live love each day as best we can, when we manifest hope and joy, these qualities endure in the perpetuity of immortality. Nothing destroys our higher essential qualities—the gift of love lives on in us. Again, this is the "hope for the future of all who pass this way," as the plaque at the nature center in David's honor so simply says. And as Elizabeth Edwards put it shortly before her passing:

"You all know that I have been sustained throughout my life by three saving graces—my family, my friends, and a faith in the power of resilience and hope. . . . These graces have carried me through difficult times, and they have brought more joy to the good times than I ever could have imagined."

Each day, take a few moments to reflect on hope and love, and their connection to immortality. Recall a time when hope and love abounded in you. It is there inside us all, sometimes outside of our awareness. Reflection brings these back. Remember, hope and love do not die; we just go away from them. This is a way of knowing our immortality.

---

D r. David Daniels, MD, is clinical professor of psychiatry and behavioral sciences at Stanford Medical School, a leading developer of the Enneagram system of nine personality styles, and coauthor of *The Essential Enneagram*. In private practice for more than three decades, David brings his knowledge of the Enneagram to individuals, couples, and groups, as well as to a wide range of applications. Find his articles at www.opentohope.com.

# Turning Points

## Traveling to Planet Grief and Back
### By Mitch Carmody

I am continually amazed at the choreography that I experience at the Compassionate Friends National Conference and the huge impact it has on my body, mind, and spirit when I walk off the dance floor and return home.

From spending four or five days on "planet grief," we return to the mundane realities of the real world and try to blend in with its preoccupied inhabitants who, for the most part, know nothing of our secret planet. They don't wear buttons of a dead child pinned to their clothing, they don't wear name tags around their neck identifying their loss, and they don't wear butterfly clothing or the Compassionate Friends T-shirts with a broken red heart.

When I return to work, I get surprised looks from people who are caught off guard when I hug them good morning without thinking. I feel a deep separation anxiety when I part from my fellow travelers to planet grief, with their honest hugs, cathartic kisses, and deep dialogues. The heart I wore on my sleeve now feels vulnerable and exposed to the harsh elements of the daily routine and the machine of the workaday world.

I am *jonesing* for my friends, my family of wounded survivors who succor my soul and I theirs in our dance of recovery. In a word, I feel drifty and lost for a few days; like getting your land legs back slowly after a week at sea, I feel unsteady and unbalanced, and I weep easily. I miss my family from planet grief and feel the impact of its loss for another year.

Today, I am decompressing, degriefing so to speak, remembering and cherishing the magic moments of the weekend and thanking God for the privilege to be there and serve the bereaved with every quark of my being. I help facilitate healing in the most sacred of places, the human heart and soul, and I'm always humbled and healed myself by the experience.

We all come to planet grief from many different worlds, a plethora of differences in race, age, religion, occupation, economic class, intellect, and political views. Yet we congregate as one family and find a common ground in compassion and love. It is in helping to heal that we are healed ourselves. Like one beggar sharing his bread with another beggar, so both are sustained for another day.

On Sunday, it was revealed to us that the Compassionate Friends had to register our Sunday walk as a protest if we were to walk the streets of Washington, DC. That's all right; we *are* protestors. We have our signs, our banners, our bibs, our

T-shirts, our name tags and buttons. We are the Compassionate Friends. We need not walk alone, and we don't. We walk in unison. We all arrived from a network of paths and losses as varied as the stars, and together on common ground we protest to the world society's ignorance of our forever journey and the injustice to our hearts.

We are changing the worldviews of grief and loss. We are educating the fortunate others about our journey and how we survive. We are intentional survivors who are working on our grief proactively, living our loss, not letting go, not getting over, not becoming bitter, but becoming better. We are the Compassionate Friends.

God bless you all until we meet again. Dear planet grief appears for a few days in the summer, and for a short time we find the camaraderie of hope to sustain us for another year.

---

Mitch Carmody's nine-year-old son died of cancer in 1987. He published *Letters to My Son: A Journey Through Grief* and now lectures and conducts grief workshops nationally for the Compassionate Friends and Bereaved Parents USA, in addition to writing articles for many national bereavement periodicals. Mitch is a trained hospice volunteer. He lives in rural Minnesota with his wife. Read more articles by Mitch at www.opentohope.com.

# Being Available for
# Turning Points
### By Pamela Prime

After my son's death, there were many turning points along the way in my grief. I could not make them happen all by myself, but I could make myself available. At each turning point, there was a sense of Divine Grace; it was only in quiet reflection or in sharing the experience with a good listener that I could say "thank you."

I remember well the first time I could look at Sean's picture without breaking down in sobs. His suicide was shocking, terrifying, and beyond heartbreaking.

That memorable day, I sat on our sofa and looked at his face. Sweet, gentle tears rolled down my cheeks as I felt unbounded love flood my heart. I wrote in my journal, but it took a few days for me to name that extraordinary moment of grace and give thanks to God. The love I felt then still remains in my heart. It is what I have of Sean, and no one can take that from me!

Sitting on my closet floor one day, months after Sean's death, I slowly opened the suitcase in which I had saved some of his belongings. At that time, I did not recall what I had saved. I was in too much pain and confusion.

I held his clothes to my face, hoping to remember how Sean smelled. I touched his poetry books, his baseball mitt, and his sunglasses with gentle caresses, hoping to recall how Sean felt. I folded up in tears on the closet floor with his things all around me and fell asleep.

I awakened, surprised by a sense of Sean's presence embracing me. I sat stunned by what had happened and felt so close to my son that I wondered if the veil had completely disappeared for a moment. Again, I wrote in my journal, but it was not until I shared this with my spiritual director that I wept in gratitude for that moment of pure grace.

There are many turning points on the journey of grieving the death of a loved one. Each is a reminder that we are not alone in our grief and that our loved ones are with us in spirit, as is our God. Our journeys are much greater than the healing of grief. They are awakening us to the presence of love in our midst and inviting us to participate in love, to become love itself, and to walk side by side with others who suffer with love in our hearts.

---

Pamela Prime's four-month-old daughter died of sudden infant death syndrome, and her son, at the age of sixteen, died of suicide. Pamela is a spiritual director, an educator, and a writer. Her first book is *When the Moon Is Dark We Can See the Stars*. Pamela is a mother and a grandmother and lives in California. To read more of her articles, visit www.opentohope.com.

# Growing Through Grief
By Fran Dorf, MA, MSW

Around one thirty in the afternoon, December 7, 1993—by coincidence, Pearl Harbor Day—I put my three-year-old son, Michael, down for his nap, went to my office, turned on the intercom, and began to work on my third novel. The intercom was silent, and I wrote steadily.

Around four o'clock, mildly concerned that Mikey was sleeping too long, I went to wake him up. I found him in the midst of a silent, deadly seizure. I started to scream, my husband came running, and although we didn't really know it then, we had arrived with our baggage at the gates of hell. We had no choice about making the journey, but who voluntarily agrees to walk with you through hell?

A true friend does.

Nancy had been one of my closest friends for more than ten years. We had that rarest of friendships—personal, family, and couple. Our daughters were best friends; our husbands were close. We talked at length nearly every day on the phone, the way women do. We examined and re-examined small moments and big ones; supported each other whether we were troubled or cheerful; shared secrets, worries, regrets, hopes, and dreams. We adored each other and had fun together. We made each other giggle and helped each other cry.

There were others who walked with my husband, Bob, and me on our journey through hell, each in his own way, but these special friends, Nancy and her husband, Nick, did us the service and honor of listening. Every Friday night for the next six months, they gave us dinner and a place and a time to reflect on, and speak aloud of, the hell that had become our lives.

They listened as we described our roller coaster of hope and despair, guilt and pain. They listened as we described in gruesome detail the accoutrements of hell: our beloved son in some unreachable, unbearable state; the arrogant doctors with all their opinions; the invasive tests and needles; the flat EKGs; the Pediatric Intensive Care Unit with its technological paraphernalia hovering over the beds, those suck-hissing, click-clicking machines; every awful place that came after that.

They listened as we tried to make the decisions that had to be made. They listened as we slowly came to the realization that it was all going to end only in despair. Mikey was our little guy, his demise was ghastly and horrific, and they listened.

Why is it important to speak of suffering in the presence of an empathic listener? Here's why:

Dr. Bessel Vander Kolk, a prominent researcher in the field of trauma, has pointed out that traumatic memories are primarily imprinted in the senses and emotions located principally in the right hemisphere of the brain. This is opposed to the left hemisphere, from which an individual constructs an orderly narrative of life's events, completes tasks, and thinks logically.

Speaking about trauma helps people identify and categorize their emotions and sensory experiences, and then organize and order these experiences as narratives with beginning, middle, and end. By speaking about emotional suffering, a person begins to integrate it into a personal history and thus move the experience more into the left brain functions, lessening emotional reactivity and/or the reliving of disturbing sensory experiences.

This is why traumatized people need to tell their stories, over and over, to an empathetic listener. It takes courage, concern, stamina, and grit to be such a listener.

Nancy and Nick were among those who gave us this gift of empathic listening, and even when our son died the following June, Nancy persisted in trying to walk with me through the strange and isolated country of grief—also hell, but a different region.

Fast-forward about a year and a half. I had spent most of that time shut inside my home, wandering around in my bathrobe, my husband and daughter like vague floaters in my field of vision.

Nancy was on the phone. "Hey honey, how are you doing?"

"The same, I guess," I said.

"You won't believe what happened," she said, and started to talk about something in her life that had upset her, just the way she would have talked before all this began. After a few moments she abruptly stopped.

"Oh my God," she said. "I'm so sorry. I feel really bad telling you about this after what you've been through. It's ridiculous."

That was the moment, possibly the first since it all began, in which I was able to observe myself again as a human being in the world among other human beings. I realized in that moment that I no longer "shared" friendship with Nancy. Our friendship had become about Nancy supporting me, listening to me, holding me, witnessing my grief. But that wasn't friendship. That was something else entirely.

And that was the moment when I realized how self-absorbed I'd been in my grief, how utterly unavailable to her or to anyone, really—even my husband and daughter. In order to move back into the world, I had to make an effort to *be* in the world again. And that meant honoring other people's experience of the world, not comparing their experience to mine. Nancy had the right to her experience, her feelings, her life, didn't she?

I thanked my friend for being so sensitive, for having given me all anyone could have given, putting a mutual friendship on hold, having demoted her own needs to the relentless needs of my grief. I told her to tell me what had happened that upset her.

I'm sure there were many other important moments when I turned a corner, but that was the one when I really started looking outward and forward again, when I started to see who I could be, even without my son, who I could be *because* I had lost my son.

I conduct writing workshops to help people heal from grief, trauma, and loss, one of which is called "Growing Through Grief." In grief, there *is* the opportunity for growth and wisdom. This is a truth that is, or should be, difficult to say to those who are in grief's initial stages, but it is still the truth.

A wise man, a psychologist named Irvin Yalom, said: "Once an individual recognizes their role in creating their own life predicament, they realize that they and only they have the power to change the situation."

This certainly applies to grief. When you lose a child (or anyone close), you could easily go on being bereaved forever. I believe that a bereaved person must, at a time of his or her choosing, figure out how to compartmentalize grief and make a conscious decision to go on living. Only then can you begin to determine what "going on" means, the shape and substance of it, the who and why and how of it.

In grief we walk alone. Though others may care, we are lonely inside. We face grief alone, experience it alone, master it alone. In grief we are narcissistic, self-reflective, self-involved, selfish. Grief is all about the self.

But in reflecting on the self, we eventually must ask: Who was I before? Who am I now? Who will I be in the future?

There is no way to answer these questions without looking outward and forward again, toward some future that we alone can make.

---

Fran Dorf, MA, MSW, is the author of three acclaimed novels, including *Saving Elijah*, inspired by the death of Fran's three-year-old son, Michael. Fran writes articles, essays, and poetry and is finishing a memoir called *How I Lost My Bellybutton and Other Naked Survival Stories*. A philanthropist and therapist, Fran conducts "Write to Heal" workshops to help people use writing as a path to inner healing. Learn more at www.opentohope.com.

# Rediscovering Laughter
By Lisa Buell

I heard the sound coming from somewhere close, swelling from the deepest part of my being. I was almost startled when I felt it resonate through my body, felt the vibration, lungs rising and falling to keep up with the demand of my spirit. How long had it been since I had felt laughter?

The noise was both familiar and startling. The overwhelming sense of loss that guarded the gate to my soul must have been on a lunch break. Loss and I had made an agreement after my daughter died that I could never be happy again. But now, before my conscious mind could react, it had already happened— happiness had bubbled up through me, spilling up over the sides of myself.

I had been holding on for so long. Weeks had turned into months, the pit in my stomach grew, my heart had been stretched to its capacity. The moment my daughter took her very last breath, all the joy, love, and sense of fulfillment was sucked out, leaving me with a sagging sense of loss. I knew there would never be a time that I would feel happiness again. How could I when my child was gone?

Slowly, over time, I recovered some semblance of interest in actively participating in my life again. Little sparks of interest for life were catching fire. One day, I woke up with the goal to get dressed before noon. I started to pay attention to the details—what I was eating, how I was spending my time.

It happened bit by bit; the process back to living was painfully slow and full of self-judgment. When the antidepressants didn't seem to work, I marched into the kitchen to whip up a batch of vanilla frosting, eating until the top of my head tingled and I could take a full breath again.

The world was still too bright. People's concern felt suffocating, and I found myself back in bed pulling the covers over my head, snuggled in my cocoon of loneliness, my thoughts circling through the last months of my daughter's life. I spent hours in bed with my "magical thinking." I changed her ending; there was no cancer, Madison's legs weren't bowed, her long shiny hair reflected the sunlight as we walked hand in hand to the beach.

Over time, I was able to stop the obsession of what Madison's life could have been, should have been. My focus shifted to internal matters; I began to find little parts of myself that I had thought were lost forever. My interest was caught in a dark theater, hooked by movies like *American Beauty*, *Shakespeare in Love*, *A Map of the World*, themes that dealt with love and loss.

The athleticism that I had grown up with was rediscovered on a trail in the forest of my childhood. The trail still there, waiting for me to soak in the colors of fall, as I pushed my body uphill—muscles burning, every pore crying, hair wet, my heart pounding.

Spontaneity was discovered in the bottle of wine I drank with friends at a dinner. After we got home, I stripped myself of clothes, and lit by the stars of evening, I washed the car while naked. I don't remember the name on that wine, just that it left me reckless. The unspoken rule of washing cars with clothes on had been broken. I was free.

I found lust and possibility in a kiss, one that transported me to another universe where I could be exposed, vulnerable, and loved anyway.

The process of reclaiming pieces of myself after my daughter died was daunting. I was paralyzed by dread, guilt, and lack of ambition. How could I possibly live without her? I didn't have a lot to hold onto. Madison was our first and only child. Was I still a mother even though my child was gone? Was I still a friend even though I never returned calls? Was I still a wife when every part of me wanted to move away and start over?

How could I live with so much anger and confusion . . . and yet I did. But really, I wasn't living, I was merely existing. I was flying below the radar of my life, doing just enough to get by, and all the while medicating myself with food and antidepressants so I wouldn't draw too much attention. I stifled my creativity, painting my life with small strokes and washed-out color. Where was the bright bold palette I had worked so hard for?

And then it happened. I don't remember the circumstances. I don't know who was with me or what it was about. But what I do know is that it was the moment I found myself again. It was there in the midst of a full-blown belly laugh, mouth agape, trying to catch my breath, tears streaming down the sides of my cheeks.

I was both surprised and elated! It was a pure expression of happiness and it bubbled from deep within me—the person who never thought she would ever be able to feel something as magnificent as happiness again. My laugh didn't turn into a cry. My eyes filled with tears but didn't sting, there wasn't a lump in my throat, my chest wasn't tight, and my mouth wasn't forming into a little square. It was my first real emotional leap; the ground felt solid under the weight of my emotion, and I let it hold all of me. I laughed so hard I peed, which made me laugh even harder.

Over the years I have continued to find pieces of myself. Some have waited a long time for sunlight, and I embrace them like a long-lost friend. Sorrow used to rule the roost of my emotions, spreading out like it owned the joint. It is still part of what I feel, but now it is squeezed over by joy, hope, excitement, and love.

Bitterness is still sometimes very bossy, but gratitude just offers it a hug. Willingness slides in, slapping bitterness on the arm. Longing is there, flanked by understanding. Acceptance remains tough for me; I don't yet have the courage to let it in. The best I can do is accept that I am not ready for acceptance. So it stands outside my consciousness, respectfully waiting for an invitation.

After many years I have a spectrum of hard-won emotions. More recently I have discovered the subtle difference between pain and suffering, and I have made a choice not to suffer. What I find most encouraging is discovering the richness that my life's experiences have brought and feeling like I made the right choice when I decided to really live again.

---

Lisa Buell is a writer, activist, mother of three, and parent of two. Her daughter, Madison, died of cancer at two and a half years of age. Lisa is the founder of Sharing Wisdom, an online resource for care-giving and bereaved families, works with Children's Hospice and Palliative Care Coalition, and travels across the country speaking about palliative care. Lisa is writing her first book, entitled *Call Button*, a collection of essays. Find Lisa's articles at www.opentohope.com.

# Belly Laughs and Crème Brûlée

By Harriet Hodgson

"Mom, we didn't move into the pub," my daughter said and laughed. "We went there to cool off and eat." No wonder my memory was hazy. My husband and I were still recovering from the loss of our elder daughter, my father-in-law, my brother, and our former son-in-law. Four deaths in nine months were overwhelming.

The pub topic came up during a family dinner at a French restaurant. We were reminiscing about a trip we and our younger daughter had taken to London and the Isle of Man. I told the story about calling the hotel desk clerk to report the lack of air conditioning and his reply: "It hasn't worked for ten years." The story sent my daughter into gales of laughter, and I laughed with her.

I had ordered scallops, stir-fried vegetables, and a glass of white wine. As I sipped the wine, savored the food, and swapped stories with my daughter, I thought to myself, "This feels so good."

Our waiter, who had been hovering in the background, asked if I wanted another glass of wine. "I'm thinking about it," I replied. He moved away discreetly and our storytelling continued.

"Mom said we could walk to the Victoria and Albert Museum from our hotel," my daughter recalled. "She didn't tell me it was four miles down and four miles back. It's a shock to realize your mother is in better condition than you are!" We laughed so hard I thought we might be asked to leave.

The waiter approached again. "Another glass of wine?" he asked. I said I was still thinking. The stories continued all through dinner. My husband joined the storytelling and we talked about our British and Manx heritage. As the waiter cleared our dishes he asked, "Another glass of wine?"

"Still thinking," I said and patted his hand. We ordered coffee and I decided to skip dessert. But when the waiter brought my coffee he also brought a crème brûlée. "This is for you," he said with a smile. I was very surprised and thanked him. Why had he given me a free dessert?

Maybe he thought the "still thinking" reply was a running joke. Seeing family members enjoy one another may have given him pleasure. I didn't know the reason behind his gesture, but I knew I hadn't laughed like this in two years. Thanks to lots of grief work, I was feeling good again, raising my grandchildren, and living a new life. The time had come to honor my deceased loved ones in a special way, and I created Action Memorials, a process of identifying the deceased person's positive traits and weaving them into daily life.

My daughter had a marvelous sense of humor, so I decided to laugh more. My father-in-law was an ethical person, so I pledged to stand up for ethics. My brother loved to read, so I promised myself more recreational reading time. My former son-in-law loved nature, so I vowed to observe it more closely.

Action Memorials have changed my life. First, they shifted my thinking from negative to positive and continue to do this. Second, they link me with my loved ones every day.

I often think about that wonderful dinner, because it was a turning point in my grief journey. Powerful as grief had been, it was no longer powerful enough to quell the joy of belly laughs and crème brûlée.

---

Harriet Hodgson, BS, MA, is a prolific writer—author of hundreds of articles and twenty-eight books. After her twin grandchildren lost both parents in separate car crashes, Harriet and her husband became GRGs (grandparents raising grandchildren), and her writing focused on loss, grief, and recovery. Harriet has appeared on more than one hundred and sixty talk shows. She lives in Rochester, Minnesota, with her grandchildren and husband, John. Read Harriet's articles at www.opentohope.com.

# Floating Downstream:
## Putting Joy First
By Monica Novak

During summer breaks, my twelve-week reprieve from the regimented early-morning school schedule, my three girls and I love to sleep in and lounge around in our pajamas all morning. (OK, they lounge while I do dishes and laundry and try to get them to pick up their stuff that's strewn all over the house.) We spend our afternoons at the pool enjoying the sun with friends or visiting family in Indiana. Our evenings are spent listening to free outdoor concerts or curling up on the couch for movie night, which, in the summer, can be any night we want!

Sometimes we take a jaunt into downtown Chicago, most recently to brave the new Willis Tower (formerly Sears Tower) Skywalk, a glass box that juts out of the building's Skydeck, allowing you to seemingly "walk on air" one hundred and three stories above Wacker Drive.

Tomorrow is our annual trip to Six Flags Great America, where we'll see which roller coasters the girls are brave enough to go on this year. And some days it's just about driving Alex to the mall, Casey to a party, Anna to a friend's, and Grandma to adult day care. When I'm lucky enough to have a few moments to myself, I head to my garden for some therapeutic rosebush pruning or grab a book (like Peter Mayle's *A Year in Provence* or Don Aslett's *Clutter's Last Stand*) and stretch out on the back deck basking in some peace and quiet. Today I'm sitting at my desk writing.

Are you wondering what any of this has to do with grief? The point I'm trying to make is that sometimes you just have to do what feels good and brings you joy with the people you love (or the people around you). Sometimes you have to adjust your priorities and tell the to-do list to chill for a while. Sometimes you have to remind yourself that all of your other responsibilities will always be waiting for you, but your time here is not guaranteed.

That's what "death" and grief taught me. I've had fourteen years to assimilate this new thinking into my life after loss. If your loss is fresh, you probably aren't in the basking mode yet, but life will continue to call you to it and it's up to you to say yes.

Put joy first. Give yourself permission to do the things you want to do more often than the things you think you should do. Somehow, the important stuff gets done anyway, and if it doesn't, then it wasn't that important after all. So, as my favorite spiritual teacher says, "You might as well go with the flow. Floating downstream is a lot easier than trying to paddle upstream."

*Author's Note*: Quotations are used around the word death because I do not believe in death in the sense that life ends, only that death is a transition from physical to non-physical.

Monica Novak became a bereaved mother in 1995 with the stillbirth of her daughter Miranda. She captured the emotions of her grief journey in her memoir, *The Good Grief Club*, about her friendship with six bereaved mothers. Monica writes and speaks on the subject of pregnancy loss and infant death with local and national organizations. The mother of three daughters, Monica lives in the Chicago area. Visit www. opentohope.com for more.

# Spirals of Hope:
# We Can Help Each Other
By Megan Prescott

I just finished my weekly phone chat with my friend Nancy. Last year, Nancy's mother, father, and brother all passed away within six weeks of one other, each from different illnesses. Her brother, Brian, was my dear friend, and after his passing I kept in close contact with her. Since then, we have become very connected, like sisters. Our biggest and most intense bond is that in the twenty years before Nancy lost her family, I had already lost mine.

Nancy and I are similar in several ways no one wants to be: both our parents have died, we endured losing our favorite sibling very close to the passing of our parents, and neither of us have children to help with a sense of continuity in our family or even the world. I truly understand her when she shares with me that she feels like a lone wolf at times—traumatized by death, trying to process the change of losing her pack, and learning how to survive without it.

But we are not the same in a very important way, as we are on different ends of the grief process. Nancy reminds me of the feelings and experiences I had more than twenty years ago when the deaths of my mom and brother were new, and I didn't understand that I was about to embark on a long bereavement journey. Nancy reminds me of where I started.

And I am a symbol to Nancy that she can survive her losses even now, at this most intense and raw stage. I'm a living example of where she will go.

Around and up the spiral turns, and I find that we give each other hope. I hadn't thought about those earlier years for a while until my recent relationship with Nancy, and I am ironically grateful to travel back to those difficult days through her. I am not alone this time. Now I am with a friend, and we are visiting each other's darkness together. We are a wolf pack of two.

Nancy casually mentioned the publishing house that would end up publishing my children's story that addresses life and loss, *Squirrel and Oak: A Story of Hope*. My mother was my high school English teacher and the one who taught me how to write a good sentence and even love diagramming them! Years later, this would circle back around to my writing and illustrating a book that helps grieving children and adults all around the country. It was a dream that started as an idea shortly after my mom and brother died and was completed following the passing of my father.

I am still amazed that I have survived long enough to make something hopeful come out of my loss, a spiral from sadness to inspiration that I couldn't imagine in those first days. Beautifully and with wonderful serendipity, my new friend Nancy was part of that circle.

May you all have many "spirals of hope" appear in your life to confirm that there really is a miraculous order in the chaos of life and death. Remember too that the Universe and the Angels give special gifts to help those who have suffered loss, so be open and ready to receive yours.

I would like to dedicate this article to all of you who have had to say good-bye to someone you loved. I hope my words bring you inspiration and encouragement wherever you are in your journey.

---

Megan Prescott has used words and images to document her own bereavement journey for more than twenty years. At age nineteen, Megan experienced the death of both her mother and brother within a month of each other. Since then, she has brought the healing power of the arts to schools, shelters, grieving families, and herself. Megan is an artist, a teacher, and the author of *Squirrel and Oak: a Story of Hope*. For more information, visit www.opentohope.com.

# This Day Is All We Have
## By Luellen Hoffman

While working in Miami Beach, I decided to take a break from the madness of my job and planned to get up earlier than usual to see the sunrise on Sunday morning. I set my cell phone alarm to ring just before dawn, so I could jump up and head to the Atlantic Ocean.

It was pitch black when the alarm went off, and I quickly threw on some comfortable clothes and walked outside. The air was warm and still, and there was no sound except for the faint roar of the distant ocean. As I arrived on the beach, I saw two guys and a gal all huddled together like best friends sharing a special moment in time. They were busy talking to each other in excited whispers, as if they were having a slumber party and waiting for the feature presentation.

A few minutes later a young man appeared, walking barefoot across the sand in a disheveled tux. He seemed too distraught or exhausted to care about anything around him. Then for no apparent reason, he collapsed on the sand just a foot away from the surf. He seemed, even through the darkness, to be deeply tired and lonely.

I perched myself up on an old-fashioned wooden lifeguard station in hope of getting a better view of the ocean, and probably to feel safer. Then I started to pray. Soon the light began to change and the darkness began to lift, as if in layers.

As the light grew, everything around us began to change, and what I had seen before in the darkness seemed to melt away. Then a red sliver of fire started to crown on the horizon, inching up slowly to form a half ball of fire—a fire bursting with energy and so much power and color that it is hard to describe.

So many things will happen on this day. Someone will be born and someone will die. Someone will marry and someone will divorce. Someone will hear good news and be happy, and someone will hear bad news and cry. This day, someone will celebrate his or her good luck, and someone will suffer bad luck. During this day, so many things will happen that will mark this day for many people around the world. For some, this day will never be forgotten, while for others it will hardly be noticed.

No matter what we have or don't have, all we really know is this day, this moment in time. Now is where we are and now is where we can see things, say things, and do the things that we want to do for ourselves and for the people in our life.

The greatest gift we can give anyone is time. Life is short. We are all here for only a short time, and we can share, love, and appreciate what this day is and what it means to us and to the people in our lives. This day is given to us as a gift. Remember this day is it. Once this day is gone, it is gone forever.

---

Luellen Hoffman's husband, Michael, died unexpectedly in 1994, which led her to write *Special Dream: Personal*

*Accounts after the Death of a Loved One* in hopes of reaching out to help others. She is an adjunct professor at George Mason University in Fairfax, Virginia, and has won top awards from VNU/Nielsen Business Media for her outstanding people and communication skills. She has two sons. Find more at www.opentohope.com.

# Despite Loss of My Son, It Remains a "Wonderful World"

By Laura Klouzek

I love the song "What a Wonderful World" by Louis Armstrong. I used to have it as a ringtone on my cell phone. I took it off my phone in 2008 when my son, Lucas, passed away. I heard it every time someone called during those two weeks to check on Lucas's progress or to see how we were faring as we lived in the waiting rooms at the hospital.

Lucas didn't get to come home with us when we left there. He had already left to be with his Father in Heaven. After that day, I had to take that song off my phone. I just didn't think it was such a wonderful world anymore.

I had always thought it was a pretty wonderful world.

God has always given me a hopeful, thankful outlook on life, and I have enjoyed more blessings than I can count. That ringtone just described how I felt most of the time. We had our share of hurts, trials, and struggles, but I could always look at my children and their families and find many blessings.

Then, in July of 2008, one of those wonderful blessings was ripped from us. Lucas was thirty-three years old and had been having some aches and pains. He had been in a minor car accident and believed his aches were just due to some injury that wouldn't quite go away. By June of that year, he was almost unable to work. Doctors couldn't find a problem. You don't usually look for cancer in a strapping thirty-three-year-old man, who looked healthy and acted OK, except for the complaints of pain in his shoulders and then in his hip.

By the beginning of July, he had to rely on crutches and decided to see an orthopedic doctor since no one else could help him. The doctor ordered an MRI, took one look at it, and told Lucas he needed to see a different kind of doctor. We got him in to an oncologist within two days, and within two weeks he left us. He died from complications during surgery due to the cancer. My life would never be the same.

Lucas was my first child. He was also a husband and father. This was the child who made us laugh, then made us cry, and brought so much joy into our young marriage. I could picture his curly little head, and remember the tears I cried when he was born. And now God had decided Lucas should be with Him. No, it wasn't such a wonderful world. Even now, two years later, I break down in tears as I remember his life and his death. That is not the end of the story, though.

God has allowed me to cry, to scream at Him, to mourn, to remember. He has surrounded my husband and me with loving, supportive families. We still have our other children and their families, and we still get to see Lucas's wife, her new husband, and our grandchildren. Friends have walked alongside us, cried with us, and been there with a hug, a special word, or a card. I got to attend a grief support group with a special friend who had lost her husband. I have been able to walk with others who have had losses in their family.

Through our families, friends, and church, God has brought laughter back to our hearts. I believe we are more caring and compassionate due to our loss. Helen Keller once said, "What we have once enjoyed we can never lose. All that we love deeply becomes a part of us."

Yes, Lucas will always be a part of my heart and soul. I will always miss his love, his smart-aleck remarks, his smile. I will continue to cry, to sometimes be angry, to mourn, and to draw strength from others who have walked this same path. And I have changed the ringtone on my phone again. It goes, "And I think to myself, what a wonderful world."

---

Laura Klouzek's son, Lucas, died in July of 2008 after a short fight with cancer. His death and her journey through grief have prompted her to help others through her writing and speaking. Laura and her husband live in rural Missouri and are the parents of five children and the grandparents of eight, in addition to twelve years of life as foster parents. For more about Laura, visit www.opentohope.com.

# About the Authors

Dr. Gloria C. Horsley, PhD, MFC, RN, and Dr. Heidi Horsley, PsyD, LMSW, MS, are internationally recognized grief experts. This mother/daughter team founded the Open to Hope Foundation and are hosts of the "Open to Hope" Internet radio show. In addition, Dr. Gloria is a board member for the Compassionate Friends, and Dr. Heidi is an adjunct professor at Columbia University, with a private practice in Manhattan. Together they have written a number of articles and several books, including *Teen Grief Relief* and the award-winning *Real Men Do Cry*, which they coauthored with Eric Hipple. Dr. Gloria also wrote *The In-Law Survival Guide*. Find more at www.opentohope.com.

Drs. Gloria and Heidi are deeply indebted to the authors who graciously shared their journeys through grief in this book and the many more on the Open to Hope website.